JAILS

Reform and the New Generation Philosophy

anderson publishing co.
2035 reading road
cincinnati, ohio 45202
(513) 421-4142

Linda L. Zupan
Illinois State University

JAILS
Reform and the New Generation Philosophy

ISBN 0-87084-975-1

Library of Congress Catalog Number 90-82317

Kelly Humble *Managing Editor*   *Project Editor* Ellen S. Boyne

To John and Pauline Zupan

ACKNOWLEDGMENTS

While researching and writing this book, I was blessed with the good fortune to work with a number of wise and talented individuals. Without their support and assistance this work would not have been possible.

The administrators, supervisors, and corrections officers of the New Generation detention facilities visited in the course of this research are to be commended for their willingness to share their time and expertise. A special note of thanks is extended to Captain Don Manning, former Commander of the Spokane County Detention Center, who kindled my interest in the New Generation concept and provided unending enthusiasm and support for this research. I am also indebted to Director Gordon Yach, Assistant Director Paul Martin, and Sergeant Frank Tucker, Las Vegas Metropolitan Detention Center; Major Russell Davis and Captain John Alese, Pima County (Arizona) Detention Center; Sheriff Robert Skipper and Captain Joseph Golden, Multnomah County (Oregon) Detention Center; Director Larry Ard and Leslie Glenn, Contra Costa County (California) Detention Center; Director Samuel F. Saxton and Al Cohen, Prince George's County (Maryland) Department of Corrections; Director Fred Crawford, Assistant Director Kevin Hickey and Captain Joseph Zappia, Dade County (Florida) Corrections and Rehabilitation Department; and Director Anthony Pellicane and Richard A. van den Heuvel, Middlesex County (New Jersey) Department of Corrections and Youth Services, for opening their facilities to this indepth examination.

Grateful acknowledgement is also extended to the National Institute of Corrections; this research was supported, in part, by Technical Assistance Grants #GD-9 and #87J01GGV.

Two other individuals contributed immeasurably to this book and deserve to share the credit for its completion. Much of the research presented herein was conducted with the assistance of Ben A. Menke, an exceptional colleague, collaborator and friend. Our frequent, and oftentimes fervent, discussions and debates have had an indelible influence on this work. Nicholas P. Lovrich has been an invaluable role model and source of sage advise. Without his commitment to the world outside of academe, this study would never have evolved.

Finally, a special word of thanks is extended to my parents, John and Pauline Zupan, for their unwavering support.

CONTENTS

LIST OF TABLES

Chapter One

Introduction

Jail: An unbelievably filthy institution in which are confined men and women serving sentence for misdemeanors and crimes, and *men and women not under sentence who are simply awaiting trial.* With few exceptions, having no segregation of the unconvicted from the convicted, the well from the diseased, the youngest and most impressionable from the most degraded and hardened. Usually swarming with bedbugs, roaches, lice and other vermin; has an odor of disinfectant and filth which is appalling; supports in complete idleness countless thousands of able bodied men and women, and generally affords ample time and opportunity to assure inmates a complete course in every kind of viciousness and crime. A melting pot in which the worst elements of the raw material in the criminal world are brought forth blended and turned out in absolute perfection (Fishman, 1923:13-14).

Since their introduction to this country by seventeenth-century English settlers, American jails have been denounced by social commentators and reformers as brutal and degrading "human dumping grounds." So vilified has been the jail that one scholar was moved to note that if "verbal condemnation alone would do the work, the jail as an institution would have crumbled long ago" (Robinson, 1944:ii).

In the first years of this century, the Illinois State Charities Commission complained of the "waste, extravagance, inhumanity, inefficiency, neglect, indifference, petty partisan and factional politics" that transformed jails into "schools of crime" (1911:34-35). More than a decade later, Joseph F. Fishman, sole prison inspector for the federal government in the 1920s, described the na-

1

tions' jails as "giant crucibles of crime" into which "are thrown helter-skelter the old, the young, the guilty, the innocent, the diseased, the healthy, the hardened and the susceptible, there to be mixed with the further ingredients of filth, vermin, cold, darkness, stagnant air, over-crowding and bad plumbing; and all brought to a boil by the fires of complete idleness" (1923:251-252). Almost half a century later, an associate administrator of the Department of Justice's Law Enforcement Assistant Administration lamented that "jails are without question brutal, filthy, cesspools of crime—institutions which serve to brutalize and embitter men to prevent them from returning to a useful role in society, if they ever had one" (quoted in Burns, 1975:172).

Despite the criticisms of over two centuries, the jail has remained by-and-large unchanged. Modern jails tend to be overcrowded, underfunded, understaffed and underresearched (Mattick and Aikman, 1969; Flynn, 1973). Jail architecture is typically obsolete, physical facilities generally antiquated, custodial personnel nearly always underpaid and untrained, and medical and mental health care woefully inadequate. Programs for inmates tend to be modest or nonexistent, and the environment for both inmates and staff generally is charged with stress, violence and hostility. In sum, American jails are commonly regarded as "the worst blight in American corrections" (Fogel, 1980:74), "the most irrational element in the entire criminal justice system" (Flynn, 1973:73), and—in a colorful mixed metaphor—"a millenarian albatross that has remained stubbornly immune to successive attempts toward reform" (Advisory Commission on Intergovernmental Relations, 1984:3).

For the 9.7 million people who annually pass through the nation's 3,316 local jail facilities, incarceration inflicts more than the mandated loss of liberty and freedom. Personal testimonials and journalistic exposés that comprise the bulk of what is known about jail conditions attest to the fact that our nation's jails tend to represent arenas of fear and filth, inhumanity and degradation. Idleness, excessive noise, lack of privacy and personal space, crowded and unsanitary living conditions, isolation from friends and family, subjection to rape and sodomy, assault, extortion, robbery, and thievery make incarceration a psychologically painful as well as physically hazardous experience. Fishman (1922:793) summarized the aspects of jail conditions that make incarceration painful:

> What the public does not know is that when the judge says, "Thirty days in jail," he is sentencing the prisoner to many more things than mere confinement in an institution. If the facts were known, in most instances the sentence would actually read: "I not only sentence you to confinement for thirty days in a bare, narrow cell in a gloomy building, during which time you will be deprived of your family, friends, occupation, earning power, and all other human liberties and

privileges, but in addition, I sentence you to a putrid mire, demoralizing to body, mind, and soul, where every rule of civilization is violated, where you are given every opportunity to deteriorate, but none to improve, and where the tendency to wrong-doing cannot be corrected but only aggravated.

What the public believes is that jails are "country clubs" in which the least deserving are provided, at taxpayer's expense, comforts and luxuries most law-abiding citizens *must* work long and hard to attain. Corresponding to the public's misperceptions about the jail is a misguided opinion that anyone incarcerated in a jail must be guilty of a crime, even if they have yet to be formally adjudicated by the courts. There is also the subliminal belief that "criminals" should suffer from their incarceration more than just a loss of liberty. Subjection to inhumane jail conditions is viewed by some citizens as a meaningful component of the "criminal's" punishment.

For those people who work within the nation's jails, the situation is not much better. Research reveals that, in general, corrections officers are a disaffected group. Symptoms of their plight include low job satisfaction, cynicism, alienation, job stress, high attrition and absenteeism (Farmer, 1977; Poole and Regoli, 1981; Shamir and Drory, 1982; Cullen, et al., 1985; Jurick and Winn, 1986).[1] In part, the same factors that make jail incarceration a violent and brutal experience for inmates make the work and the work environment violent and brutal for custodial personnel. Although officers are separated from inmates by heavy metal bars, they are not protected from the gibes and jeers of inmates, the occasional cup of urine thrown at them as they patrol the housing units or the fear that comes from having to work in an environment that appears to be uncontrolled and uncontrollable. Nor are they immune to the frustrations attendant on the meager salary and low status associated with custodial work.

Although for years American jails have successfully eluded reform efforts, the costliness of maintaining the status quo is increasingly apparent. Lawsuits initiated by inmates and staff, intervention by activist courts, vandalism and property damage, and high staff turnover are all costs associated with antiquated

---

[1] While many who write about jails and jail conditions argue that custodial personnel within these facilities suffer from low job satisfaction, cynicism, alienation, job stress, high attrition and absenteeism, their claims have yet to be empirically validated. The fact is that very little research has been conducted on the problems experienced by custodial personnel in jails. There does exist, however, an extensive body of literature on custodial work and custodial workers in prisons that can be reasonably, and cautiously, generalized to jail personnel. Many similarities exist between custodial work in both institutions—particularly in regard to the nature of the work, the clientele, the organization and the work environment. If anything, these personnel-related maladies would be magnified in the jail due to the numerous and pervasive organizational, administrative and environmental problems. These problems will be discussed in more detail in Chapter 3.

physical facilities and deficient inmate management practices. For a small number of jail administrators, consultants and architects, the pressures toward jail reform provided an opportunity to question traditional assumptions about incarceration and to reevaluate the practice of inmate management in local detention facilities. From this reevaluation emerged the New Generation, podular/direct supervision design for jail facility architecture and inmate management.[2] The introduction of the new philosophy represents a radical departure from past custodial practices and is the most thoroughgoing innovation in institutional corrections in decades. Proponents claim that the podular architectural design and the direct supervision inmate management system prescribed by the new philosophy alleviate many of the deficiencies of traditional architecture and inmate management, and, in consequence, provide a safer and more humane environment for inmates and staff.

The New Generation Approach

Between 1973 and 1983, during the height of the jail reform movement, 1,000 new jail facilities were built in the United States (Nelson and O'Toole, 1983). Despite claims that the newly constructed facilities were "state-of-the-art" and on the "cutting edge," most were designed in a traditional linear/intermittent surveillance style that dates back to the eighteenth century. Linear refers to the architectural design of the facility while intermittent surveillance refers to the style of inmate supervision. Typically, linear facilities are rectangular in shape with single or multiple-occupancy cells aligned along corridors; the corridors are situated at acute angles to create a spoke-like effect. The nature of the linear architectural design has important implications for the operations of the facility, particularly with regard to how inmates are supervised and managed by the custodial staff.

In the traditional linear facility, continuous supervision of inmate activities by custodial staff is difficult, if not impossible. There are extended periods of time during which inmates are left unsupervised by staff. The underlying assumption of the linear/intermittent surveillance design is that heavy metal doors, bars and various security devices prevent inmate escapes and assaults on staff,

---

2   While many in the field of corrections refer to all newly constructed jail facilities as "New Generation," this use of the term is incorrect. "New Generation" refers only to jail facilities with a "podular" architectural design and direct inmate supervision by custodial staff. Within the context of this study, the term "New Generation" will be used to denote a philosophy of correctional thought that includes a distinctive set of theoretical assumptions, concepts and principles. "Podular/direct supervision" or "direct supervision" will be used to denote the application or implementation of the New Generation philosophy. Hence, "New Generation" is theoretical while "podular/direct supervision" is applied.

and that indestructible furnishings and fixtures prevent serious inmate vandalism. Experience has shown, however, that the physical structure of the facility is limited in controlling inmate behavior. It cannot prevent assaults, rapes, or even homicides between unsupervised inmates assigned to multiple-occupancy cells or who are in isolated areas of the common dayroom or tank. It cannot prevent formation of inmate groups or gangs, inmate suicides, vandalism or property damage. In sum, the linear/intermittent surveillance architectural design cannot prevent the types of behavior and activity that make jail incarceration a brutal and violent experience for inmates, and, in fact, the structure of the facility actually contributes to institutional disorder by providing opportunities for inmates to engage in aberrant behavior without fear of detection.

In contrast to the traditional, linear/intermittent surveillance jail design, the podular/direct supervision style of architecture and inmate management is designed to reduce opportunities for aberrant inmate behavior while simultaneously reducing the "need" for inmates to engage in such activities. Underlying the New Generation philosophy is the assumption that inmates engage in violent and destructive behavior in order to control and manipulate a physical environment and organizational operations which fail to provide for their critical human needs. Proponents of this philosophy argue that through appropriate architecture and inmate management practices providing for critical needs (safety, privacy, personal space, activity, familial contact, social relations and dignity) the inmates' inclination and need to engage in illegitimate behavior will be greatly reduced.

The architecture and interior design of the podular/direct supervision facility are based on a body of knowledge concerning the effect of architecture on human behavior; the facility design reflects this body of knowledge and differs significantly from the design of traditional linear jails. First, inmates are divided into small and manageable groups of between 16 and 46, and housed in living areas called modules. Second, the modules are designed to enhance custodial staff observation, supervision and interaction with inmates. Third, furnishings and accoutrements within the modules function to reduce inmate stress associated with crowding, idleness, noise, lack of privacy, fear of victimization, and isolation from the outside world. Fourth, bars and metal doors are noticeably absent from the modules, effectively reducing noise and the dehumanization typically associated with coercive, custodial institutional designs.

In addition to significant architectural differences, traditional and podular/direct supervision facilities differ in the level and quality of supervision imposed on inmates. The inmate management style of the New Generation philosophy is predicated on the belief that inmates must be continuously and directly supervised by custodial staff to prevent opportunities for illicit inmate behavior and activities, and to reinforce *institutional* as opposed to *inmate* control. To achieve continuous and direct custodial supervision, the living modules are staffed around the clock by corrections officers who receive extensive training in interpersonal communication and relations, as well as principles of supervision, crisis and conflict management, problem-solving and other human relations subjects. In tandem, the architecture and inmate management style of the podular/direct supervision design function to reduce both opportunity and need for inmates to engage in illicit behavior.

Although jails ascribing to the New Generation philosophy have been in operation within the federal prison system for almost 15 years, and in various local jurisdictions for as long as 10 years, little is known about how the philosophy has been operationalized and implemented through the architecture and operations of on-line podular/direct supervision facilities. Of critical concern is how custodial personnel implement direct-supervision inmate management. The extant literature on the New Generation philosophy suggests that effective inmate management is achieved through the ability of the custodial staff member to maintain "total control," to "communicate effectively," and to be a "good leader" (Nelson and O'Toole, 1983). Yet little is known about how corrections officers implement these general principles in the day-to-day supervision of inmates. Little is also known about the impact of the new architectural design and inmate management style on inmates and the custodial staff. Although proponents claim that podular/direct supervision facilities provide a safer and more humane environment for both inmates and staff, this assertion has yet to be empirically validated.

The lack of knowledge about the New Generation jail philosophy and its effectiveness is particularly critical given the growing popularity of the philosophy. In the last several years a number of local jurisdictions have committed resources to erecting New Generation, podular/direct supervision facilities. Multnomah County, Oregon; Clark County, Nevada; Contra Costa County, California; Pima County, Arizona; Prince George's County, Maryland; Bucks County, Pennsylvania; Larimer County, Colorado; New York City, New York; and Dade County, Florida, are but a few of the communities that have built or are in the process of building direct supervision facilities. The lack of quality literature and research on the philosophy is surprising, given the fact that these and other jurisdictions throughout the country are investing millions of dollars to construct New Generation detention facilities on the still unverified claim that they are safer and more secure than traditional jails.

The New Generation philosophy of jail architecture and inmate management was developed in order to resolve age-old custodial dilemmas that make safe and humane incarceration problematic. While it is imperative that research evaluating the effectiveness of the new approach be presented, the exact nature of the solution offered by the New Generation philosophy must first be thoroughly defined. Although a fairly coherent body of prescriptive literature exists on the New Generation philosophy, what is lacking is a thorough evaluation of how this philosophy is operationalized and implemented in the architecture and daily operations of on-line podular/direct supervision jail facilities. In essence, the paucity of research on New Generation jails raises questions as to how the theoretically oriented philosophy is converted into a coherent program for implementation. Therefore, this work presents evaluations focusing on two critical issues: how the New Generation philosophy is implemented in the architectural design and inmate management style of the jail facility; and, how the philosophy impacts the quality of institutional life experienced by both inmates and staff within the new facilities.

Before turning to a discussion of the New Generation philosophy, it is first necessary to review the problems currently plaguing American jails and the history of their development. The modern jail is surely a product of its past. As such, the problems that the New Generation philosophy presumes to resolve are deeply rooted in centuries of neglect, mismanagement, and misuse.

Four distinctive themes in the history of modern jails help to explain their current state. The first theme concerns the origin of the problems plaguing jails. From their earliest days, jails were violent, brutal and unsanitary institutions in which prisoners were degraded and violated by their conditions. In large part, administrative and fiscal arrangements were responsible for these conditions. A second theme concerns the "dumping ground" nature of the jail. Soon after their introduction, jails emerged as catch-all institutions into which were thrown those for whom no other care or treatment facilities were available. Children, the physically ill, and the insane were often imprisoned in jail along with common criminals. The third theme pertains to the role played by the jail in the control of the poor and other perceived enemies of the ruling class. From its earliest years, the jail was used to control a new class within English society, the vagrant. Over time the jail continued to serve as a powerful tool of social control, particularly against those in society who were seen as threats to the establishment. A final theme concerns the stubborn immunity of the jail to change. Throughout its history, attempts at reform were undertaken to correct and improve jail conditions. Despite these reform efforts, the jail institution remained relatively unchanged.

Chapter Two

The Origins of the Jail

As with many social institutions in America, the origin of the jail can be traced to medieval English practices. Jails originally developed out of the need to house accused offenders until the King's court could be convened in the county and were also used to hold convicted offenders until punishment could be meted out. Although the jail (referred to in early English society as the "gaol") can be traced back to the tenth century, Mattick (1974:782) writes that "wherever the chief or other effective governmental authority was able to exercise the power or right to impose punishment, a concomitant necessity was to provide or build holding places until the punishment could be imposed or carried out." Hence, from the earliest times there was a need to detain individuals and "unscalable pits, dungeons, suspended cases, and sturdy trees to which prisoners were chained pending trial" (Mattick, 1974:782-783) were among the earliest forms of pretrial detention preceding the jail. Once the jail was introduced, it rapidly replaced other modes of detainment. In 1166, King Henry II "enjoined all sheriffs to ensure that in all counties where no gaols existed gaols should now be built" as places in which the accused could be held (Pugh, 1968:4). By the middle of the twelfth century, jails were in use in most counties and in many cities. Private jails were also maintained by the church. Known as Bishop Prisons, these institutions were run by archbishops, bishops or other church officials, and housed servants of the church and individuals accused of committing ecclesiastical offenses (Babington, 1971).

Although the gaol originated as a place to hold the accused until their trial, as early as 1272, a number of statutes authorized imprisonment as punishment for certain offenses (Babington, 1971). In 1285, for example, the punishment for a lawyer who perjured himself before the court was one year in the gaol

(Babington, 1971).   The typical period of imprisonment dictated by these statutes was a year or a year and a day.

At their inception and thereafter, jails were locally erected and administered institutions. Although formally under the jurisdiction and control of the crown, the king offered no monies for construction or operation of the gaols. As the king's chief administrative officer within the shires (later known as counties) the sheriff was charged with the responsibility of detaining the accused. The sheriff was usually a member of the noble, landowning class who was appointed to office by the king. The position itself was usually passed from generation to generation within select families. But despite the pomp and ceremony attendant on the office, it entailed little work or responsibility (Burns, 1975; Moynahan and Stewart, 1980). Consequently, sheriffs contracted with "keepers" to maintain custody of inmates and to ensure that they did not escape. The contract was either purchased by the keeper or was granted as patronage by the sheriff. Although the keeper was paid no salary, the contract was considered desirable in that it provided the keeper an income from fees charged inmates and the contract itself could be sold for an exorbitant price.

Jail operations were financed through a system of fees imposed upon inmates and paid to the keepers. In addition to these fees, the keeper profited by selling goods produced by inmates or by selling their labor. While the contract was profitable for the keepers, their responsibilities towards inmates were minimal. Keepers were under no obligation to keep the jail clean or in repair. Nor were they responsible for providing adequate care to inmates. Their sole responsibility was to keep inmates from escaping.

For the most part, inmates in early English jails were forced to support themselves. In order to earn the money necessary to pay the keeper's fees and to survive incarceration, inmates were allowed to beg and could accept money from friends and charitable donations. It was not uncommon for charitable individuals, aware of the conditions of deprivation existing in the local gaols, to bequeath sums of money in their wills for the provision of food and clothing for prisoners. Infrequently, the county provided inmates with small allowances. Industrious and hardworking inmates could produce and sell their own handiwork.

The history of the "fee system" is one of continuous abuse. Although the fee system was not initially sanctioned through statute, it was an ancient custom practiced in most jails, though its applications varied from jail to jail. The system required inmates to pay for every service and good provided by the keeper. They were required to pay a fee to be booked into the jail. An additional sum was charged if they desired mattresses, and there were yet more fees for beds and bedclothes. Even after courts mandated their release, inmates were required to pay a fee before the keeper would allow them to leave the confines of the jail.

In what amounted to extortion, the keepers could make incarceration for the rich a minor irritation, while incarceration for the poor could be fatal. In essence, the fee system required people to "pay for the privilege of being in jail" (Burns, 1975:148). Although the amount of the fees was determined by the inmate's economic status and the seriousness of the offense, the fee system put its greatest burden on the poor. Individuals of means who found themselves incarcerated in the jail could virtually ensure that their imprisonment be without deprivation. If one had the funds, the keeper could even be paid to allow prisoners to live outside the jail or to live with their families in private, opulently furnished suites. Other inmates paid their keepers a fee to be temporarily released to steal the money necessary to afford incarceration. For those who could not afford to pay the fees, jail meant complete deprivation. Although begging proceeds or charitable donations provided some relief, many poor prisoners died from starvation (Harding, et al., 1985:41).

Early English gaols were commonly constructed of wood. In some towns, the gaol consisted of a shed set under the city walls or attached to a castle (Babington, 1971). The structure was often insecure and escape was quite easily accomplished. To compensate for the structural deficiencies, prisoners were often weighed down by manacles, fetters and shackles, and iron collars, for which they also paid the keeper a fee for the privilege of wearing. So confining were the bonds, prisoners had difficulty in lying down or even sitting comfortably.

The typical gaol was divided into two sections. The "master's side" was primarily for the more well-to-do prisoners. The accommodations offered graduated levels of luxury and comfort according to the amount of money a prisoner could afford to pay for rent (Babington, 1971). The "common side" was for the penniless prisoners. For these prisoners, the living conditions were often literally intolerable. Young and old, men and women, healthy and ill, felons and debtors were forced to live communally. The lack of segregation, particularly according to sex, and the excess of liquor that could be purchased by prisoners from the keepers, produced what one scholar called an "orgy of sexual promiscuity" among prisoners. In some cases, women prisoners benefited from the consequences of sexual freedom in the gaol. In one documented case, the execution of a female prisoner was delayed for over 18 months. Each time she was to be executed, she was pregnant (Harding, et al., 1985:40). More often than not, women prisoners suffered from the lack of segregation. It was not uncommon for female prisoners to be raped by their male keepers or by other inmates (Harding, et al., 1985:40).

The lack of even the barest necessities for survival gave rise to the practice of "garnishment" among inmates. On arrival to the gaol, a new prisoner was required to pay a fee to other prisoners. The practice of garnishment was accepted by the keeper, who often took a portion of the garnish for himself, along with all the other fees he collected from the new prisoner. If the fee was not paid or if the person could not afford to pay, other prisoners would literally strip the clothes from the back of the new inmate. Since it was not uncommon for prisoners to wear the same set of clothing for years until they were mere shreds of material, the only hope the more impoverished prisoners had for acquiring less threadbare clothing was by taking it as garnish from new arrivals.

It was not unheard of for untried prisoners to wait for years to appear before the court. During the reign of Henry II (1154- 1189), itinerant judges began to hold court in the local counties at regular intervals. However, inadequacies in transportation and communication made it difficult for the itinerant judges to fulfill their schedules. And, in one location, the local Assize Court met only once every seven years (Howard, 1960).

Overcrowding was also a critical problem in English gaols. Not only did overcrowding aggravate the conditions in which prisoners lived but it severely taxed the resources of the gaol, particularly the food supply. Even though inmates were required to pay for their food, local famines, poor harvests, and the presence of robbers who regularly stole food that was enroute to the jail, severely strained the gaol's food supply. As a result of both the food shortage and overcrowding, many prisoners died in the gaol before reaching the courts. In 1306, the Warwick gaol was "so full of prisoners that many of them have died and die from day to day" (quoted in Harding, et al., 1985:41). Newgate gaol, in 1341, was so "full of prisoners that they are continually dying of hunger and oppression" (quoted in Harding, et al., 1985:41).

Another continuing problem in the gaols was that of disease—particularly "gaol fever" (now believed to be a form of typhus). Whether illness was brought in by other prisoners, diseased rats or other vermin that frequented the gaol, or whether it fermented within the gaol as a consequence of inadequate ventilation and sanitation, the damp and cold conditions in which prisoners were housed and the lack of adequate diet made them particularly susceptible to illness and disease. Prisoners were also not immune to the various epidemics or health threats that existed outside the jail, as evidenced at the Fleet gaol in London.

> The moat which has been constructed around the Fleet in the fourteenth century, ten feet wide and deep enough to take a boat laden with a tun [sic] of wine, was filled with effluent from various latrines and sewers while butchers used it to deposit cattle entrails, the whole becoming so clogged that it was possible to walk across it. The consequent threat to security and danger to the health of the inmates was a cause of some alarm. Public health measures were the concern of the London council but general legislation was needed in 1388 to deal

with those who cast "annoyances, dung, garbages, entrails and other ordure" into water courses (Harding, et al., 1985:42).

As early as the thirteenth century, jails emerged as "dumping grounds" for social outcasts, misfits and those for whom there were no alternative institutions able to provide care and treatment. Children as young as 4 years of age were incarcerated in gaols for such offenses as theft, sheep stealing and homicide because there were no alternative institutions (Harding, et al., 1985).[1] Also incarcerated were the insane and the diseased, particularly lepers. Superstition and charity forbade their execution. Instead, they were isolated from the community in the local gaol where they would often spend the remainder of their lives.

While the gaol was evolving into a catch-all institution for confinement of the young and the ill, it was also developing as a weapon with which English rulers could control a new class of citizenry, the vagrant. Irwin (1985:4) argued that the jail emerged as a tool of royal social control concurrent with the breakdown of traditional feudalism and the passing of the Dark Ages:

> The need for this new institution arose from a great increase in the number of detached persons. At this time, England, along with all of Europe, was moving out of feudalism with its isolated, mostly autonomous fiefdoms. By the late eleventh century Muslim control of the Mediterranean had ended, and trade once again began to connect European populations and to result in the cultivation of urban centers. New towns appeared, and towns grew into cities. European kings began reestablishing and extending their hegemonies. After having remained stable for centuries, the population in most parts of Europe was increasing. At the same time, the feudal system was unraveling. More and more persons were cut loose from the land and from the two basic social organizations of the agricultural society, the family and the tribe.

The economic upheaval of the era and the resulting dissolution of ties to the land and the family produced a troublesome number of "outlaws who lived by robbing, plundering, poaching, and smuggling," and who, once arrested, could not be trusted to appear in court (Irwin, 1985:4). Consequently, detain-

---

[1] Harding, et al, (1985:36) recount two cases of the very young incarcerated for murder. In one case, "Katherine Passeavant, aged four, was imprisoned in 1249 after accidentally killing another child by knocking it into a vat of hot water by opening a door." In a second case cited by the authors, "Alice le Ster who was six when she accidentally knocked a stone over a cliff with fatal consequences had to wait fourteen years between her remand to gaol and the granting of her pardon."

ment of these individuals within the gaol was necessary to insure their presence when judgment was passed against them.

As time passed, however, the problems associated with the growing number of displaced, unemployed and poor persons increased. In order to control this rabble, "English rulers passed more and more laws designed to...stop their incursions on private property, and, when shortages of labor existed, to assign them to low-paid productive work" (Irwin, 1985:6). Between 1349 and 1743, a series of vagrancy laws were passed to make it easier to imprison the unemployed and the poor. Through the use of jail incarceration, the state could manage the threat such persons might pose to the established order.

Attempts to improve jail conditions were undertaken as early as 1702. In that year, the Society for the Promotion of Christian Knowledge investigated the conditions of gaols in London. Their exhaustive proposals, however, were never published (Howard, 1960). A government committee, appointed in 1729 to report on the condition of all the kingdom's gaols, also had little effect (Howard, 1960). The most well-known and influential champion of reform was John Howard (1726-1790). As the Sheriff of Bedfordshire, Howard saw first-hand the suffering prisoners endured while confined to local gaols. Howard's recommendations for reform are now legendary:

(1) segregation of prisoners by age and sex and severity of crime;

(2) cells for prisoners so moral and physical contamination could be reduced;

(3) salaried staff to prevent the extortion of prisoners;

(4) appointment of chaplains and medical officers for the spiritual and physical well-being of the prisoners;

(5) prohibitions against the sale of ale and liquor to prisoners; and,

(6) provision of adequate clothing and food to prisoners to ensure their continued good health (Howard, 1960).

Although Howard's writings aroused public and political interest in gaol and prison reform, it was not until years after his death that improvements were made in gaol conditions (Howard, 1960).

Introduction of the Jail to the New World

The jail was introduced to the New World by English settlers who also brought with them their homeland's system of shires or counties and the practice of local jail administration by a county sheriff. As with the British gaols, the first American jails were used to detain alleged criminal offenders before trial or sentencing. In addition, the jail was used to house the convicted offenders until a sentence of death could be carried out. The first jail system in America was established in Virginia soon after the founding of Jamestown in 1606 (Burns, 1975:149).

The fee system was introduced with the jail. In 1626, the fee for admission to, or release from, a Virginia jail was two pounds of tobacco (Burns, 1975:149). With the fee system came many of the abuses that were prevalent in England. County sheriffs charged exorbitant fees. The rich could escape from jail incarceration altogether or, at the least, spend their time in luxury. Charles Sutton (1874:95), warden of the New York County Jail, commonly referred to as "The Tombs," wrote admirably of the conditions under which one well-to-do prisoner in The Tombs waited for the outcome of his murder trial:

> In a patent extension chair he lolls, smoking an aromatic Havana, while he reads the proceedings of his trial the day previous in the morning's paper. He has an elegant dressing gown on, faced with cherry colored silk, and his feet are encased in delicately worked slippers, the gift of one of his lady friends. His clothes are neat, and up in style to the latest fashion plate. He is cleanly shaven, and has a general air of high-tonedness about him which is quite refreshing. To one side of him is his bed—a miracle of comfort...Then comes his lunch—not cooked in the prison, but brought in from a hotel. It consists of a variety of dishes, such as quail on toast, game pates, reed birds, ortolans, fowl, the newest vegetables, coffee, cognac, etc.; and then it is back again to easy chair, book and segar [sic].

While rich prisoners often lived in opulent splendor, "it was not uncommon for individuals with no resources to die of starvation" (Burns, 1975:153). As in the English gaol, the poor suffered the most deprivation during their incarceration.

Conditions in most American jails equaled those found in English gaols. In addition to extortion by jailers, inmates were subjected to "demoralizing idleness and the corrupting intermingling of all classes" (Burns, 1975:153-154). Segregation according to age, sex, race, offense, criminal history, and mental or physical state was unheard of in early American jails. In theory, prisoners were to be cared for and treated in accordance with common law tradition. Sir William Blackstone defined this to mean that prisoners be treated with the "utmost humanity, and neither be loaded with needless fetters, or subjected to other hardships than such as are absolutely requisite for the purpose of confinement only" (quoted in Jordan, 1970:145). In practice, however, humanitarian treatment was difficult at best, given the scant resources allocated for prisoner care. Although by the late eighteenth century the fee system had been modified so that the local government paid for inmate provisions, the monies were often inadequate.

> Tennessee sheriffs, for example, in 1796 were paid 25 cents a day per prisoner and for this sum were required to provide a daily ration of one pound of wholesome bread, one pound of good roasted or broiled fish, and a sufficient quantity of fresh water. During the 1820s, prisoners in Alabama county jails were fed on 50 cents a day. Some twenty years later, Louisiana sheriffs were given 37 1/2 cents a day and ordered to provide a daily allowance of one pound of beef or three-quarters of a pound of pork, one pound of wheaten bread, one pound of potatoes or one gill of rice, and one gill of whisky. Jailers were also obligated to furnish each prisoner, at the beginning of the winter season, a blanket capot, a shirt, a pair of woollen trousers, and a pair of course shoes. In summer, a shirt and a pair of trousers of coarse linen were to be provided. It is interesting to note that Nebraska, in 1867, allotted sheriffs not more than 25 cents a day for feeding prisoners, the same sum that Tennessee paid seventy-one years earlier (Jordan, 1970:146).

In addition to the inadequacy of the monies paid for the maintenance of prisoners, problems arose with keepers pocketing a substantial portion of the fee at the inmates' expense.

> Instead of being paid a salary, the jailer is given a certain sum a day to feed the prisoners in his charge, retaining, as part of his compensation, such portion of his allowance as is not paid out in food for the prisoners. For instance, if a jailer receives fifty cents per day per prisoner and has a daily average of fifty prisoners in his jail, he will get $25 to pay for food. Every cent that he does not pay out for food goes into his own pocket. A more vicious system it would be impossible to conceive—that of one man lining his own pockets in the same degree in which he withholds food from another (Fishman, 1922:797).

In the late eighteenth century, the jail system underwent its first major change in over eight centuries. As a result of the influence of European humanists and rationalists such as Beccaria, Voltaire, Bentham and Romilly, the punishments assessed for criminal offenses underwent considerable change both in America and abroad. The movement was away from the use of corporal and capital punishment for criminal offenses and toward the use of imprisonment as an alternative form of punishment. Prior to the nineteenth century, major criminal offenses were punished by death, mutilation, branding and whipping; minor offenses were punished by public ridicule and humiliation through the use of stocks, the pillory and the ducking stool.[2] The reform of criminal punishment replaced corporal punishment with incarceration in houses of correction or local jails.

In the New World, the earliest penal reform was instituted by the Quaker colony in Pennsylvania founded by William Penn. Prior to the reform, over 200 crimes were punishable by death. The "Great Law of Pennsylvania," enacted in 1682, sought to abolish the use of stocks, the pillory, branding irons and the gallows. Corporal punishment was replaced by imprisonment and fines.

While the reform law itself was without a doubt humanitarian and much needed, it had profound and far-reaching impact on American jail practices. With the abolition of corporal and capital punishment for many minor and major criminal offenses came the need for places to house convicted offenders sentenced to incarceration. In the years following reform, this responsibility fell chiefly to the local jail. Without adequate facilities to allow for the segregation of those awaiting trial from those serving sentences, a new problem developed—the potential "contamination" of the unconvicted by the convicted. In their 1829-1831 study of the American penal system, Gustave de Beaumont and Alexis de Tocqueville (1964:49) criticized the jail on this very point.

He who has not yet been pronounced guilty and he who has committed but a crime or misdemeanor comparatively slight, ought to be surrounded by much greater protection than such as are more advanced in crime and where guilt has been acknowledged. Arrested persons are sometimes innocent and always supposed to be so. How is it that we should suffer them to find in the jail a corruption which they did not bring with them?

In later years, the establishment of houses of corrections and modern day penitentiaries would slowly relieve the jail of its responsibility for all convicted offenders. However, even today the jail remains a place where short-term sentences are served by offenders.[3]

---

[2] A common perception is that stocks and the pillory are nonviolent methods of punishment designed to bring public humiliation to the offender. But, on the contrary, a sentence to stocks or pillory often entailed more than mere confinement for the offender. Burns (1975:82) writes: "If the prisoner or his offense were unpopular, he was likely to be stoned and pelted with rotten vegetables, rotten eggs, and the like. Occasionally, persons were stoned to death. The victim might also be whipped or branded while in the stocks or pillory. When that person was released, he would be compelled either to tear his ears loose from the nails or have them cut away carelessly by the officer in charge."

[3] Some states, such as Washington, have contracted with local jails to house state prisoners (those sentenced to serve a term in prison) in order to deal with overcrowding in prisons. In other

The movement from corporal punishment to the use of imprisonment represented the first and last criminal justice reform to have a significant effect upon the jail (Flynn, 1973:51). With the exception of minor changes such as the juvenile reformatory movement and the establishment of hospitals for the criminally insane in the late nineteenth and early twentieth centuries, and the rise of community-based corrections in the late twentieth century, the jail has remained virtually immune to change throughout its long history. While these changes resulted in the siphoning off of portions of the jail population (e.g., juveniles, the criminally insane and convicted offenders deemed appropriately trustworthy to live in the community under the supervision of a probation officer), their impact on jail conditions was minimal.

This is not to imply that jail reform was not attempted; just that it was limited to the local level and, even then, the improvements were often short-term. The most comprehensive and noteworthy reform effort took place at the Walnut Street Jail in Pennsylvania. Erected in 1773, the Walnut Street Jail was originally built to serve the county and city of Philadelphia. Until 1790, the Jail housed primarily pretrial detainees and prisoners awaiting imposition of their sentences. From 1790 until the Jail closed in 1835, it functioned as both a local detention facility and as a state penitentiary for sentenced offenders.

In its early years, conditions within the Walnut Street Jail were similar to those found in other American jails and English gaols. No effort was made to segregate offenders according to age, sophistication, offense, or even sex. Little attempt was made to restrain the behavior of inmates beyond preventing their escape, and even that often proved too difficult for the jail. To the consternation of city residents, escapes were numerous and often. The fee system was in existence and many inmates existed in a state of near starvation. However, prisoners of means could easily purchase "spirituous liquor" from the jail bar and sexual intercourse from prostitutes who "secured their own arrest upon fictitious charges in order that they might ply their trade among the inmates of the jail" (Barnes, 1927:148).

Spurred by the reform activities of the Philadelphia Society for Alleviating the Miseries of Public Prisons, a group of citizens concerned with prison welfare, laws were passed in 1789 and 1790 to improve conditions within the Walnut Street Jail. Male prisoners were segregated from female prisoners. Debtors were segregated from criminals. A rudimentary classification system was implemented. The sale and use of alcohol was prohibited. The fee system was abolished and food and clothing were provided to all inmates regardless of their ability to pay. Medical care was provided during a physicians weekly visit.

states where prison overcrowding is severe and where the courts have ordered prisons to reduce their populations, local jails have been forced to hold state prisoners only because the prisons refuse to accept them. The effect of the spillover from state prisons to jails will be discussed in more detail in Chapter 3.

Religious services were held every Sunday and all inmates were required to attend. Prison industries were instituted. Inmates were paid a wage for their labor and were allowed to keep all earnings above their maintenance costs. Progressive discipline was implemented and a system of rewards and punishments was used to control inmate behavior. A Board of Inspectors was appointed by the mayor and aldermen of Philadelphia to supervise the prison and to inspect the conditions and operations of the jail on a weekly basis.

Soon after implementation of these changes, the Walnut Street Jail was optimistically being heralded as a successful and pioneering experiment in jail reform. It was claimed that the new system had both a reformatory and deterrent effect on prisoners (Barnes, 1927:151). Visitors to the jail expressed surprise at the cleanliness of the facility and the industriousness of the prisoners. Productive inmates were earning money not only for their future release but also to help support their families.

By 1816, twenty-six years after passage of the reform acts, conditions within the Walnut Street Jail had deteriorated to the point that they were little better than before the reform effort, the only exception being that liquor was still prohibited and prisoners were still segregated by sex and offense. The deterioration is credited to two factors: the failure of local officials to provide appropriate accommodations for the burgeoning jail population and inmate idleness caused by a fire that destroyed the jail's industry shops.

Modern American Jails

If, as Winston Churchill suggested, "the sophistication of a society may be judged by the way in which it treats its prisoners," many communities in the United States would be deemed provincial. Although in the past century, new and massive jail facilities have been built, complicated locking systems implemented and elaborate surveillance techniques devised as a reflection of the increasingly complex technological society in which we live, the modern jail still retains elements of the inhumane conditions and custodial practices that prevailed in early English goals.

One of the most disparaged jails in the United States is Chicago's Cook County Jail. In 1923, federal prison inspector Joseph Fishman (1923:247) described the Cook County Jail as a "synonym for everything that is vicious in our jail system." For Dorothy West, who spent eight weeks in 1968 in the jail on the charge of armed robbery, the experience included her assault and rape by other inmates. Her degradation began when she and six other women were booked into the jail. All were given vaginal examinations by a doctor who did not bother to sterilize the instruments between patients. Her living quarters consisted of a filthy, cramped cell that she shared with five other inmates, "plus an assortment of cockroaches, rats and waterbugs" (1972:155). Upon her arrival, her cellmate searched her purse, taking her money, toothbrush and a change of underwear. Dinner that first evening consisted of pig's tails, undercooked lima beans and cocoa. That night an inmate in West's area began to hemorrhage and was taken to the infirmary. Sometime before morning the woman died without ever receiving medical attention.

Soon after West was admitted to the jail, there was a "shakedown" of the facility during which each cell was searched for illegal weapons and contraband. A rumor surfaced that the search was instigated after West had informed on other inmates. That evening her mattress and hair were set on fire by other inmates. Following this attack, other rumors circulated that she was being held in jail as a state witness in a well-publicized murder case. Fearful because of threats from other prisoners, West requested that the matron place her in protective custody. The matron laughed and told her she was being a "silly girl." The night before she was to appear in court, while the four matrons on duty were in other areas of the jail, West was attacked by eight other inmates.

> Ruby's first blow caught me on the side of my head. As soon as she hit me, a scream went up from the others. "Kill the stool-pigeon bitch." All eight of them fell on me at once. Somebody set fire to my skirt, and my nylon petticoat went up in flames. I tried to beat at my burning legs, but they were banging my head against the bars. I felt my nose crumple, and start to gush blood. I fell and they kicked me repeatedly in the left eye. They kicked my breasts and jumped up and down on me. Then somebody pulled off my panties, thrust them into my mouth as a gag, and I was raped. My hair was burning and I could feel the skin on my forehead crack and begin to peel. I'm told the beating went on for an hour (1972:157).

The matrons responded to the attack by calling West a "troublemaker." They poured iodine on her wounds and locked her in the "hole" without further medical attention. When West attempted to file a complaint with the warden of the Cook County Jail she was accused of being a "nut" who had hurt herself while attempting suicide. Given a suspended sentence and probation for the armed robbery charge, West was released from the jail with "bruises all over [her] body, a broken nose, a bad concussion and infections from the burns" (1972:157). For some time after her release, West suffered from impaired vision and needed to wear dentures to replace her broken teeth.

While West's experience is shocking in its savagery, it is far from unique. In a 1968 expose on the jail, journalist Bill Davidson (1968) uncovered a shocking number of examples of violence and mayhem in the Cook County Jail, including: a 14-year-old boy who was housed with adult males and continually raped while jail guards paid no attention to his screams; a series of unaccounted-for deaths that were ruled suicides but were, by all indications, homicides; a newly admitted inmate who died from pneumonia due to a lack of medical attention; guards who unlocked cell doors to permit "barn bosses" to rape other inmates; organized crime figures who had the run of the jail, one of whom had his laundry handwashed by guards, was given specially prepared meals and was allowed to conduct his illegal operations from the chaplain's office.

Although in all accounts Cook County Jail is the most notorious of American jails, studies and reports indicate that conditions in other facilities are not much better. Attorney Ronald Goldfarb (1966) toured the Washington, D.C., jail and later wrote that the facility resembled a "human stockyard." The jail was seriously overcrowded. There was one guard for every 350 prisoners. Homosexuality was rampant, as was sodomy and rape. Inmates who could not afford bail seemed to be altogether forgotten by jail officials. Two men were in jail for almost a year without ever having been indicted.

A court-ordered investigation of the Philadelphia Prison (Jail) System, conducted by the Philadelphia District Attorney's office and the Police Department in 1968, revealed that sexual assault, particularly gang-rape, among jail inmates was a relatively common occurrence (Davis, 1968). The investigators documented and substantiated 156 incidents of sexual assault among a 20% sample of inmates who passed through the jail system between June, 1966 and July, 1968. It was suggested that if the investigators had studied all inmates admitted to the jail during the 26-month time period they would have discovered hundreds of additional assaults. The investigators also learned that in one case, a guard ignored the screams of a prisoner being gang-raped in his cell and that many of the guards actively dissuaded victims from reporting the assaults for fear that it would make the officers look bad.

In the 1960s, the arrest and subsequent jailing of middle class youths during civil rights and Vietnam War protests and demonstrations stimulated a number of reports on local jail conditions. One such article was written by Gloria Wade Bishop, a black woman who was arrested in 1964 during a civil rights demonstration in Atlanta, Georgia. Bishop recounted the conditions she and her fellow protesters were subjected to during their brief stay in the Atlanta jail:

> The cellblock in which we were confined was composed of two sections: a front eating area of two benches and four solitary-confinement cells, and a back sleeping area of sixty-two beds. The beds were covered with bug-infested mattresses and filthy blue sheets. In the sleeping area were four seatless, unclean, and tissueless toilets. Tissue is issued only when the prisoner requests it from the matron, who must then go to a supply room, secure the tissue, and bring it to the

cellblock. Meals in the jail corresponded to the physical condition of
the cells. For breakfast we were given strips of salty, shriveled-up,
greasy, fried fatback; for lunch, overcooked, unseasoned, souplike
beans, and for dinner, the same beans. Most of us found the food
inedible, but we accepted our share and gave it to other cellmates.
Cellmates who were not demonstrators were mostly drunks and lesbians, many of whom came into the cell without shoes and wearing
torn and badly soiled clothes. Most disturbing to us was not the
swearing drunks and the strong odor of cheap wines, but the flirting
lesbians who fondled some of the teen-agers. One night we saw two
highly intoxicated women make love on a back bunk, and numerous
times we were told by one lesbian or another, "I'm gonna git you
tonight." Such a threat was almost carried out when one of the lesbians pulled a teen-age girl from a top bunk in an attempt to make
love to her. Complaints were made against the lesbians, but the jailer
made no effort to separate them from the young girls (Bishop,
1964:68-69).

The protesters were transferred to the "stockade" in the middle of the night,
where, when they protested over starting work at 1:30 in the morning, they were
thrown into "the hole."

Located behind the white men's dressing rooms, the hole is a small
windowless, bedless room of approximately four by eight feet and approximately ten feet high. Overhead, a bright light burns constantly,
making it difficult to sleep or to distinguish night from day. The fea-
ture of the hole that disturbed us most was the lack of toilet facilities;
we had to use the concrete floor and had no tissue. Two of us were
placed in one hole, two in another, and three in still another. The hole
in which sixteen-year-old Patricia and I were confined smelled like a
recently used rural outhouse. On the floor were many cigarette butts,
two tobacco pouches, fallen plaster, and other trash. Large black
roaches crawled around boldly. Two hours after being in the hole, we
were given our first meal: one biscuit and a cup of water. The bis-
cuits were placed on the floor on top of the fallen plaster, cigarette
butts, and dried urine (Bishop, 1964:69).

After spending four and a half days in jail, 25 hours of which was spent in the stockade, Wade and the other protesters were released. She concluded the account of her jail experience with the comment:

> What a relief that the door was shutting us, not inside as before, but outside where the air was free from the odor of urine and the smell of too obvious inhumanity...I was once again free (Bishop, 1964:70).

Chapter Three

The Persistent Problems Plaguing Modern Jails

The Law Enforcement Assistance Administration defines the jail as "any facility operated by a local government for the detention or correction of adults suspected or convicted of a crime and which has authority to detain longer than forty-eight hours" (quoted in Flynn, 1973:55). As the "hybrid" of American correctional institutions, the jail's role is two-fold: to act as a "way-station" for those awaiting action by other components of the criminal justice system, and to act as a penal institution for those who have been convicted and sentenced to less than one year's incarceration. This dual role gives the jail jurisdiction over a broad range of people. Inmates of a jail may include people awaiting trial, arraignment or sentencing; those serving sentences of less than one year; and persons who are awaiting transfer to other jurisdictions or correctional institutions. On any given day, 49% of the people in jail are serving sentences while 51% are pretrial detainees who have yet to be convicted of a crime but are detained because they cannot raise the funds necessary for bail or because they are deemed a risk by the courts (U.S. Department of Justice, 1990:4).[1]

---

[1] For years, in keeping with the judicial axiom that an individual was presumed innocent until proved guilty, bail was routinely granted to any criminal offender. In cases where it was probable that the defendant would not appear in court, bail was set exceedingly high to ensure that it could not be met. However, the 1984 Bail Reform Act included provisions for "preventative detention," that allowed courts to deny bail to some federal suspects. The law was directed at organized crime suspects and drug dealers who, in most cases, could afford to meet high bail. In May, 1987, the U.S. Supreme Court upheld the preventative detention aspect of the Act, paving the way for states to pass similar laws (*Time*, 1987:69).

Although the jail is the oldest of American penal institutions, it is the least studied of all correctional institutions.[2] Only since 1970 have statistics on jail populations been systematically collected at the national level. In 1970, the National Criminal Justice Information and Statistics Service completed the first comprehensive census of county and city jails. Subsequent censuses were conducted by the Bureau of Justice Statistics in 1973, 1978, 1983, and 1988, and are planned for subsequent five-year periods.

From these censuses we know that approximately 9.7 million people are incarcerated annually in the nation's 3,316 jails. About 343,000 people are in jail on any given day—roughly equivalent to the entire 1984 population of Toledo, Ohio (U.S. Department of Justice, 1990). We also know that ethnic minorities, the poor, and the undereducated make up a major proportion of the jail's population. According to the 1978 Census of Jails conducted by the Department of Justice, the typical inmate is a young, minority male with an annual income slightly above the "poverty line" as defined by the U.S. government. Fifty-six percent of jail inmates are black or Hispanic (U.S. Department of Justice, 1990). While 1 out of every 10 persons in the general population is black, four out of every 10 male inmates and 5 out of 10 female inmates are black. Forty-five percent of jail inmates have annual incomes below the "poverty line," while one out of four have no source of income and are dependent on welfare, social security or unemployment benefits (U.S. Department of Justice, 1980a:2-7). A majority of jail inmates are high school dropouts. Only 40% of the jail population have completed high school. In contrast, 75% of the general population of comparable age have high school diplomas (U.S. Department of Justice, 1980a:4).

Although sociodemographic data of this nature is necessary to determine who is in American jails, it says little about the nature of jail incarceration or the

---

2   The number of inmates annually incarcerated in jails is approximately 30 times the number of prisoners handled by state and federal prisons (Irwin, 1985:XI). The jail is also the first, and often only, experience people have with incarceration. Yet the jail has been virtually ignored by correctional scholars. In a review of the *Criminal Justice Periodical Index*, Mays and Thompson (1988) find that in a four-year period, fewer than ten articles about jails appeared in scholarly journals. It is not clear why there is such a lack of scholarly interest in jails, as compared to prisons. One reason may be because the transitory nature of inmates makes it difficult to undertake long-term studies of inmate cultures. Another reason may be because jails are such troubled institutions that few want to undertake the task of unraveling their problems. A final reason may be because of difficulty in gaining access to these locally run facilities. Whatever the reasons, Irwin (1985:xi) argues that studies on jails, rather than prisons, are more urgently needed: "First, many more people pass through the jail...Second, when persons are arrested, the most critical decisions about their future freedom are made while they are either in jail or attached to it by a bail bond. These decisions, like the decision to arrest, are often highly discretionary and raise disturbing questions about the whole criminal justice system. Third, the experiences prisoners endure while passing through the jail often drastically influence their lives. Finally, the jail, not the prison, imposes the cruelest form of punishment in the United States."

conditions within these facilities. The information that does exist comes from journalistic exposés, personal narratives of those who have been incarcerated, court documents in cases involving jails, and a handful of scholarly studies. All four sources concur in depicting conditions in most jails as bleak indeed.

In an attempt to understand the nature of the jail situation, the Advisory Commission on Intergovernmental Relations (1984:5) concluded that the " 'jail problem' is not simply a problem—if it were, its solution would probably not be so hard to attain. Rather, the 'jail problem' is a complex collection of problems, including jurisdictional authority and responsibility, constitutional rights, sociological and medical opinions, basic public safety, and perhaps most difficult, the allotment of increasingly scarce resources for the benefit of an exceedingly unpopular constituency." The most commonly cited and serious problems affecting modern American jails are misuse and overuse of detention; decrepit and substandard physical plants; overcrowding; administrative arrangements; staffing and personnel deficiencies; and substandard inmate care and treatment.

Misuse and Overuse of Detention

Soon after their development jails evolved into catchall institutions into which were thrown the ill, the addicted, the young, and other social misfits. Today, jails continue to serve as dumping grounds for society's more troubled members. Alcoholics, the mentally ill, juveniles, and women are among the individuals routinely detained in jails. In many instances, these individuals are incarcerated for offenses that are not fundamentally criminal; their primary offense is that they offend public tastes rather than threatening the safety or well-being of the community. Rather than detaining these individuals because they are a danger to the community or because they might flee prosecution, the jail functions primarily as a mechanism of social sanitation, concealing from public view those members of society who offend and repulse.

The jail, however, is ill-equipped to deal with the special and varied problems of alcoholics, the mentally ill, juveniles, and women. Geared primarily to the goals of custody and security, jails have neither the staff nor the resources to provide for the physical, medical, psychological or social needs of these individuals. The warehouse mentality of the jail makes physical and psychological deterioration inevitable as well as leading to a vulnerability to suicide, medical trauma and victimization by staff and other inmates.

Alcoholics

Street alcoholics, particularly skid row drunks, are vulnerable to arrest by virtue of their being drunk in public. Consequently, they make up a substantial proportion of the jail population. In 1970, the Law Enforcement Assistance Administration estimated that of the 67,000 inmates incarcerated on any given day in the nation's 4,037 local jail facilities, 30,000 were alcoholics (Law Enforcement Assistance Administration, 1971). It is believed that 20% to 40% of the jail population nationwide is incarcerated for public intoxication. The large number of alcoholics in jails is the consequence of a large number of arrests for public drunkenness. One out of every ten arrests in the United States is for public intoxication. According to the Federal Bureau of Investigation's Uniform Crime Reports, an estimated 933,900 arrests were made for drunkenness in 1986. This figure does not include the increasing number of arrests annually made for driving while intoxicated or disorderly conduct, for which public inebriates are often jailed in states which have decriminalized public intoxication. Frequently, the same individuals are arrested and booked into jail over and over again.[3]

The impact of these arrests on the jail is immense, particularly in terms of cost and wasted jail space. It is estimated that 400 million dollars is expended each year in trying and jailing public inebriates (American Correctional Association, 1985). Given the critical problem of jail overcrowding, jailing public inebriates has been criticized as a waste of precious jail space that could be used to detain more serious offenders (American Correctional Association, 1985).

Alcoholic inmates also pose special problems for the jail, particularly with regard to their medical needs. Even a short stay in jail may produce *delirium tremens*, which can be fatal if medical attention is not available. And, not surprisingly, alcoholic inmates suffer from a wide range of other medical problems. In a study of 3,000 public inebriates in New York, researchers found that 50% had wounds, cuts or burns; 25% suffered from seizure disorders; 20% had bone fractures; 20% experienced hallucinations; 20% had severe brain damage; 20% had severe gastrointestinal bleeding; and, 15% had cardiopulmonary problems (American Correctional Association, 1985). Yet the level of medical facilities available to these, as well as other, jail inmates is surprisingly poor. A 1972 American Medical Association (1973:ii) survey found that "65.5% of the responding jails had only first aid facilities, while 16.7% had no internal medical facilities. In only 38% of responding jails were physicians available on a regularly scheduled basis, and in only 50.6% ...were physicians available on an on-call basis. In 31.1% no physicians were available." A more recent study conducted by the National Institute of Justice (U.S. Department of Justice, 1980b:209) reported that 77% of American jails had no medical facilities, 70% did not give inmates medical examinations upon entry into the jail, and only 15% gave medical examinations to those inmates who were "obviously" ill at

---

[3]   At a medium-sized jail in Texas, I was shown the booking record of a middle-aged male who had been arrested and booked into the jail 72 times for public intoxication. On a few occasions, the man was arrested just hours after his release from the jail.

the time of their incarceration. By 1980, only 67 jails in the country were ac-credited by the American Medical Association for meeting the minimum stan-dards of health care. The National Sheriff's Association jail study in 1981 found that only 16.6% of the responding jails had an in-house infirmary and that slightly more than 40% conducted initial medical screening of inmates or took inmates' medical histories.

Alcoholics are also vulnerable to suicide during their jail incarceration. Suicides are more common among inmates in jail for public intoxication and under the influence of alcohol at the time of their incarceration (Hayes, 1983).

Many criminal justice reformers have argued that public drunkenness is a type of offense that is not fundamentally a crime and therefore, should not be under the purview of the criminal justice system (Miller, 1978). Rather than threaten the safety and well-being of the public, street alcoholics offend public tastes. It is recommended that alcoholics be treated for their disease rather than incarcerated. On the heels of this recommendation, many states have acted to decriminalize public drunkenness and to establish public health centers for the detoxification and treatment of alcoholics. However, despite these efforts, pub-lic inebriates continue to be arrested and jailed for such offenses as disorderly conduct, disturbing the peace or littering.[4]

Juveniles

On June 30, 1988, 1,676 juveniles were incarcerated in the nation's jails (U.S. Department of Justice, 1990). Even though many states forbid the practice of incarcerating juveniles in adult detention facilities, over 100,000 juveniles annually pass through adult jails (U.S. Department of Justice, 1988). A study

---

[4] Drug addiction among jail inmates is also a critical issue in jail administration. The 1978 *Pro-file of Jail Inmates* reported that 40% of jail inmates were drug addicts or daily users, 8% used drugs less than daily but at least weekly, and 20% took drugs less than weekly (U.S. Department of Justice, 1980). More recent studies of the extent of drug use among jail inmates are unavail-able; however, data compiled from other sources suggest that the proportion of inmates who use drugs is high. The results from the National Institute of Justice Drug Use Forecasting, for ex-ample, indicates that between 56% and 84% of males arrestees in 16 large cities test positive for drugs and between 58% and 88% of female arrestees test positive (U.S. Department of Justice, 1989). The study also reports that "recent drug use in arrestees is more than 10 times higher than is reported in surveys of persons in households or senior high schools" (U.S. Department of Justice, 1989:2). While many alcoholics are arrested simply because they are intoxicated, most drug users are arrested because they *commit a criminal offense while on drugs*. As with alco-holics, drug-addicted inmates pose special problems for the jail in terms of their medical needs and their susceptibility to suicide. Although narcotic withdrawal is less likely to be fatal than alcohol withdrawal, drug addicts are more likely to successfully commit suicide than are nonad-dicts (U.S. Congress, 1970).

conducted in Minnesota (Schwartz, Harris and Levy, 1988) found that 4,000 juveniles were admitted to the state's jails and police lockups in 1986, a 5% increase in the number admitted the previous year. More surprising was the fact that many were very young. Two hundred and fifty of the youths were 13 years old or younger. The same study found that the majority of the juveniles had committed no crime or only petty offenses.

The incarceration of juveniles in adult jails has been criticized for a number of reasons. First, the co-mingling of adults and juveniles places young people in greater risk of being physically, sexually and mentally abused by adult offenders and defendants (Advisory Commission on Intergovernmental Relations, 1984:12). Juvenile girls, in particular, are vulnerable to sexual assault by jail guards (Chesney-Lind, 1988; Soler, 1988; Children's Defense Fund, 1976).[5] Juveniles are also more susceptible to suicide. For every 100,000 juveniles incarcerated in adult jails, 12 commit suicide. Flaherty (cited in the Advisory Commission on Intergovernmental Relations, 1984:12) noted that "the rate of suicide among children held in adult jails and lockups [is] significantly higher than among children in juvenile detention centers and children in the general population of the United States." Reports indicate that the suicide rate among juveniles in adult jails is 7.7 times higher than among juveniles in juvenile detention centers and 4.6 times higher than among juveniles in the general population (U.S. Department of Justice, 1983b).

The higher rates of suicide can be attributed to a number of factors. First, in jails which have made efforts to conform to the 1974 Juvenile Justice and Delinquency Prevention Act's mandate that juveniles and adults be completely separated during confinement, juveniles are often placed in isolated parts of the jails where they receive little staff support or supervision (Steinhart, 1988). Second, jail staff are typically not trained to recognize signs of severe depression in juveniles. Finally, juvenile girls with a history of sexual and physical abuse may be more vulnerable to depression and suicide while incarcerated (Chesney-Lind, 1988).

The nature of the alleged offenses for which juveniles are incarcerated is also an issue of concern. According to the Children's Defense Fund (1976:3-4), "17.9% of jailed children...had committed 'status offenses,' i.e., actions which would not be crimes if done by adults, such as running away or truancy." The same study found that 4.3% of incarcerated juveniles had committed no crimes

---

5   A number of cases involving the victimization of juveniles in adult facilities have received national media coverage, as well as stimulating litigation against the jails. In Ohio, a 15-year-old girl, ordered by the judge to 5 days in jail to "teach her a lesson," was raped by a jail guard. In Wisconsin, a 13-year-old boy, held in jail for 11 days, was repeatedly beaten by other juveniles while the guard ignored the assault. In Idaho, a 15-year-old boy, jailed for failing to pay $73 in traffic fines, was tortured and beaten to death by other inmates. For a discussion of these cases, see Soler (1988).

but were taken to jail by the police for their own protection and because there were no alternatives available other than jail. Only in 11.7% of the cases were youths incarcerated for having committed serious criminal offenses. In the Minnesota study (Schwartz, Harris and Levi, 1988), most of the juveniles were being held for minor or petty crimes. Twenty-eight percent were confined for public order offenses (e.g., vandalism, possessing or receiving stolen property, driving while intoxicated); 17% for status offenses (e.g., running away, truancy, incorrigibility, loitering, curfew violations); and 10% for probation violation or contempt of court.

In 1975, Congress passed the Juvenile Justice and Delinquency Prevention Act which placed restrictions on the confinement of juveniles in adult facilities in states participating in the federal juvenile justice program. Initially, the Act allowed the incarceration of juveniles if they were housed in a part of the jail where they were out of sight and sound of adult prisoners. In 1980, the Act was amended to totally eliminate the practice of jailing juveniles in adult facilities. A deadline for removing juveniles was set for 1985, but was later extended to January, 1988. However, by 1987, 22 states participating in the program had failed to comply with this mandate (*Criminal Justice Newsletter*, 1987).

A number of reasons have been offered as to why the practice of jailing juveniles in adult facilities continues. In interviews with key juvenile justice and jail figures in Minnesota, Schwartz, Harris and Levi (1988) found that the lack of available alternatives for the detention of juveniles was the most important obstacle. Also cited were: the perception among key criminal justice figures that it was not a real problem; the belief that jailing juveniles was necessary for public safety; and the belief that jail serves a deterrent effect among juveniles. Steinhart (1988), in an analysis of a California law abolishing the jailing of juveniles, found that political leaders in smaller counties opposed the ban because they had so few juvenile offenders that the construction and operation of a juvenile detention facility would be cost prohibitive. They also were reluctant to transport juveniles to detention facilities in other counties because of the manpower and transportation costs.

Mentally Ill

The mentally ill are also overrepresented in the jail population. It is estimated that the lifetime prevalence of psychiatric disorders in the general population is 33%, yet among the jail population anywhere from 35% to 60% of inmates suffer from some form of mental illness (U.S. General Accounting Office, 1980:1).[6] The National Institute of Corrections estimated that 60% of all inmates suffer from mental disorders (cited in U.S. General Accounting Office, 1980:1). In a study conducted at the Philadelphia County Prison (Jail) system, psychopathology was diagnosed in 75% of the 493 newly admitted inmates systematically selected by the researchers (Guy, et al., 1985). In a study of 445 inmates referred for mental health evaluations in the Denver County Jail, 22.9% (102) were diagnosed as suffering from functional psychosis, 14.4% had previously been hospitalized for less than one month for mental problems and 27.9% had experienced long term or multiple hospitalizations (Swank and Winer, 1976). So numerous are the mentally ill in the nation's jails that an American Medical Association representative reported that "the jail is turning into a second-rate mental hospital" (cited in Wilson, 1980:14).

Some researchers have suggested that the jail is replacing the mental hospital as a "dumping ground" for the mentally ill. A number of reasons have been offered for this shift, including a general movement toward deinstitutionalization,[7] stricter commitment laws, less stringent discharge criteria, and reductions or curtailment of public funding for residential and outpatient treatment programs. According to one report:

> One of the most serious problems in the L.A. County Jail is a backlog of mental health cases waiting for transfer to state mental health facilities. In California, as in most other states, the closing of state mental hospitals, together with a general tightening of the civil commitment laws, has meant that increasing numbers of mentally ill people are on the streets. According to the [American Medical Associations' Joseph] Rowen, that has meant that growing numbers of former mental patients, as well as people whose bizarre behavior might have landed them in a hospital bed a few years ago, are now being arrested and are ending up in jail (Wilson, 1980:14).

---

[6] Gibbs (1987) questions the validity of studies that have accessed the prevalence of psychopathology among jail inmates. Typically, these studies are conducted on newly admitted inmates who are still experiencing the stress of adapting to the jail environment and incarceration. Gibbs argued, with some empirical support, that the symptoms of psychopathology prevalent in the inmate population may actually be "situational," and produced by the harsh environment and conditions of the jail. His own research indicated that inmates with no history of mental illness displayed symptoms of psychopathology in the early stages of their incarceration.

[7] In the first half of the twentieth century, the number of patients confined to mental hospitals steadily increased. Yet, beginning in the 1950s, patient numbers have steadily decreased. From 1955 to 1975, the number of mental patients decreased to 25% of maximum hospital capacity (Pollack, 1977).

Poor planning on the part of the federal government and local communities, further exacerbated the problem:

> Federal mental-health planners envisioned the flowering of a network of support services to care for deinstitutionalized patients at the community level through the stimulus of Federal seed money. But 1,300 of the 2,000 community mental-health centers projected for 1980 have failed to materialize and many that did have failed to service this chronically ill population. Deinstitutionalization, and ostensibly humane treatment programs, has denigrated into a tragic crisis...Planners, without real consultation, assumed strong communities would accept the chronically ill. When few welcomed large numbers of these troubled people, patients were steered to transitional neighborhoods that would not put up a fuss, but the strong community support factor essential for successful aftercare was absent. The result was city streets became wards of mental hospitals, and it was out of the snakepits and into the gutter for victims of deinstitutionalization policy (cited in Advisory Commission on Intergovernmental Relations, 1984:14).

Most jails have neither the personnel nor the facilities to humanely deal with the mentally ill. The American Medical Associations' (1973) survey of medical care in jails found that only 14.2% of the 1159 responding jails had facilities for the mentally ill while only 15.2% of the jails made a psychologist available to prisoners. In the absence of appropriate personnel and facilities, some jail officials and staff have resorted to inhumane techniques to restrain mentally ill inmates. In an Allegheny County (Pennsylvania) jail, for example, mentally ill inmates "clothed in hospital gowns or left naked, were bound to canvas cots with a hole cut in the middle. A tub was placed underneath the hole to collect the body wastes. Prisoners also were required to sleep in canvas cots, many of which were discolored by vomit, feces, and urine" (U.S. General Accounting Office, 1980:9).

Women

Women comprise only a small percent of the total inmate population; however, census data reveal that their number is increasing at a faster rate than males. On June 30, 1983, less than 7% of the total jail population were female (U.S. Department of Justice, 1988). Five years later, on June 30, 1988, women comprised almost 9% of the total jail population. In real figures the number of women incarcerated in jail climbed from 15,652 to 30,299 in the five-year period—an increase of approximately 94% (U.S. Department of Justice, 1988). In contrast, the number of males increased by 51% during the same period.

The typical female inmate is a poor, undereducated, young, minority (American Correctional Association, 1985). Sixty-six percent of female jail inmates were unemployed prior to their incarceration and 47% have one or more children dependent upon them (American Correctional Association, 1985). Some scholars suggest that many women in jail do not pose a threat to the community but are incarcerated because their limited financial resources makes raising the necessary bail difficult, if not impossible. An examination of the offenses for which women are incarcerated demonstrates that many were arrested for victimless crimes. A 1981 study of women booked into the San Francisco jail reveals that 40% were arrested for prostitution, 30.3% for property crimes (theft, shoplifting, forgery, fraud), 12.1% for drug offenses, and 6.1% for violent offenses (cited in American Correctional Association, 1985).

Jailed women seldom have access to programs and services provided to male inmates. Furthermore, because so few women are incarcerated in jails, special programs designed specifically for their unique needs are not offered:

> Many women in jails are mothers with sole responsibility for the support of their children. Separated from their children, they live in fear of losing custody of their offspring to the state. Many jails do not permit children to visit their mothers in jail or severely restrict those visits. There is a lack of gynecological care for jailed women and seldom any special health care for pregnant women; use of contraceptive pills is often interrupted because they are not available in jail (American Correctional Association, 1985:24).

Another deficiency in the treatment of female inmates concerns jail staffing. In a number of the nation's jails, female corrections officers are not employed by the jail or too few are employed to ensure around-the-clock supervision of female inmates (Kerle, 1985). A 1982 study found that in almost 23% of the 2,664 responding jails, women corrections officers are not always on duty when female inmates are housed in the facility (National Sheriffs' Association, 1982). While the lack of female employees is understandable in small jail facilities where resources and personnel are often limited, it also exists in a number of large facilities. In over 13% of the largest jails in the country (63 beds or more), women officers are not always on duty when female inmates are detained (National Sheriffs' Association, 1982). In many of these facilities male corrections officers are deployed to supervise female inmates.

The absence of female staff, even if only for limited periods of the day or night, leaves women inmates particularly vulnerable to exploitation and abuse by male staff. Take, for example, the controversial case of Joan Little. Little, a

20-year-old black woman, was the only woman inmate in the Beaufort County (North Carolina) Jail.   She had been in the jail for 81 days on a charge of breaking and entering, and was awaiting transfer to a state prison for women (Reston, 1975).   During her stay in the jail, she was supervised entirely by males; the jail did not employ female guards for women prisoners (*Newsweek*, 1975:86).   According to Little, in the early morning hours of August 27, 1974, 62-year-old Clarence Alligood, a white jail guard, entered her cell and sexually attacked her.   Little claimed that in self-defense she killed Alligood with an ice-pick he had brought into the cell.   In her trial for murder, the prosecution claimed that Little had willing engaged in sexual intercourse with Alligood on previous occasions in return for special privileges and sandwiches, but that on the morning of August 27th, Little "had taken the ice pick from Alligood's desk while making a telephone call, cooperated in a sexual act and then murdered him" (*Time*, 1975:19).   The trial became a *cause celebre* for feminists and civil rights activists, and in the end, the jury found Little not guilty of murder.

Physical and Sanitary Conditions of Jails

Although the "typical" American jail has been described as a "relatively small institution with less than twenty-five cells, built between 1880 and 1920, located in a small town, frequently the county seat of a rural county (Mattick, 1974:785-786) the description is somewhat misleading.   Although 44% of the nation's jails are small (less than 25 cells), they hold only 4% of the nation's inmates.   In contrast, only 4% of the nation's jails hold over 45% of all jail prisoners.   Typically, these large facilities are located in major metropolitan and urban areas (Advisory Commission on Intergovernmental Relations, 1984:6).   Decrepit and decaying physical facilities are common to both the small and large jails.   While these conditions exist in small, rural facilities because of fiscal and administrative neglect, they exist in large, urban facilities because of overuse and overcrowding (Flynn, 1973:64).

A common complaint leveled at the modern jail concerns deficiencies in its architectural design.   In his scathing commentary on prison and jail architecture, Norman Johnston (1973:54) concluded that:

[T]he history of prison architecture stands as a discouraging testament of our sometimes intentional, sometimes accidental degradation of our fellow man.   Prison structures have continued to be built in a way which manages by one means or another to brutalize their occupants and to deprive them of their privacy, dignity, and self-esteem, while at the same time strengthening their criminality.   The 19th century contemporary prison seems to allow mechanical contrivances to dominate the prisoner. Architects in the future must share some responsibility for the unintended indignities made possible by their works.

Deficiencies in jail architecture can be traced, in part, to the assumptions that have traditionally directed institutional designs. William G. Nagel (1973:18-19), in the definitive study of modern jail architecture, argued that facility administrators, consultants and architects develop jail and prison designs with four assumptions in mind:

(1)   Jailers are not wise enough to recognize which inmates might try to escape. They, therefore, must apply maximum custody provisions to all.

(2)   Jails must be designed to compensate for the inadequacies and transience of personnel.

(3)   Jails receive the most destructive elements of society, who have, during confinement, much idle time for the venting of their destructive impulses. The masonry, hardware, and furnishings, therefore, must be virtually destruction-proof.

(4)   Jails must be built as cheaply as possible. Since the concrete and hardware needed to provide the desired level of physical security are expensive, costs must be kept down by housing detainees in wards and by keeping the amount of activity space provided to a minimum.

The impact of these assumptions on the architecture and interior design of jails is immense. Jails are massive, concrete and metal constructions resembling fortresses on the outside and cages on the inside. The implicit belief that prisoners must be restrained and constrained is overemphasized in the architecture and furnishings. The bars, the strategically placed video cameras and the deliberately located eavesdropping equipment are all geared to the effective and efficient supervision, control, and surveillance of inmates.

In the typical jail facility, inmates are housed in two-, four-, six-, and eight-person cells or in multiple-occupancy dormitories. Although both the American Correctional Association and the National Jail Association recommended single-occupancy cells, few jails are designed to provide them (American Correctional Association, 1981:30). Even in some facilities featuring single cells, overcrowding has forced double- or even triple-bunking. Ironically, inmate living space is even less in double-bunked single cells than in multiple-occupancy cells.

The linear/intermittent surveillance design of the Calhoun County, Alabama, jail. In a linear design jail, multiple-occupancy cells or dormitories are aligned along a corridor. Corrections officers must continuously patrol the corridor in order to supervise inmates; however, their range of vision is limited to the cells directly in front of them. (Photograph courtesy of Brent Smith.)

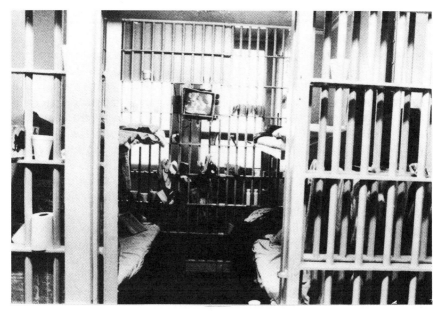

A multiple-occupancy cell in the Shawnee County, Kansas jail. In most jails, inmates are not allowed televisions within the cells. (Photograph courtesy of Ken Kerle and American Jail Association.)

Single-occupancy cells are recommended over multiple-occupancy cells (particularly dormitories) for a number of reasons. First, they provide greater security against escapes. Second, they allow greater flexibility in the classification and segregation of different categories of inmates. Third, they provide better security for jail personnel. Fourth, they prevent homosexual activities among inmates. Fifth, they assist in reducing aberrant inmate behavior such as assaults, extortion, etc. Sixth, they fulfill inmate privacy needs (Nagel, 1973:24). A majority of jail experts and administrators acknowledge that the most critical problem associated with the lack of single cells is the violence that occurs between inmates in multiple-occupancy cells and dormitories.

The most economical housing arrangement, in terms of building costs and space utilization, is the use of dormitories. Over 51% of confinement space in local facilities is composed of dormitory units that house between 11 and 50 prisoners (U.S. Department of Justice, 1980b:80). In many jails, dormitories provide inmates with less than the 60 square feet of floor space recommended by the American Correctional Association and the Commission on Accreditation for Corrections (American Correctional Association, 1981:30). Revealingly referred to as "jungles" by correctional personnel and inmates, dormitories are the most detrimental of housing arrangements in terms of their impact on staff and inmates. According to Nagel (1973:24), dormitories provide greater opportunities for sexual exploitation, moral contamination and physical exploitation among inmates; they deprive inmates of privacy, prevent appropriate classification or separation of prisoners, and pose serious threats to the safety of staff.

As discussed previously, most jails, regardless of their age, were built in a traditional, linear/intermittent surveillance architectural style. The inability of the custodial staff to adequately supervise inmates and their activities is a consequence of this architectural design. In more modern facilities, sophisticated electronic equipment has been installed to improve institutional surveillance of inmates. However, overreliance on these technological mechanisms significantly reduces contact between inmates and staff and promotes the impression that "inmates are literally held in the system—they are mere items" (Nagel, 1973:29). For inmates, the effect of mechanical bugging devices and short-circuit television systems is often dehumanizing. One inmate, for example, complained that the jail "is the only place in the world where a man can urinate, defecate and masturbate knowing full well that some bastard is watching him on the boob tube" (quoted in Nagel, 1973:64,67).

In the typical jail cell at least one wall consists of bars; the other three are cement or cinderblock. The bars give the cell its cage-like appearance and effectively reduce inmate privacy. Where cells are equipped with toilets, no effort is made to shield inmates from the view of others. Anyone walking by the cell can look in on inmates as they use the toilets. Toilets are left unscreened for purported security and surveillance reasons.

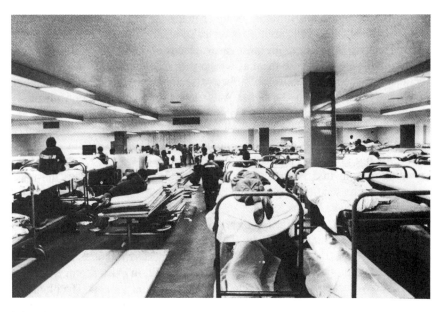

A dormitory in the Los Angeles County Jail. In some correctional facilities, dormitories house up to 100 inmates. (Photograph courtesy of Ken Kerle and American Jail Association.)

The dayrooms in the Calhoun County, Alabama, jail serve a variety of purposes including recreation area, library and shower/toilet areas. Inmates have little privacy when using the shower and toilet facilities. They must stand or sit on the floor while in the dayroom as seating is not available. (Photograph courtesy of Brent Smith.)

Rugs, curtains, soft furniture or other materials that absorb sound are absent from most cells. Jail furniture is typically made of heavy, durable metal to prevent inmate vandalism. In most cases, pieces of furniture are bolted to the floor so inmates cannot use them as weapons to throw at other inmates or staff members. Because of the lack of effective sound absorbing components, noise levels are often exceedingly high. Without appropriate absorption materials, sounds from the locking and unlocking of the metal doors, from televisions and radios, and from the inmates themselves are magnified. One inmate commented that "all night the jail sounds like a nuthouse. All the junkies are screaming their guts out going through cold turkey" (quoted in Reid, 1976:369). After spending a night in a Boston jail, a federal judge complained that "the noise seemed to increase after midnight and approached a virtual bedlam which lasted until dawn" (*Inmates of the Suffolk County Jail v. Eisenstadt*, 1973:680-681).

In many modern facilities, cells are equipped with stainless steel toilets and sinks. Often, the toilet can only be flushed from outside the cell by corrections officers and toilet tissue is provided only upon request. In some older facilities, cells are not equipped with either toilets or sinks. Still in existence in some jails is the "honey bucket" system wherein a bucket serves as a toilet. The plumbing is so antiquated in other facilities that toilets may not flush or may occasionally back up. In these cases, persistent and unpleasant smells permeate the cells.

Adequate lighting is also a problem in many facilities. Since many jails are designed without windows, natural light may be totally absent. The assumption is that windows threaten the security of the facility. There is, however, little evidence to support this belief. Artificial light may also be inadequate for inmate activities. In many facilities, the lack of light gives a dark, dreary and depressing appearance to the living area.[8]

In a survey sponsored by the National Sheriff's Association (1982), 11%, or 262 of the 2,373 responding jails were built in the 1800s; 26% or 612 of the responding facilities were built sometime between 1900 and 1920. Older jails have myriad problems involving, in particular, inadequacies in the physical plant. Many of these facilities have antiquated ventilation and heating/cooling systems. While the jail is hot in the summer, it is inevitably cold in the winter.

---

[8] While conducting research in Washington state jails in the spring of 1983, I visited one small jail in the western part of the state. The jail consisted of a ship's brig set into a large, double-story room. While the conditions of this jail were deplorable for a number of reasons, they were made worse by a serious lack of light. The only source of natural light was a small window located at the uppermost part of the room; this light was supplemented by one small, bare light bulb hanging from the ceiling. Neither the window nor the light bulb provided sufficient light to enable inmates to read.

The compact multi-purpose dayrooms of the Shawnee County, Kansas, jail serve 12 inmates in the cell block. (Photograph courtesy of Ken Kerle and American Jail Association.)

As is typical of many older traditional jails, shower and toilet facilities are located in the dayrooms and afford inmates little privacy from other inmates or from those outside the cellblock area. (Photograph courtesy of Ken Kerle and American Jail Association.)

Nonfunctioning ventilation systems have been credited with the spread of aerobic viruses that cause illnesses among inmates and staff. A typical problem in aging facilities is plumbing that leaks water onto the floor. In a number of these facilities, overcrowding forces inmates to sleep on floors, and, consequently, in puddles of water.

Common to many jail facilities is a lack of cleanliness—both of the facility and of inmates. As succinctly stated by Mattick (1974:802), "if cleanliness is next to godliness, most jails lie securely in the province of hell." Jail inmates suffer high rates of venereal disease, tuberculosis and infectious hepatitis (Mattick, 1974:802). Yet the lack of cleanliness and sanitation makes it inevitable that these diseases are passed from inmate to inmate, or even from inmate to staff. In some facilities elementary personal hygiene materials such as soap, towels, toothbrushes, clean clothes and bedding are in short supply or, in some cases, absent. Even shower facilities may be inadequate. Often the ratio of showerheads to inmates is so high that it is necessary for inmates to compete for the opportunity to shower. In addition, communal showers provided in many facilities make showering a dangerous task. Often unsupervised, the shower area is a common site for sexual assaults.

The age and decrepit condition of the facility also contribute to its uncleanliness. In older facilities, any remedial measure taken cannot overcome the physical deterioration that contributes to an unclean and unsanitary environment.

> Extensive cleaning is not possible in some old jails because the iron-work is rusted, the cement floors are broken, and the walls would disintegrate. Such jails are havens for rodents, body lice, and other vermin that can successfully survive sporadic attempts at extermination. Where jails can be cleaned, this is usually done by the inmates themselves (Mattick, 1974:802).

A final problem concerning the physical plant of modern jail facilities is the lack of space for inmate programs such as counseling, educational and vocational classes, recreation, and visitation. In a survey of 2,452 facilities, the National Sheriffs' Association (1982) reported that only 35.1% have space for medical services; 29.2% have space for counseling or educational programming; 28.6% have space for outdoor recreation; 27.9% have space for contact visits; 25.6% of the responding facilities have specifically designated space for library services; 25.4% have space for indoor recreation; 17.8% have space for dining; and 7.1% have space for vocational programming.

Even more surprising is that only 45% of the facilities have dayroom space.[9] As a result of the lack of space, inmate programming is minimal at best, and, in many cases, nonexistent.

In the last two decades there has been a movement for greater state involvement in jail administration, largely as a consequence of burgeoning inmate litigation challenging the constitutionality of jail conditions, particularly those concerning the physical plant of the facility. The focus of this involvement has been primarily on the establishment and enforcement of minimum standards for the operation, construction and renovation of local jail facilities. In 1966, 40% of states had adopted comprehensive standards. Twelve years later, 45 states had implemented jail standards, the majority of which were mandatory.

In most cases, the standards adopted by states are those delineated by federal courts in actions brought by inmates and by professional correctional associations such as the American Correctional Association and the National Sheriffs' Association (Advisory Commission on Intergovernmental Relations, 1984:97-98). The most comprehensive set of standards was promulgated by the American Correctional Association. These standards focused on such issues as minimum floor space provided to inmates, lighting, noise levels, air circulation, temperatures, toilet and shower facilities, recreation, visitation and inmate program space, and other aspects of the physical environment of the jail.[10]

While it was hoped that these new standards, particularly those that were mandatory, would improve jail conditions, the evidence suggests that their impact has been modest at best. Establishment and enforcement of minimum standards is a highly political exercise. Products of political bargaining and consensus-building, the standards adopted by states are often vague and unenforceable. Some argue that accreditation by the state is based more upon "who you know" than upon actual compliance with the standards. One jail administrator commented that "the only difference in this state between an accredited jail and one that isn't, is the plaque on the wall of the Sheriff whose jail is accredited" (cited in Advisory Commission on Intergovernmental Relations, 1984:103). In many states, jail inspection amounts to a "bad joke" (Allinson, 1982:22).

Although no one has yet made a comprehensive evaluation of the impact of state standards on jail conditions, indirect evidence suggests that full compliance has yet to be attained. According to a joint study conducted by the Advisory

---

9   Dayrooms are typically adjacent to the living cell area, and, like the cells, are separated from the remainder of the facility by bars. Usually, inmates have unlimited access to the dayroom during the day but are locked in their cells at night. Many dayrooms are equipped with television and recreational equipment (e.g., card and board games). In most facilities, dayrooms are furnished with metal or hard plastic furniture that make it less than comfortable for inmates.

10   The standards established by the American Correctional Association cover a broad range of issues including fiscal management, personnel training and staff development, inmate records, safety and emergency procedures, food service, security and control, inmate rights, inmate rules and discipline, classification, and so forth (American Correctional Association, 1981).

Commission on Intergovernmental Relations and the National Association of Counties, 16 states with mandatory minimum standards had jails under court order to revise conditions (cited in Advisory Commission on Intergovernmental Relations, 1984:103). This evidence suggests that even where states have adopted standards, local jails have failed to live up to them.

Overcrowding

Survey after survey has revealed that overcrowding is the most critical problem facing urban jail administrators today. In a survey of 35 jail administrators and social services providers, Gibbs (1983) found that overcrowding was listed as the most serious of 24 jail problems. In a study conducted by the National Sheriffs' Association, 795 out of 2,452 jails listed overcrowding as the greatest problem affecting their facility.

Prior to 1980, jail populations remained relatively stable. The average annual population of the nation's jails in the 1970s hovered at around 158,000. In the 1980s, there has been a dramatic upswing in the jail population. The Bureau of Justice Statistics (U.S. Department of Justice, 1983a) reported that by 1982 the national annual jail population jumped to approximately 212,000, an increase of about 26% between 1978 and 1982. Between 1983 and 1988, jail populations grew from a daily rate of 223,551 to 343,569 inmates—an increase of 54% (U.S. Department of Justice, 1990).

The 100 largest facilities in the United States have been the hardest hit by the overcrowding problem. In these facilities inmate populations consistently exceed designed capacity (U.S. Department of Justice, 1983a:2). In some cases the problem is so pronounced that many inmates are forced to sleep on the floors or in dayrooms when cell capacity is surpassed. Although smaller facilities seldom exceed their capacities, they nevertheless feel the effects of too many inmates. In the National Sheriffs' Association (1982) jail survey, small facilities rated overcrowding as the most serious problem affecting their facility even though they were the least likely to be operating at capacity. On closer examination, the authors of the report concluded that:

> many participants cited overcrowding as an issue which at times didn't square with the figures cited as their daily inmate population. What some of these people probably mean is there aren't enough staff on shift to handle the workload properly. Even if a jail does have a bed space for every prisoner, jail officers think of it as overcrowded if, due to staff shortages, the inmate counts, bed checks, and cell searches are overlooked and inmate programs such as outdoor recreation are postponed (National Sheriffs' Association, 1982:231).

The jail overcrowding problem involves a number of factors, including: a judicial movement toward stricter penalties for crimes, such as mandatory sentences for driving while intoxicated; state restructuring of sentencing, particularly from indeterminate to determinate sentencing, that has resulted in the diversion of many offenders from prisons to jails; general increases in crime rates; and, finally, overcrowding in state prisons.[11] The U.S. Department of Justice (1983a:3) concluded that "during 1981, the number of states under court orders to reduce overcrowding rose from 28 to 31, while the number involved in litigation about overall prison conditions increased from 32 to 37." This litigation has had a tremendous impact on local jails.

When prisoners are forced to reduce the inmate population, many simply refuse to accept sentenced prisoners. Consequently, jails must retain inmates until the prison will accept them. In 1981, 8,576 state prisoners were being held in local jails (U.S. Department of Justice, 1983a:3). In New Jersey during the same year, 945 (11%) of the state's 8,692 prisoners were housed in 21 county jails that were themselves overcrowded (Carney, 1982:24). In Mississippi, the prison system was so overcrowded that 1,300 inmates were backed up in local jails awaiting transfer to prison.[12] Some jail administrators and sheriffs have become so frustrated with the overflow of state prisoners that they have taken extraordinary steps to alleviate the problem, including suing the state to force them to accept their own prisoners. In one case, the sheriff in Pulaski County, Arkansas, chained 19 state prisoners housed in his jail to posts and fences outside of two prisons. He had been forced to house the prisoners until the state could meet a court order to alleviate overcrowding in the prisons. By 1988, the problem intensified. On June 30, 1988, 28,481 state prisoners were being held in local jails because there was no bed space available in state prisons (U.S. Department of Justice, 1990).

While many jails grapple with the problem of "spill-over" from overcrowded state prisons, the courts have made it clear that overcrowding in jails will not be tolerated. In the 1979 case of *Bell v. Wolfish*, the U.S. Supreme Court concluded that "a detainee may not be punished prior to an adjudication of guilt."[13] Because, on the average, around 60% of all persons in jail are pretrial

---

[11] Since passage of the 1984 Bail Reform Act, federal detention facilities have witnessed a 36% increase in pretrial detainees. Preventative detention, permitted by the Act, has increased the demand for space in federal lockups (Clear and Cole, 1986:213-214). The U.S. Supreme Court recently upheld the preventative detention clause in the Act. If other states follow the precedent established by the U.S. Congress and pass similar laws, local jails may experience further increases in population, adding to the already burdensome problem of overcrowding.

[12] In many cases, jail conditions are so poor compared to those in prisons that inmates "have actually protested in an effort to get *into* prison" (cited in *Newsweek*, 1980:76).

detainees—who under our system of law are presumed to be innocent—the courts have stipulated that any condition of detainment which in effect punishes pretrial detainees violates their constitutional rights. In the case of *Gross v. Tazewell County Jail* (1982), the U.S. District Court summarized its rationale for prohibiting overcrowding in jails:

> It is abundantly clear that extreme overcrowding in a local jail is of greater practical effect and constitutional consequence than in a larger institution or a common road camp. Perhaps more importantly, the local jail houses a high percentage of pretrial detainees...As a matter of common sense and fundamental fairness, the criminal justice system must insure that pretrial detainees are not housed in more deprived circumstances than those accorded to convicted persons...Overcrowding in a local jail cannot be qualitatively equated with overcrowding in a state penal institution.

Overcrowding is the most common basis on which inmates challenge the constitutionality of jail conditions. Of the 285 facilities under court order in 1982, overcrowding was the primary cause for court action in 73%, or 209, of the cases (National Sheriffs' Association, 1982:45). Of the nation's 612 largest jails, 23%, or 139, were under court order in 1986 to reduce inmate populations (U.S. Department of Justice, 1987).

While overcrowding has a number of consequences for jail administrators, it also has tremendous impact on the inmates housed in overcrowded facilities.[14]

---

[13] The case of *Bell v. Wolfish* represents a dramatic shift from over a decade of court intervention into the administration of correctional institutions. In this case, the Supreme Court decided that double-bunking in the Federal Metropolitan Correctional Center (MCC), a podular/direct supervision facility, did not violate the Due Process Clause of the Fifth Amendment that prohibits the punishment of pretrial detainees. The Court cited several facts specific to the situation at the MCC in its decision. First, inmates in the facility spent relatively few hours in the confines of their cells. Prisoners usually were confined only for sleeping. The Court believed that 75 feet per cell was adequate space for two prisoners to sleep. Second, the inmates in the facility were exposed to the conditions of the facility for relatively short periods. Eighty-five percent of the pretrial detainees were released within 60 days. Finally, the court noted that the MCC was unlike most traditional jail facilities. Legal scholars are uncertain of what the Court meant by this. According to Call (1983:25-26), "It is unclear whether by this implied reference to MCC as a nontraditional jail the Court meant to suggest that the modern design of MCC and its cells with doors rather than solid walls also militated in favor of its decision." Following the *Wolfish* decision, lower courts continued to find overcrowded jail conditions unconstitutional. These courts either ignored *Wolfish* or made brief mention of it without analysis of its applicability to the case at hand. In an assessment of the impact of *Wolfish*, Call (1983) concluded that the decision had little effect on subsequent lower court actions. These courts continued to find overcrowding unconstitutional.

First, overcrowding places excessive strain on the resources of the jail, particularly with regard to programs, goods and services provided to inmates. The availability of telephones, televisions, recreation and visitation time, counseling and educational programs, and medical and mental health treatment is significantly reduced as a result of overcrowding, and in some cases, may be denied to all inmates. The amount of personal space provided to each inmate is also reduced, thereby removing any opportunity for privacy. Even basic hygiene facilities such as a shower or a change of clothing and bedding may not be readily accessible in a facility that is overcrowded.

While reductions in services, programs and goods produce feelings of frustration and perhaps anger among inmates, some scholars suggest that overcrowding stimulates aberrant inmate and staff behavior.[15] Although only a limited amount of research has been conducted on the impact of crowding in correctional institutions, existing research suggests that overcrowding has psychological and physical consequences for inmates. Clear and Cole (1986:225) summarized the effect of overcrowding on inmates as follows:

> Cells intended to hold one or two persons are holding three, four, even five. It is not uncommon for prisoners to sleep in hallways, with or without mattresses. Direct and immediate consequences of overcrowding are violence, rape, and a variety of health disorders. There is some evidence that prolonged exposure to seriously crowded conditions reduces the expected life span of inmates. Certainly tempers flare in close quarters and the vulnerable inmate becomes a more likely victim. What makes these facts even more depressing to contemplate is that many of the persons subjected to these conditions have not yet been tried and must be presumed to be innocent.

Administrative Arrangements

From the time of their inception jails were administered by county sheriffs. Through default, sheriffs have remained the titular heads of most local facilities. Only in six states are local jails administered by state officials rather than by county sheriffs. These states include Alaska, Connecticut, Delaware, Hawaii, Rhode Island, and Vermont. In a small number of local jurisdictions, jails are administered by county-level departments of correction. In Kentucky, all coun-

---

[14] In some cases, overcrowding has resulted in the "emergency" suspension of state standards for local jail operations. In Oklahoma, the legislature eliminated 94 of the 172 state standards. The rationale was that the standards were "frivolous" or "too excessive" (Allinson, 1982:22).

[15] Research on the effects of overcrowding is discussed in greater detail in Chapter 5.

ties (except those containing a city over 100,000) separately elect county jailers who have custody and control over the jail.

Burns (1975) suggested that the jail has remained under the jurisdiction of county sheriffs because of self-interest, particularly in regard to the monies that could be made through extortion of prisoners. In earlier days, the jails' fee systems provided sheriffs with a fairly substantial income. Under the fee system, sheriffs received a set amount of money per day for the care of prisoners. In addition to the widespread abuses previously discussed, the fee system encouraged wholesale arrests of nondangerous social outcasts in order to increase the jail population and the fees paid to the sheriff (Miller, 1978:23). The fee system provided the incentive for sheriffs to detain prisoners for as long as possible.[16] The prisoner fees paid to the sheriff made the position highly desirable and much sought after. In some localities, the local sheriff earned more money than the President of the United States (Burns, 1975:157)!

Today, jail administration by county sheriffs is commonly cited as the major cause of jail problems and a formidable obstacle to reform efforts. The majority of the criticisms directed at jail administration by county sheriffs focuses on the sheriffs' preoccupation with their law enforcement role and neglect of the correctional role. For the most part, sheriffs tend to have little interest in or knowledge about jail administration. Twenty years ago the President's Commission on Law Enforcement and Administration of Justice (1967) observed that "the basic police mission of apprehending offenders usually leaves little time, commitment, or expertise for the development of rehabilitative programs, although notable exceptions demonstrate that jails can indeed be settings for correctional treatment." Years later, Flynn (1973:59) commented that sheriffs "view the jail as an adjunct to their law enforcement activities and as a place for the temporary detention and warehousing of inmates."

The background, education, training and interests of most sheriffs are in law enforcement. Few have the expertise, training or incentive to spend inordinate amounts of time on jail concerns. In a study of local jails in Illinois conducted by the University of Chicago's Center for Studies in Criminal Justice, it was found that "the sheriffs and their deputies, or the police authorities, who are responsible for the jails, spend 10 percent or less of their time doing any jail work" (cited in Mattick, 1969:112). Nor is it politically expedient for sheriffs to devote time and energy to the jail. More often than not, sheriffs are elected on the basis of their crime control and law enforcement abilities, not their skills as jail administrators. It is certainly more glamorous and attractive to be a crimefighter than a jail keeper. For elected sheriffs, there is truth in Huey Long's adage: "There ain't no votes in prisons."

---

[16] For a discussion of how the fee system promotes incarceration and overcrowding in jails, see *Behind Bars: Kentucky Looks at its County Jails* (1981), an investigation of Kentucky jails prepared by the Kentucky Department of Justice.

Although every comprehensive jail study conducted within the last 60 years has recommended either replacing the sheriff as the chief jail administrator with an appointed, correctional specialist or abolishing local jail control (Fishman, 1923; Robinson, 1944; Richmond, 1965; Flynn, 1973; Mattick, 1975), jails remain firmly dominated by local political officials. These reforms would reduce the number of locally elected positions, reduce patronage opportunities, and damage the interests of local bailsbondsmen and tradesmen who regularly deal with the jail. These lost opportunities ensure that local opposition is fierce and prolonged.

Personnel

In a 1982 survey of jails sponsored by the National Sheriffs' Association (NSA) respondents were asked to identify five of the most serious problems in their facility. Of the 2,452 responding facilities, 1,209 ranked "personnel" among their top five problems (1982:225). Ken Kerle, a jail consultant and co-author of the NSA report, stated that: "personnel is still the number one problem of jails...Start paying decent salaries and developing decent training and you can start to attract bright young people to jobs in jails. If you don't do this, you'll continue to see the issue of personnel as the number one problem of jails for the next 100 years" (cited in Advisory Commission of Intergovernmental Relations, 1984:7).

Clear and Cole (1986:221) summarized the jail personnel conundrum as follows: "Local corrections workers are among the most poorly trained, least educated, and worst paid employees in the criminal justice system." The personnel problems cited by authorities in the field include inappropriate selection and training programs, substandard salaries, understaffing, and low job prestige (Advisory Commission on Intergovernmental Relations, 1984; Mattick, 1974; National Sheriffs Association, 1982; Miller, 1978; Flynn, 1973).

The impact of these personnel problems on the jail and its operation is tremendous. Clear and Cole (1986:221) observed that turnover in jails is extraordinarily high and that many jails report complete staff turnover once every two or three years. Mattick (1974:804) concluded that "if a jail's staff is inadequate in its initial qualifications for the job, in screening, in training, in numbers, and in motivation and morale, even the most modern, well-designed, and fully equipped penal plant will be defeated in its every function and purpose."

The personnel problem most often discussed by correctional scholars is that of understaffing. Approximately 99,000 people are employed in the nation's jails; of this number, 74% perform custodial duties (U.S. Department of Justice, 1990). A Law Enforcement Assistance Administration study (1971) concluded that there were 1.6 full-time staff members per jail per shift.[17] On average, each staff member is in charge of 40 inmates. Many small and rural counties do not employ custodial personnel, but rely instead on local police or sheriff's employees to make periodic checks of the jail to ensure that inmates have not escaped, killed themselves, or killed one another.

Understaffing, and in some cases a complete lack of staff, has been criticized for a number of reasons—primary among them the threat it poses to inmate safety and security. Many jail officials deal with inadequate staffing levels by locking inmates in their cells to prevent escape and ease the handling of prisoners. Without appropriate staff supervision, however, little can be done to protect inmates locked in multiple-occupancy cells from one another. Inmates themselves express concern over the lack of adequate supervision. According to one inmate in the San Francisco jail, "I was here three days and didn't sleep a wink because I was scared. You know what was scariest of all? Never seeing a guard" (quoted in *Newsweek*, 1980:77).

A second personnel dilemma concerns the lack of adequate systems for the recruitment, selection, training, and compensation of correctional staff. The National Sheriffs' Association's comprehensive study of jails provided a number of insights into the deficiencies of most personnel systems.

> *On Recruitment:* "Too often, there are no standards for recruitment and warm bodies are taken off the street, put into uniform, given a set of keys, and told to go to work. At times, one finds line officers in the golden age category—a job men and women take to supplement a social security or retirement check. Most people in the over 60 bracket are not physically capable of handling the younger inmates who act out in a physically violent manner" (1982:231).

> *On Screening Job Applicants:* "Most [jails] are deficient in the areas of physical, written, and psychological testing...Many jails which we have examined have no educational requirement at all for the jail officer position although a few states require a high school diploma or a GED (general equivalency diploma) certificate" (1982:119).[18]

> *On Training:* "...jail training is still an extremely low priority in local facilities. Jail training today is where police training was 20 years ago. Until sheriffs and county governing personnel understand the ne-

---

[17] This figure does not take into account vacation, sick leave or other absences by the correctional staff. If these were included, the ratio would be much smaller.

[18] In many jails, staff selection is based on patronage. When the sheriff leaves office, so do the jailers who were appointed by him/her. In some areas, sheriffs are prohibited from holding office for two consecutive terms. Hence, complete staff turnover occurs very four years (Flynn, 1973; Mattick, 1974).

cessity of a well-trained jail staff, problems will continue to plague jails.[19] Training seems to be the most expendable item in budgets and frequently budget cuts are given as the excuse for not conducting training...Most state and local governments have defaulted on their responsibility to give training to jail officers on any consistent basis" (1982:125-127).

On Salaries: "Jail officer careers will never achieve the status they deserve so long as counties continue to pay jail officers less money than the officers assigned to police duties.[20] Part of the problem facing counties today is not only the lack of sufficiently trained staff, but the lack of qualified staff in terms of education. Education relates to salaries. No person wants to make a career where the reward is lousy wages. You can't attract the people who have the potential to be the best officers by paying them wages in the poverty range" (1982:151).

With an apparent lack of quality control in most jails' personnel systems, it is more than likely that people unfit for correctional work are hired and retained. An example of unfit officers was found in the 1969 investigation of the Nassau County (New Jersey) Jail. To investigate the validity of rumors concerning brutality and corruption among corrections officers, undercover private investigators were sent into the jail to pose as inmates. The investigators found that, in general, the facility was well run; however, they also uncovered a number of problems concerning staff attitudes and performance.

Investigative reports dealing with the attitude and performance of the guards revealed that, while most did their jobs with insight, understanding, and courtesy, some performed indifferently and behaved arrogantly. As the investigation proceeded, it became more and more obvious that the entirely unprofessional attitude and behavior of this latter group had a serious detrimental effect on the best interests and concerns of the institution. These guards seemed less intent on doing their jobs than on demonstrating their superiority and dominance over the inmates. Although at times this behavior appeared consciously directed at specific individuals purely for purposes of harassment, it was just as prevalent as a simple reflexive response to any inmate's request or expression of human sentiment (Cahn, 1973:8).

---

[19] In discussing the inadequacies of corrections officer training, Miller (1978:28) characterizes most jail training as " 'good luck' on-the-job training."

[20] The survey results revealed that, on average, the starting salary for corrections officers is 14% less than for sheriff's patrol officers.

Among the behaviors exhibited by the unprofessional officers were threats issued against inmates, insults, profanity, name-calling (e.g., "chump," "punk," "honky"), ignoring or responding with sarcasm to legitimate requests and complaints, belittling and degrading comments, minor physical abuse, and general harassment.[21] The most serious form of abuse found by the undercover agents was the granting of special privileges to organized crime figures. In addition to treating these prisoners with dignity and respect, the officers delivered illicit liquor and narcotics to them. In one case, a female prisoner was supplied to a mobster for his sexual pleasure.

Inmates reacted to the degrading treatment with anger, frustration, resentment and aggression. When officers continued to ignore complaints that coffee or Kool-Aid was not being delivered with meals, inmates staged a hunger strike to get their attention. It is apparent that if inmates are pushed too far by uncaring and rude corrections officers, a hunger strike can easily erupt into a more serious demonstration.

A more serious case of officer misconduct occurred in the Okaloosa County (Florida) Jail. While checking the detoxification unit at about 10:00 one evening, a female corrections officer found a male inmate with one end of a shoestring tied around his neck and the other end tied to the bunk directly above him. After removing the shoestring and determining that the inmate still had a pulse, the officer left the man in his cell. The officer did not notify her supervisor or call for medical assistance. The next morning, the inmate was found dead. The autopsy showed that the inmate had died about two hours after he was found hanging by the officer. An investigation into the suicide revealed that the inmate had threatened to kill himself when booked into the jail and that the officer had failed to notify her supervisor of the threat or to initiate 15-minute observations required for suicidal inmates. The officer was suspended without pay for five days and received a written reprimand (*Daily Home Sun*, 1989:23).

Available research on correctional employees tends to suggest that, in general, corrections officers are largely a disaffected group.[22] Symptoms of their

---

21 Cahn (1973:9) recounts examples of harassment where "inmates on their way to the visiting room would have to wait for ten minutes for a door to be opened while the officer with the key stood a few feet away chatting with a colleague." In the meantime, the inmates lost ten minutes of visitation time that could have been spent with their families or friends.

22 The plight of corrections officers in local detention facilities has been virtually ignored by correctional scholars. Consequently, much of the following section relies on research conducted among corrections officers in prisons. Although some scholars argue that the two types of institutions are vastly different, in several respects they are highly similar—particularly in regard to the nature of their clientele, the work performed by officers, and their organizational and work environments. While caution must be exercised in generalizing the results of personnel-related research findings from the prison to the jail setting, they at least provide some hint of the problems that may be plaguing corrections officers in jails.

plight include high levels of stress (Stinchcomb, 1986), cynicism (Farmer, 1977), alienation (Toch and Klofas, 1982; Poole and Regoli, 1981), and occupational tedium (Shamir and Drory, 1982); low levels of job satisfaction (Hays and Tompkins, 1986); and high turnover rates (May, 1980; Jurik and Winn, 1986; *Corrections Compendium*, 1987; Benton, Rosen and Peters, 1982).

Scholars have offered a variety of reasons to explain why corrections officers are such a troubled group. Some authorities suggest that the nature and design of the work performed by corrections officers is an important factor in the problems they experience (Brief, Munro and Aldag, 1976; Toch and Grant, 1982). Herzberg, Mausner and Snyderman (1959) argued that people find satisfaction in their work when it is interesting and challenging, when it provides genuine responsibility, and when it presents opportunities for achievement, personal growth and individual advancement. The design of the job performed by corrections officers has been criticized by several scholars as incapable of providing these sources of satisfaction.

The work performed by corrections officers in jails is best described as fragmented, routinized and menial—in a word, impoverished. An examination of officer activities, tasks and assignments illustrates this point. The following tasks have been emphasized for a New York corrections officer: "Checks inmate passes and records inmates' movements in and out of areas"; "Watches for unusual incidents and reports any to his supervisor either verbally or in writing"; "Makes periodic rounds of assigned areas checking for faulty bars, gates, etc. and checks areas for daily fire report"; "Supervises bathing"; "Announces sick call" (Toch and Grant, 1982:85-86). These obligations appear to be bureaucratic chores that require little or no judgment, initiative or skill on the part of officers. Consequently, the nature and design of the job can frustrate fulfillment of officers' personal needs for recognition, challenge, responsibility, and achievement, and produce officers who are dissatisfied, apathetic, unmotivated, alienated from their jobs and uncommitted to the goals of the jail.

Another source of dissatisfaction for jail guards is the lack of well-defined and clearly articulated organizational goals. In part, this lack of goals is due to an ambiguity about the role of the jail within the criminal justice system and within society as a whole. By default, security and custodial convenience have emerged as the underlying forces that direct the operations of the jail.[23]

The persistence of incoherent and ambiguous goals has important consequences for custodial personnel. First, it prevents officers from clearly identifying the obligations of the job and the organization's expectations of their per-

---

[23] Flynn (1973:66) defined custodial convenience as the facility's preoccupation with ensuring that inmates do not escape: "As much as possible, jails are geared to the fullest possible supervision, control, and surveillance of inmates. Physical structures, program choices—if any—and operational policies optimize security and administration convenience and restrict the inmate's movement to the point of removing all of his control over his environment."

formance. Deprived of these guidelines, officers must second guess the organization or rely on co-workers (or even inmates) to provide clarity. In either case, the risk is high that the officer will perform tasks in direct opposition to what the facility's administration desires. Second, officers lack the ability to assess whether their performance has a positive effect on attainment of the organization's goals. In essence, the performance of officers under these circumstances is without direction or purpose.

A third source of dissatisfaction is the classical hierarchical authority structure of the jail organization. As with most police agencies, the jail hierarchy is organized along paramilitary lines, with graded levels of authority that are assigned specific military ranks. Corresponding to Weber's organization model, authority, power and control increase as one ascends the hierarchy. Jail guards, who occupy the lowest level of the hierarchy, are vested with little authority and control. Likewise, jail policies formulated by those at the upper levels of the hierarchy direct and control the behavior of those at the lower levels.

In the hierarchical organization of the jail, first-hand factual reports about what is occurring in the facility are communicated upward by corrections officers, and policies, directives, and orders are communicated downward by the administration. Schrag (1961) argued that this arrangement alienates corrections officers in three ways. First, although corrections officers are closest to the situations involving inmates and know the most about them, they have little input in the decision-making process. Their role is to follow orders, not to evaluate them. Second, because the administration is so far removed from situations involving inmates, they must rely on officer reports that may be distorted in the communication process. Consequently, their decisions may be inappropriate to the situation. The decisions, however, are communicated in the form of commands and officers have no recourse but to follow orders. Finally, because communication between the administration and subordinates is limited, officers are not privy to reasons and rationales for the various rules and regulations that direct their every action. Without an understanding of the reasons for the rules, officers are more inclined to unofficially reinterpret them or to simply ignore them.

Another source of guard dissatisfaction is the overabundance of formal institutional rules and regulations for the control of inmate and staff behavior. There are few activities or situations involving inmates which are not covered by an institutional rule or regulation. Corrections officers, whose primary responsibility is to control inmates, are also governed by an exhaustive list of rules that prescribe expected behavior in all situations.

Cressey (1968) observed that the organization's concern for obedience to rules and regulations places corrections officers in a precarious position. Although his observations were specifically intended for prison organizations, they are applicable to the equally rule-bound jail organization. As managers of inmates, corrections officers need flexibility and discretion to deal with the myriad situations they encounter. However, the organization's preoccupation with rules does not provide this necessary flexibility and discretion. Cressey (1968:494) summarized the situation as follows:

> Prisons differ significantly if not uniquely, from other organizations, because their personnel hierarchies are organized down to the lower level of the administration of the daily activities of men. The guard, who is the lowest level worker in a prison, is also a manager. He is managed in a system of regulations and controls from above, but he also manages, by a corresponding system of regulations, the inmates who are in his charge. Essentially because he is a worker, he cannot be given full discretion to produce a desired end product such as inmate docility or inmate rehabilitation, and essentially because he is a manager his activities cannot be bureaucratized in a set of routine procedures.

A consequence of the overabundance of jail rules is the conflict that results when obedience to rules is not compatible with other organizational expectations. This incompatibility is often found in the potentially conflicting expectations of rule enforcement and order maintenance. While officers are expected to enforce all facility rules, they are also expected to maintain order among inmates. The two expectations can conflict when excessive rule enforcement leads to inmate unrest. Another source of conflict among organizational expectations of rule enforcement was offered by Schrag (1961). He argued that it would require the repeated use of force and the issuance of a number of official rule-infraction reports for officers to enforce all facility rules. Such a flurry of activity would cause administrators to question the competency of the officer and his or her ability to control inmates.

Another source of dissatisfaction is the lack of adequate organizational resources available to officers for performing the required tasks of the job. One of the most important resources in short supply are the means necessary to control inmate behavior. Although officers are legitimately empowered to use coercion (e.g., force, threats and physical punishments) to control inmates, administrators actively discourage its use. Coercion is costly in terms of manpower and resources; its use breaks down any chance of peaceful control, and public opinion will eventually condemn its excessive use (Schrag, 1961). Consequently, officers are caught in a quandary. Because inmates do not view officers as possessing legitimate control, coercion is the only means of control that they possess (Sykes, 1958). However, if coercion is used too often, officers risk disciplinary action by the jail administration.

Some scholars have argued that the involuntary and hostile nature of the clientele with whom corrections officers routinely interact is a source of irritation for the officers (Lipsky, 1980). Client-centered organizations such as jails require officers to work intensively and intimately with other people. Over an extended period of time such contact can be particularly wearing and stress-inducing (Shamir and Drory, 1982). The situation is made worse by the fact that officers receive very little esteem from their work with inmates. The job performed by officers places them in intimate contact with inmates who tend to be neither respectful, appreciative, nor supportive of their work.

Inmate Care and Treatment

A final component of the jail problem concerns the care and treatment provided to inmates. As noted previously, the decrepit state of the jail's physical plant, overcrowding and inadequate personnel place undue stress on prisoners. Inmate stress is further aggravated by the difficulties many prisoners experience while adapting to the jail environment and by the treatment they receive in the facility.

Jail incarceration is a totally disrupting event for those who must endure it. The shock that accompanies initial entry into the jail and the rapid transition from freedom to captivity are particularly difficult (Gibbs, 1982; Toch, 1975). Flynn (1973:68) described jail entry as a watershed where a "person first loses contact with family, employer, friends, personal belongings and clothes, and with every other symbol of his individuality and humanity." Those who have been arrested but not convicted must wrestle with a number of questions concerning how long they will be in jail, the chance of securing bail, the abilities of their attorney, and the extent of their legal predicaments. However, their inability to freely contact and consult with others leaves many of these questions unanswered. In *The Felon*, Irwin (1970:39-40) described prisoners' reactions to processing by the criminal justice system and the jail experience:

> These experiences—arrest, trial, and conviction—threaten the structure of his life in two separate ways. First, the disjointed experience of being suddenly extracted from a relatively orderly and familiar routine and cast into a completely unfamiliar and seemingly chaotic one where the ordering of events is completely out of his control has a shattering impact upon his personality structure. One's identity, one's personality system, one's coherent thinking about himself depend upon a relatively familiar, continuous, and predictable stream of events. In a Kafkaesque world of the booking room, the jail cell, the

interrogation room, and the visiting room, the boundaries of the self collapse.

While this collapse is occurring, the prisoner's network of social relations is being torn apart. The insulation between social worlds, an insulation necessary for the orderly maintenance of his social life, is punctured. Many persons learn about facets of his life that were previously unknown to them. Their "business is in the streets." Furthermore, a multitude of minor exigencies that must be met to maintain social relationships go unattended. Bills are not paid, friends are not befriended, families are not fed, consoled, advised, disciplined; businesses go unattended; obligations and duties cannot be fulfilled—in other words, roles cannot be performed. Unattended, the structure of the prisoner's social relations collapse.

The rapid transition from street to jail is so highly disruptive, debilitating and traumatic that it can result in serious psychological disturbances in prisoners and even lead to self-injury and suicide (Gibbs, 1982). In 1988, 287 jail inmates killed themselves (U.S. Department of Justice, 1990). According to a national study on jail suicides, "for the approximately 200,000 inmates in county jails and police lockups on any given day..., at least one person will kill himself" (Hayes, 1983:480). The suicide rate in jails is 16 times greater than in a city with a population comparable in size. The typical jail suicide is a 22-year-old, single, white male who has been arrested for an alcohol-related offense. The suicide usually occurs within 24 hours of arrest (Hayes, 1983:467-470). Research findings indicate that suicide is more prevalent in jails than it is in prisons (Danto, 1973), and that self-injury is greater among pretrial jail prisoners than in those serving sentences (Esparza, 1973; Heilig, 1973). Bowker (1982:312) argued that inmates react to the psychological stress associated with jail incarceration be becoming either resentful and uncooperative or depressed and suicidal.

The stress caused by the rapid transition from street to jail and uncertainty over legal matters is further aggravated by the treatment prisoners receive during the booking process. In addition to the loss of freedom and contact with friends and family, inmates are forced to undergo a series of degradations that include strip searches and delousing conducted by facility personnel. Barbara Deming (1972:152), arrested in Albany, Georgia, for participating in an integrated cross-country peace march, provides an example of the indignities prisoners experience when booked into jail:

A policewoman takes us into a small room in the building where we are arraigned. She searches our handbags for sharp objects; we take off most of our clothing for her, unfasten the rest as she peers at us.

The guard outside the temporary detention cell examines our bags for a second time, removes a few more possessions. At the House of Detention, a third guard empties the bags, keeps every remaining article. We have packed a few things with which to keep ourselves decent: comb, toothbrush, deodorant, a change of underclothes. She takes them all—even, in my case, some pieces of Kleenex. And if I have to blow my nose? "Find something else to blow it on," she tells me cheerfully. She explains then: I might be smuggling in dope this way. I am led into a large shower room and told to strip. Another guard shakes out each piece of clothing. Hands on her hips, she watches me closely as I take my shower, and I struggle hard now for self-possession. Her stance reminds me a little of that of an animal trainer. Now she asks me to hold my arms wide for a moment, turn my back and squat. I ask the reason. She, too, is searching for dope—or for concealed weapons. One of my companions has been led in by another woman and has stripped and is sitting on the toilet there. Her face is anguished. She explains her predicament to the guard: she is menstruating, but her extra sanitary napkins have been taken from her. "Just don't think about it," the woman tells her. I don't know how to help her; catch her eye and look away. I am given a very short hospital gown and led now into a small medical-examination room. Another of my companions is just leaving the room and smiles at me wanly. I climb up on the table. I assume that the examination performed is to check for venereal disease. The woman in the white smock grins at me and then at her assistant, who grins back. No, this too is a search for concealed dope or dangerous weapons.

Once in jail, prisoners are exposed to a number of irritants to which they must adapt, the most common of which is prolonged inactivity. In a survey of jail administrators and social service providers (Gibbs, 1983), insufficient activities for prisoners was ranked as the third most serious problem encountered in jails. Overcrowding and inmates with psychological problems were the only other problems ranking higher than inmate idleness. Almost half of the respondents indicated that boredom was the most serious problem facing jail prisoners.

For inmates, boredom and idleness are constant sources of irritation and stress. Some spend inordinate amounts of time worrying about their situation and about what is occurring outside the jail. In the words of one inmate:

You're in the cell most of the day. You're locked in. And you have nothing to do but think. You get tired of playing cards. That's all they got here is cards. You get tired of that after a while. You get sick of that. And you got to think. And what do you think about? You think about home, girl friends, things that you'd be doing, like if it was Friday night or Thursday night, what you'd be doing. And, like, when I lay down, I think of things like that. I try not to, but I can't help it. And I see things that I would be doing. I know what I'd be doing, and I can see this...I just couldn't take it (cited in Toch, 1975:148).

In the investigation of the Nassau County Jail, undercover agents sent into the facility recounted their experiences as inmates. For one female operative, the enforced boredom was almost unbearable.

My immediate feeling that [first] morning was of excitement, and in less than fifteen minutes, my cell was straight and I was dressed...and then it struck me that I had nowhere to go, nothing to do or see...that my freedom of choice for the rest of the day consisted solely in whether I ate or didn't eat the food that would be slid under my door, and whether I passed the time by sleeping, or reading one book or the other. My eagerness to be involved in the jail, just like any other desire, was utterly irrelevant. I think I could have become frightened at this first emotional realization of incarceration, but I was helped out, as at many later bad moments, by my knowledge of why I was here...that my responses were to be noted, not feared; emotions were grist to my mill, so I shrugged and noted it, and lay down on my bed with *Kiss Me Again, Stranger*, until breakfast arrived (Cahn, 1973:4).

An accounting of inmate services offered in the nation's jails indicates that only the largest jails offer educational, counseling and recreational programs to inmates; smaller jails have neither the facilities nor the money to provide inmate programs. The National Sheriffs' Association (1982:193,199) survey found that of 2,452 facilities only 49.6% offered personal counseling; 38.1% offered substance abuse counseling; 29.1% offered the GED (general equivalency diploma); 21.7% offered group counseling; and 14.4% offered adult basic education.

The same study found that a majority of jails (55.5%) allowed inmates only one or two visits from friends and relatives per week.[24] On average, inmates were provided 14.5 hours of outdoor recreation per week and 6.3 hours of indoor recreation per week.[25] Analysis by the size of the facility indicated that, in general, the larger the jail facilities, the wider the variety of programs for in-

[24] Almost 15% of the surveyed jails had unlimited visitation while 17.2% allowed from three to five visits per week.

[25] Although it could be argued that 20.8 hours per week is an adequate amount of recreation time, it must be remembered that with the exception of sleeping, eating, reading and watching television, there are few activities to fill the remaining 315.2 hours of the week.

mates. The smallest facilities had the fewest inmate programs. In summary, jails offer few activities for inmates except for "ubiquitous television viewing, card playing, perhaps ping-pong" (Flynn, 1973:63).

A commonly cited obstacle to offering educational and counseling programs to inmates in jails is the diversity of the inmate population. Types of jail inmates run the gamut from sentenced to unsentenced; women to men; young to old; employed to unemployed; educated to uneducated. The problems that these people face also vary and include alcohol and narcotic addition, personality disorders, psychiatric disorders, learning disabilities, mental illness, physical illness and disabilities, lack of education and job training.

Another reason given for the lack of adequate programs is the belief that they threaten the security of the facility. It is assumed that when inmates are provided with opportunities to leave the living area and to associate with other inmates during the counseling or educational sessions, facility security is reduced. Some, however, including the American Correctional Association, argue that programming and activities enhance facility security.

> Perhaps, in the final analysis, the soundest and safest security measure of all *is the existence of a positive program of inmate activities.* Such a program includes all the things such as work, recreation, and education...Such multifaceted programs are sometimes referred to as "calculated risks" against security. Actually, these positive programs have become important security factors in well-managed institutions of all types and have become primary security features in many institutions...Prisoners who are receiving decent food and humane treatment and who are busily engaged in self-improvement, seldom resort to disturbances or escape attempts. No matter how modern the buildings, how secure the facilities, how efficient the operating procedures may be, or how well the personnel may be trained, it should be emphasized that security cannot be assured if it is predicated entirely on procedures which are operated wholly against the will of the prisoners. If the prisoners are committed to inactivity, moral degradation, humiliation and mental stultification, then the desire within them to escape or throw off the shackles of these unnatural restraints will become so strong that security facilities and procedures will be breached sooner or later (American Correctional Association, 1966:367).

In addition to idleness and inactivity, prisoners are exposed to a number of other stress-inducing irritants in the jail environment. Jails have been aptly characterized as "revolving doors" because of the high number of people that pass through them and the relatively short duration of most incarcerations. The average inmate stay in a jail is 11 days (U.S. Department of Justice, 1983a).

Such a high rate of turnover makes it difficult for inmates to establish and maintain relationships with other inmates and, consequently, produces an environment perceived by inmates as both unstable and unpredictable.

The poor quality of the food provided by the facility is another source of irritation. In many cases, jail food tends to be unpalatable, contaminated and insufficient (Flynn, 1973). More often than not, by the time the food is served to inmates it is lukewarm. In cases where trustees are serving inmate meals, favoritism often prevails; the amount of food inmates receive depends on their relationship with a trustee or on what they can give the trustee in return.[26]

Another problem that inmates must deal with is unsafe conditions within the jail. Four factors contribute to inmate feelings of personal danger and insecurity: overcrowding, inadequate inmate classification, jail architecture and the lack of staff supervision. Overcrowding reduces the amount of space and privacy provided to inmates and forces them into close physical proximity with each other. Because of overcrowding, cells designed to hold one prisoner are used to house two or more. According to one court (*Inmates of the Suffolk County Jail v. Eisenstadt*, 1973:676,679), "it is impossible for two men to occupy one of these cells without regular, inadvertent physical contact, inevitably exacerbating tensions and creating interpersonal friction." In addition, multiple-occupancy cells provide ample opportunities for abusive inmates to prey upon more vulnerable jail residents.

In many facilities, classification for purposes of segregating inmate types is rudimentary at best, and nonexistent at worst. In most jails, classification and segregation are exclusively based on obvious inmate categories such as male/female and adult/juvenile (Mattick, 1974). No attempt is made to segregate experienced inmates from the inexperienced, predatory inmates from the vulnerable, or even sick inmates from healthy ones.[27]   Mattick (1974:812) commented that "jailers often *intentionally* fail to separate prisoner types for

---

[26] Trustees are prisoners who have been given work responsibilities in the jail. Some argue that without trustees many jails would be unable to function due to understaffing. Trustees may be responsible for cleaning, preparing meals, washing laundry, etc. In order to accomplish these tasks, trustees are given the run of the facility. Trustees are usually inmates serving a longer jail sentence who have been deemed reliable and responsible by the jail staff. In one facility I worked at, a trustee who was serving a one-year sentence on involuntary manslaughter regularly advised staff on jail and sheriffs' operations. Because the jail had no full-time jailers, sheriff's officer dispatchers were responsible for the wellbeing of inmates. High personnel turnover meant that the sheriff's office and the jail were being run by inexperienced and untrained staff. Because the trustee had been in the facility much longer than the staff, he was often able to advise them on how to perform the job. He was even able to show the dispatchers how to handle emergency police calls.

[27] Small jail facilities are often deterred from classification because, even if they had a well conceived system, the lack of space makes segregation according to inmate characteristics almost impossible.

lack of staff to supervise them; drunks and suicide risks are placed with others 'for their protection,' and juveniles may be mixed with adults so the latter can 'straighten them out'." Hence, without adequate classification and segregation, inmates are confined in close quarters with others who may be predatory, physically ill or mentally unbalanced.

The architecture of the facility and the lack of supervision interact to increase inmate safety concerns. In many traditional facilities, there are "blind spots" that make it difficult, if not impossible, for staff to observe inmate behavior and activities. Blind spots are those physical locations where staff surveillance is blocked by design features such a grillwork, walls, or dead-end corridors (Atlas, 1982). Many argue that the existence of blind spots provides predatory inmates with opportunities to assault (even murder) other inmates without being detected by staff. Even without the presence of "blind spots," the lack of adequate supervision provides opportunities for assaultive behavior. Inadequate supervision, whether a consequence of an architectural design that makes it difficult for staff to continually observe inmates, or whether a result of understaffing, often invites assaults between inmates as well as other types of aberrant inmate behavior.

A final irritant is the treatment inmates receive from staff. As demonstrated in earlier sections of this chapter, inmates do not always receive fair and consistent treatment from corrections officers. In a substantial number of cases, inmates are harassed, brutalized, and degraded by their keepers. The brutal nature of those hired as jail guards is commonly cited as a reason for this treatment.

A frequently stated homily is that guards differ little from the people they guard. Research on correctional staff backgrounds suggests strongly that this is particularly true in regard to the level of education and the socio-economic characteristics of both groups (Mattick, 1974:804). Others, however, have found that this similarity extends to psychological attributes as well. After administering a series of psychological tests to corrections officer candidates and prison inmates, psychologist Allan Berman found that each group was almost identical in regard to their "violence potential," with inmates scoring as slightly less violence-prone than the officers. According to Berman (cited in Mitford, 1973:9), the findings "imply that the officer group actually has the potential for even more unexplained lashing out than does the inmate group." He concluded that "...the officer candidates are as likely as the inmates to engage in assaultive behavior. This would carry along the correlative implication that the reasons why one group is behind bars and the other group is guarding them may be due to incidental factors..."

Others argue that authoritarian behavior on the part of guards is actually a product of the social institution of the jail rather than a reflection of the individual characteristics or pathologies of the guards. The crux of this viewpoint is that situational as opposed to dispositional factors contribute to staff brutality and aggression. Although often criticized for its methodological deficiencies, the simulated prison experiment conducted by Haney, Banks and Zimbardo (1973) supports this argument. In that research, 22 "physically and mentally stable" male college students were randomly assigned to the role of guard or inmate and situated in a simulated prison. According to the authors, extreme reactions by both groups were almost immediately apparent.

> While guards and prisoners were essentially free to engage in any form of interaction (positive or negative, supportive or affrontive, etc.), the characteristic nature of their encounters tended to be negative, hostile, affrontive, and dehumanizing. Prisoners immediately adopted a generally passive style of responding, while guards assumed a very active initiative role in all interactions. Throughout the experiment, commands were the most frequent form of verbal behavior and, generally, verbal exchanges were strikingly impersonal, with few references to individual identity. Although it was clear to all subjects that the experimenters would not permit physical violence to take place, varieties of less direct aggressive behavior was observed frequently (especially on the part of guards). In fact, varieties of verbal affronts became the most frequent form of interpersonal contact between guards and prisoners (1973:164).

Conclusions

The history of the jail provides an important lesson about the insidious nature of the problems affecting modern detention facilities. More than 350 years of intensive industrial and technological growth and development have passed, yet the modern jail still retains elements of the inhumane conditions and custodial practices that prevailed in the first jails. Early English gaols were "dumping grounds" into which were thrown children, the physically infirmed, the mentally ill, and other social outcasts deemed offensive to public taste and sensibilities. The modern American jail continues to function as a catch-all institution for the more troubled and troublesome members of society. Inadequate physical facilities, unsanitary living conditions, overcrowding, the lack of segregation, uncaring personnel, idleness and boredom were common in feudal, English goals as they are in modern American jails.

For many who pass through the portals of the contemporary American jail the experience is one of inhumane brutality. In *The New Red Barn*, Nagel

(1973:188) captured in a photograph the sentiment of prisoners and staff alike. Scrawled on the wall of a cell were these words:

> To the builders of this nitemare though you may never get to read these words. I pity you; for the cruelity of your minds have designed this hell; if men's buildings are a reflection of what they are, this one portraits the ugliness of all humanity. If only you had some compassion.

Chapter Four

Evolution of the
New Generation Philosophy

Although for decades the deplorable conditions in jails were tolerated and ignored by governmental officials and the public, federal court intervention forced an end to the malaise in local corrections. In the mid-1960s, the federal courts moved away from their traditional "hands off" policy in regard to the constitutionality of jail conditions. In case after case, the courts ruled that conditions in many local jails constituted cruel and unusual punishment, and ordered that immediate action be taken to improve jail facilities and operations (*Cooper v. Pate*, 1964; *Holt v. Sarver*, 1976; *Estelle v. Gamble*, 1976). The U.S. Supreme Court's 1974 decision in *Wolff v. McDonnel* provided support for this intervention. The court asserted that:

> Though his rights may be diminished by the needs and exigencies of the institutional environment, a prisoner is not wholly stripped of constitutional protection when he is imprisoned for crime. There is no iron curtain drawn between the constitution and the prisons of this country (555-556).

The courts' willingness to hear inmate allegations as to violations of their constitutional rights and to intervene in the administration of local jails produced a deluge of litigation as inmates challenged every conceivable aspect of the jail and its operations—from inadequate heating, lighting and ventilation to the censorship of mail. The number of petitions filed by local and state prisoners in federal courts increased from 218 petitions in 1966 to 2,030 in 1970, 12,397 in 1980, and 16,741 in 1981 (Howard, 1982:379; Advisory Commission

65

of Intergovernmental Relations, 1984:149). In 1981, "one out of every five cases filed in federal courts...[was] on behalf of prisoners" (Moore, 1981:1). The impact of this litigation on local jails was profound and far-reaching. By 1982, an estimated 11% of all jails were under court order; 16% had been involved in court actions; and 20% were a party in a pending lawsuit (National Sheriffs' Association, 1982:43-55).

In response to the threat of inmate litigation, many jurisdictions constructed facilities in order to improve jail conditions and forestall court intervention. In many cases construction was necessary given the antiquated and decrepit physical conditions of jail facilities and the need to meet minimum physical plant standards established by the courts. But in most cases construction alone did not overcome the century-old and obviously outdated institutional operations, practices and architecture which contributed significantly to unsafe, inhumane and unconstitutional jail conditions.

For a small number of local officials, the court-ordered pressures to improve jail conditions provided an opportunity to question the success of traditional jail operations. The search for a more effective alternative led many to consider the innovative architecture and inmate management style implemented in the federal Metropolitan Correctional Centers. Although a radical departure from the architecture and custodial practices of local detention facilities, the modular design and direct inmate supervision style of the Metropolitan Correction Centers represented a model for local jail officials who believed that the problems of jails involved more than just an antiquated and decrepit physical plant.

Federal Metropolitan Correctional Centers

During the mid-1960s the federal government undertook the construction of the first federally operated detention facilities for federal prisoners. The construction was part of a Presidential directive to improve the federal correctional system (Nelson, 1988b). These facilities were to be located in the metropolitan areas of New York City, Chicago, and San Diego. Up until this time federal pre-trial detainees and other unconvicted prisoners in these cities were housed in local jails on a contract basis. The worsening problem of overcrowding at the local level, however, made more evident the need for the construction of detention facilities to maintain custody over increasing numbers of federal prisoners. Under a mandate from the U.S. Congress, the Federal Bureau of Prisons sought to build "humane institutions whose environment would respect the legal and moral rights of individuals" (Wener and Olsen, 1978:1). In the architectural requirements for design and construction of the detention facilities, the Bureau of Prisons outlined the intent of the envisioned Metropolitan Correctional Centers.

Planning for the new Metropolitan Complex is based on the assumption that pre-trial detainees, being presumed innocent, should not be submitted to any restriction beyond those justified by the specific purpose of their detention...While a person is detained, the government is obliged to care for him and to protect him against dangers to his personal rights. These duties extend not only to proper feeding, clothing, and health care, but also to treatment according to general American standards of decency and full protection of human rights (cited in Wener and Olsen, 1978:3).

Inexperienced with administering pre-trial detention facilities, the Bureau of Prisons set out to study the issues and problems of short-term detention and to examine the research of penologists and psychologists. From this research, the Bureau established a set of principles that were to be incorporated into the design of the new facilities (Wener and Olsen, 1978).

First, the new federal facilities were to provide an environment wherein safe and secure detention would be assured. Second, the facilities were to be planned for purposes of detainment rather than punishment. Design features that produced a punishment effect were to be minimized. Third, inmates were to be divided into small groups of approximately 40 to 50 for housing purposes. Finally, interior features of the facility were to be designed to reduce the "trauma" of incarceration and to ensure efficient use of space. The living units were to be arranged to ensure that corrections officers could observe all areas within the unit; "blind spots" or obstructions to staff observation of the unit were to be minimized. In addition, no office, desk, or station for corrections officers was to be included in the living units so that officers would interact with inmates rather than spend their shift locked in an office or ensconced behind a desk. The living units were also to be designed with areas of open and unrestricted space to reduce the sense of confinement experienced by prisoners. Furthermore, the designs were to remove all possible "symbols of incarceration." No bars were to be used in the living units, windows were to be provided in every prisoner's room, and carpets, padded and moveable furniture, and colorful wall coverings were to be used to reduce the institutional ambience of the facility.

The most important design requirements stipulated by the Bureau of Prisons were single cells for inmates, direct staff supervision and "functional inmate living units." Functional units place all "sleeping, food, and hygiene facilities, as well as some recreational equipment, in one self-contained, multi-level space" (Wener and Olsen, 1978:4). A corrections officer is assigned to each unit to ensure direct and continuous supervision of inmates.

The concept of the functional unit originated in the mid- to late-1950s, but was used only in federal juvenile correctional centers. In early 1960, the

Demonstration Counseling Project introduced the functional unit concept in the National Training School for Boys in Washington, D.C. In this application, a case load of juvenile inmates were housed in one living unit, and a multidisciplinary staff was assigned to implement counseling and recreational programs. These efforts were so successful that functional units were implemented in other types of facilities. In 1968, for example, functional units were employed in the first drug treatment programs in federal correctional institutions. Their use spread to other correctional institutions. By 1977, functional units existed in 23 federal correctional institutions (Lansing, Bogan, and Karacki, 1977:43).

Evaluations of the effectiveness of the functional units have found that they offer a number of advantages. Among the most important:

(1) [They] divide the large number of inmates into small, well-defined and manageable groups, whose members develop a common identity and close association with each other and their unit staff.

(2) [They] increase the frequency of contacts and the intensity of the relationships between staff and inmates, resulting in:

(a) better communication and understanding between individuals;

(b) more individualized classification and program planning;

(c) more valuable program reviews and program adjustments;

(d) better observation of inmates, enabling early detection of problems before they reach critical proportions;

(e) development of common goals which encourage positive unit cohesiveness; and,

(f) generally a more positive living and working environment for inmates and staff.

(3) The multi-disciplinary unit staff members' varied backgrounds and different areas of expertise enhance communication and cooperation with other institution departments.

(4) Staff involvement in the correctional process and decision-making opportunities are increased, further developing the correctional and management skills of the staff.

(5) Decisions are made by the unit staff who are most closely associated with the inmates, increasing the quality and swiftness of decision-making.

(6) Program flexibility is increased, since special areas of emphasis can be developed to meet the needs of the inmates in each unit; programs in a unit may be changed without affecting the total institution (Lansing, Bogan and Karacki, 1977:44-45).

The Federal Bureau of Prisons sought to achieve four goals through these design requirements. First, they hoped that the functional unit design and direct inmate supervision style would encourage informal and positive interaction between inmates and staff, thereby reducing tensions and allowing the staff to assist and counsel inmates. Second, it was hoped that single rooms would reduce tensions associated with the lack of inmate privacy. Third, the soft environment of the living units was intended to encourage care for and pride in the unit, and to reduce aggressive and destructive inmate behavior. Finally, it was hoped that through such design features as windows in the rooms the sense of separation prisoners experience from the community would be reduced.

The Federal Bureau of Prisons commissioned three architectural firms to design the facility. They were forbidden to communicate with each other during the design process. The purpose was to see what plans could be independently developed from the Bureau's specifications. In 1975, the Metropolitan Correctional Centers opened in New York City, Chicago and San Diego. Although the architectural firm of Harry Weese and Associates won a major architectural award for their design of the Chicago Center, all three were given mixed reviews. ' Immediately upon opening, the facilities in New York City and San Diego were overcrowded. The New York Center was sued for overcrowding. This case produced the U.S. Supreme Court's landmark decision, *Bell v. Wolfish.* Therein, the Court declared that double-bunking was not per se unconstitutional given the fact that inmates were not locked in their cells most of the day (Call, 1983).

Several minor design problems were found in all three facilities. In Chicago, for example, there were not enough elevators to transport staff, prisoners and visitors through the high-rise facility. There was no gym for indoor recreation, and there was not enough storage space in the living units. For the most part, however, the facilities met the goals established by the Bureau: "there was little violence, tension, or vandalism; staff requirements were not excessive; and officers seemed more satisfied with their jobs" (Gettinger, 1984:11).

While the Bureau of Prisons hoped that the design and operations established in the Metropolitan Correctional Centers would be duplicated by local facilities, the concepts, particularly direct inmate supervision, were not readily accepted in other jurisdictions.[1] Even though the Centers were demonstrably

---

1   Local jail officials did, however, readily accept a number of specific design features of the Metropolitan Correctional Centers, most importantly the functional living unit concept and individual rooms for inmates. They did not so readily accept the concept of direct inmate supervision. Jails that have the functional living units but not direct inmate supervision are commonly referred to as "podular/remote supervision" facilities. This design is distinguishable from the podular/direct supervision design in that inmates are divided into smaller groups of between 12

successful in achieving their goals of safe and humane incarceration, many local jail administrators believed that the prisoners in the federal Centers were different from those in local facilities. They argued that federal detainees were "softer prisoners," while the individuals they regularly dealt with were more violent and destructive.

Despite this reticence, the first local facility designed in the new style opened in the 1970s. Officials in Contra Costa County (California) had originally designed their jail as a 642-bed traditional, high-rise facility. During the design phase of the project, local community opposition arose over both the design and the size of the new facility. To appease critics, the county executive appointed a committee to study the issue. The first act of the committee was to scrap the original architectural plans and start fresh. Their meetings included heated debates on the purpose of detention, a desirable size for their facility, and its operating philosophy. After touring a number of facilities with different designs, the committee expressed approval of the Chicago Metropolitan Correctional Center design. Satisfied with the recommendations of the committee, county officials ordered the architects to construct a smaller, 386-bed facility in accordance with the design concepts of the Chicago Center. The major design difference between the two facilities was the "open booking" intake center which had been originated in a St. Louis jail and was incorporated in the Contra Costa facility. The open booking area has been described as "unusual":

> Most booking areas are high-security places, with inmates kept in large holding pens or isolated is small barren rooms until escorted to the desk for processing. The Contra Costa County booking area is the most relaxed spot in the jail. It centers around a large lounge, attractively furnished and supplied with television sets and cigarette and coffee machines. Men and women are not separated, but mingle together. Arrestees stay in the lounge until they are called to the desk. They can telephone relatives and attempt to raise bail. Inebriated arrestees are kept in a separate room, which is staffed by volunteers from Alcoholics Anonymous. Unless they are charged with a serious crime, they are released without being booked into the main part of the jail (Gettinger, 1984:12).

---

and 16 for housing purposes. The fixtures and furnishings in the living units are made of heavy, vandal-resistant metal and are typically bolted to the walls or floor. Corrections officers supervise inmates from a glass-enclosed observation post or by intermittently patrolling the housing units. As with the traditional linear/intermittent surveillance design, the extent to which inmates are supervised by correctional staff is limited by the desires of the individual officers and design features that make observation of all areas of the living unit difficult from a fixed location. And as with the linear/intermittent surveillance design, the fixtures and furnishings of the living units are designed to compensate for the lack of inmate supervision by staff.

The Contra Costa Detention Facility became a "showplace" as soon as it opened. Not only did the facility prove cost-effective to build, but early reports indicated that it was safer for inmates and staff. Most importantly, the experience of Contra Costa County discredited the belief that the new design would work only with "soft criminals." In Contra Costa, "almost no misdemeanants are booked into the jail; the majority of inmates have been charged with burglary, armed robbery, murder, narcotics, or escape" (Gettinger, 1984:13).

The opening of the Contra Costa Detention Facility marked the material birth of the "New Generation" philosophy. The term, "New Generation," was coined to characterize a style of architecture and inmate management totally new and unique to local detention facilities. The term, as well as the architectural design and inmate management style, symbolized a new generation in correctional thought. Like most significant innovations in social technology, the precepts of the new philosophy developed over an extended time period, and hence, New Generation jail thinking passed through several stages of change and modification. Similarly, as with other social innovations, the New Generation philosophy itself represents a synthesis of a number of smaller programmatic changes which were developed in correctional institutions throughout the country.

The popularity of the New Generation design grew following the success of the Contra Costa County Jail. Tucson (Arizona), Portland (Oregon), and Las Vegas (Nevada) were among local jurisdictions opting for the new design. By late 1988, direct supervision facilities were either in operation or being planned in 41 local jurisdictions (Nelson, 1988a). The federal government, continuing with its commitment to such facilities, constructed new Metropolitan Correctional Centers in Tucson and Miami. In addition, a New Generation federal detention facility is currently being planned for Los Angeles.

A most surprising effect of the New Generation jail movement was the decision by New York City officials to reconstruct the Manhattan House of Detention, commonly known as "The Tombs," as a New Generation facility. The Tombs was closed by federal courts in 1974 for brutality, excessive noise and physical inadequacies deemed too extensive to be repaired. Instead of tearing down the structure, the building was gutted and renovated in accordance with the New Generation design. The new Tombs opened in the Fall of 1983.

Support for the new philosophy also came from various professional correctional associations. The American Correctional Association endorsed the new design in its publication, *Design Guides for Secure Adult Correctional Facilities* (1983). At about the same time, the Advisory Board of the National Institute of Corrections also formally endorsed the philosophy. In a press conference, W. Walter Menninger, Chairman of the Advisory Board and Director of Law and Psychiatry at the Menninger Foundation, stated:

> Careful studies of these new generation facilities have found significant benefits for inmates, staff and society at large. There are fewer untoward incidents and assaults in these facilities than in traditionally designed or remote supervision facilities. In addition to the greater level of personal safety for both staff and inmates, one finds greater staff satisfaction, more orderly and relaxed inmate housing areas, a better maintained physical plant (i.e., less destruction and graffiti) after years of heavy use. Finally, of no small consequence is the fact that these facilities are cost effective both to construct and to operate.
>
> From my perspective as a psychiatrist, I am not surprised that the new generation facilities have proved to be so effective. The design of the facility brings out the best, rather than the worst, in the inmate. The inmates respond positively to an expectation they will function in a reasonable and appropriate manner...
>
> Accordingly, the Advisory Board of the National Institute of Corrections (NIC) urges jurisdictions presently contemplating the construction or renovation of jails and prisons to explore the appropriateness of the podular/direct supervision (new generation) concept of jail and prison design/management for their new and renovated facilities. The NIC Advisory Board believes that the economic, social, and professional values implicit in this concept of jail and prison design and management exemplify an appropriate direction for detention of persons who require incarceration (cited in Nelson and O'Toole, 1983:35-36).

Chapter Five
Assumptions Underlying the New Generation Philosophy

The fundamental goal of the architectural design and inmate management style prescribed by the New Generation philosophy is to create an incarcerative environment in which both inmates and staff are safe from violence and predation, and where inmates are treated humanely and in accordance with constitutional prohibitions against punishing pretrial detainees. Both the architecture and inmate management style are informed by a set of theoretical assumptions about the causes of unsafe and inhumane conditions that exist in many traditional jail facilities. In their simplest form, these assumptions maintain that unsafe and inhumane jail conditions are the result of defects in traditional jail architecture and operations which create fear among inmates and staff; which provide opportunities for inmates to engage in predation without fear of detection by staff; which allow inmates to share power and control with jail staff; which isolate inmates from formal and informal mechanisms of social control; which communicate and reinforce the message that inmates are untrustworthy; and, which subject inmates to uncontrollable and unrelievable environmental stress.[1]

Inmate and Staff Fear

A number of deficiencies in the architecture and operations of the jail make detention a dangerous experience for inmates or, at the least, create a perception

---

[1] Five of the six assumptions are inferred from Stephen Getttinger's (1988:14-15) brief description of the psychology of New Generation jails. Credit should therefore be given to Gettinger for providing the initial foundation for these assumptions.

of peril and insecurity. These deficiencies have been described in detail in previous chapters. The most critical include: the linear architectural design that
provides ample opportunities for inmates to engage in violent and destructive
behavior without detection by staff; intermittent staff surveillance that leaves
inmates unsupervised for substantial periods of time; inadequate classification
systems that assign predatory prisoners to the same housing units as more vulnerable inmates; heterogeneous inmate populations that bring together ill and
healthy, strong and weak, and naive and sophisticated offenders; rapid turnover
among prisoners that creates an unstable and unpredictable environment; overcrowding which forces inmates into close proximity with those who have reputations for aggressive and violent behavior; and, understaffing which further reduces staff surveillance of inmate activities.

Although violence is not an everyday occurrence for most prisoners, many
live in constant fear that one day they will be confronted by violence from other
inmates, knowing that the institution alone cannot prevent or deter it from hap-
pening. To a large extent, inmates must depend on their own abilities to protect
themselves from victimization. However, the means available to inmates are
severely limited. In most cases there are only two options available—fight or
flight (Toch, 1977).

In many respects, the nature of the correctional institution makes violence
the only effective response to threats or acts of violence. Inmates housed in
multiple-occupancy cells or dormitories have few available means to physically
escape from victimization—particularly when the victimizer shares a cell or
dormitory with the victim. To flee from violence or its threatened use, inmates
must request segregation. However, the costs associated with such flight are
quite severe. To make such a request, inmates must first admit to themselves
that they are too weak to fight off an attack. To enter segregation is to suffer a
serious blow to one's self-esteem and to the vision of one's courageousness
(Toch, 1977). To flee victimization also requires that the facility have available
segregation space and that the staff be willing to cooperate by removing the inmate from the general population. In some cases, staff cooperation may not be
readily provided. Staff may respond to the requests of the inmate with ridicule
or with the advice that the inmate stand up to other prisoners. Toch (1977:158)
cited an interview with an inmate who was advised by staff to counter the
threats of other inmates with violence.

And they [staff] told me that you can't run away from it. You have to
knock them down, face up to them. The first person that you knock
out, you get locked up for three or four days, and then you come out
and come back down, and you're going to get a lot more respect...I
remember one thing that I said to them. I said that these guys were
big, and I would have to jump three feet to reach them. And they said

that I would have to bring them down to my size. And he told me to kick them in the nuts, and that would bring them down to my size. And he said not to be afraid of lockup...And they all agreed with each other...they said that there was a recommendation that I would have to start fighting and that that would be the only way to do things...One guy started out and said, "Why don't you knock him out on his ass?" And the others said, "Yeah, why don't you?" And then that was the solution, and then they sent me out and said, "Next, please!"

Given the lack of opportunities for flight, as well as the associated costs, fighting back may be the only means of self-protection readily available to inmates. For many, preemptive violence is the only means to survive an impending attack and to prevent future victimization. By demonstrating a willingness to use violence the inmate warns others that an attack will not be without costs.

Targets of victimization are chosen because they are deemed unmanly, and they are viewed as unmanly because they show fear or resourcelessness. A man loses his target attributes if he provides demonstrations of fearlessness, or if he sports stigmata of manliness. Violence works because it points to a misdiagnosis of the target. Violence also works because aggressors are not as sure of themselves as they pretend. A victim who reacts nonfearfully becomes an uninviting arena for proving one's manliness. He is uninviting because the confrontation can misfire into a demonstration of unmanliness. It is safer to seek other fish in the sea whose reactions are dependably fearful (Toch, 1977:162).

In addition to preemptive violence, inmates who fear victimization by others may make contraband weapons, "buy" protection from other inmates, or join gangs. While these alternatives provide some measure of protection, they also add to overall levels of disorder in the facility and reinforce the need for protection. In short, inmates who fear for their safety engage in behaviors that increase the probability of destruction and violence—thereby intensifying perceptions of danger.

Fear is also prevalent among staff. Their fear grows out of their contact with inmates who have reputations for using violence and brutality, and from having to continually deal with a population that appears uncontrolled and uncontrollable. Staff fear is further intensified by the knowledge that the tools necessary to control inmate behavior are lacking. While coercion is the primary and formal means by which the jail organization presumes to maintain order, its use by custodial staff is severely limited by institutional policies, laws and public opinion. Furthermore, force and physical violence are neither effective nor efficient means for controlling inmate behavior (Sykes, 1958; Schrag, 1961; Cloward, 1968). Since the legitimate means available for inmate control are weak and ineffectual, officers find it more expedient and safer to allow inmates to bend or break rules in exchange for at least a modicum of compliance and cooperation (Cloward, 1968; Goffman, 1961; Sykes, 1958). In succumbing to this corruption of their authority, officers demonstrate to themselves, as well as to inmates, the tenuous nature of their control.

Like inmates, officers develop strategies to cope with their fear of inmates and the threat of violence (Jacobs and Retsky, 1975). Some officers become *repressive* and respond to the threat of inmates with their own form of violence. These officers believe that by placing stringent controls on prisoners they can discourage violence. Others try to strike-up *friendships* with inmates in the hope that they will protect them from harassment and violence by others. Still others deal with their fear by *avoiding* contact with prisoners. As with inmates, the coping strategies adopted by officers increase the probability of inmate violence. More importantly, they serve to further reduce what little control officers hold. With the first approach, repression stimulates resentment and promotes expressive bursts of inmate violence against staff. The second approach places staff in the position of performing favors for prisoners. In some cases, these favors include purposely failing to report violence, bringing in contraband weapons, and even allowing inmates access to the segregation units for the purposes of victimization (Davidson, 1968). All of these favors hold a potential for additional violent behavior. The third approach, avoiding prisoners, presents inmates with opportunities to engage in violence upon other inmates without staff detection. The less supervision inmates receive from fearful staff members, the less they are deterred from using violence against others. The relationship is cyclical. The more officers avoid prisoners out of fear, the more violent inmates become—and, in so doing, the officers are reinforced in their fear of inmate violence.

Unprotected and Unprotectable Space

Within the last few decades there has been a growing interest in the effect of the physical environment on crime rates and the fear of crime (National Crime Prevention Institute, 1986:118). Several studies have been conducted to test the relationship between the physical design of buildings, streets, and neighborhoods and the frequency with which crime occurs or is feared. This research has established links between design features and crime at the site (Ley and Cybriwsky, 1974; Pablant and Baxter, 1975), street (Bevis and Nutter, 1977), and neighborhood levels (Lewis and Maxfield, 1980; Fowler, McCalla, and Mangione, 1979). Other research findings support the hypothesized relationship between environmental design and fear (Newman and Franck, 1980; Waller and Okihiro, 1978).

Supporters of the environmental design approach to crime control argue that appropriate design features can influence the incidence of crime in two ways. First, physical structures and environments can be designed to reduce opportunities for the commission of crimes and to raise the perceived risk of being detected and apprehended. Second, environments can be designed to facilitate informal social control and natural surveillance of buildings and neighborhoods by residents (Newman, 1972). Although this is a relatively new area of research and the assumptions of the model are still under debate, there nevertheless appears to be a link between crime and the physical design of the environment. Notwithstanding the obvious connection between crime and inmate victimization, very few writers have considered the contribution of incarceration facilities' design on exploitation and destruction.

The traditional, linear jail architecture is poorly designed for ensuring institutional control of inmate behavior or preventing incidents of exploitive and destructive behavior. The design severely obstructs staff observation of inmates and their activities by limiting officers' range of vision to only the cell they face. The problems of the architecture are further aggravated by an overreliance on mechanical surveillance equipment to monitor areas deemed a high risk for inmate escapes. Other areas of the jail, particularly inmate living units, are usually given scant attention. In his study of jail architecture, Nagel (1973) found that in many facilities inmate housing units were rarely observed by the correctional staff. Instead, the emphasis was on perimeter security—guarding the exterior boundaries of the facility to prevent inmate escapes. Cameras and other mechanical devices were used to oversee inmates. However, these devices were placed in such a way that numerous unsupervised locations resulted.

> In some jails the officer sat in his office and looked at the images televised from cameras focused down the corridors of the housing units. Here, the concern is perimeter security; if nothing was going on in the corridor, or elevator, all was considered well. Anything could be going on in the housing unit itself because the cameras did not provide surveillance of these areas. The safety of the individual inmate was not considered important in the design of the closed circuit television system. In fact inmate safety is diminished by replacing the physical walk-around with the television system (Nagel, 1973:29).

Brantingham and Brantingham (1978) and Brill (1979) suggested that selection of a crime site is a conscious and deliberate act. Inmates select locations for victimization that are perceived to provide the lowest risk of being observed by custodial staff. Housing units, showers, and areas of the dayrooms or recreation yard that are obstructed from staff view ("blind spots") are common locations for inmate misbehavior.

Studies of sites selected for inmate victimization bear out the notion that housing units are the least supervised and most vulnerable areas for inmate attacks. Sylvester, Reed and Nelson (1977) found that 25% of prison homicides occurred in the participants' cell; one-third of all homicides occurred in cellblocks or dormitories. Atlas (1982) found similar results in a study of the relationship between architectural and environmental factors and the incidence of inmate violence in four correctional institutions in the southeastern United States. According to his findings, most incidents of violence occurred in inmate cells (between 27% and 44%) or in dormitories (between 5% and 31%). He also found that the most serious assaults (armed assaults) occurred in areas that received only limited staff supervision. Atlas (1982) concluded his study by noting that housing was the most important factor in inmate assaults. These findings support Newman (1972), who similarly contended that opportunities for particular types of crimes are present in different parts of the building.

In addition to influencing opportunities for aberrant behavior or its detection by staff, the layout and design of the facility also determine the degree to which inmates can protect themselves from victimization. In jails where multiple-occupancy cells and dormitories are the primary housing arrangements, inmates have few available means to escape from victimization. To physically remove themselves from the threat of others, inmates must request transfer to segregation. As previously discussed, few inmates are willing to suffer such humiliation.

The design also influences the ability of inmates to develop a sense of territory, thus reducing fear and anticipatory violence. Territory, according to Brower (1965:9), is a "tendency on the part of organisms to establish boundaries around their physical confines, to lay claim to the space or territory within these boundaries, and to defend it against outsiders." Ardrey (1966), along with other environmental psychologists, argued that territory is important for all social animals for the development of a needed sense of security and safety.

Territoriality is typically associated with species of animals who mark and identify certain areas as their own. Within such an area animals feed, mate and raise offspring. They also strive to protect its perimeter from encroachment by other, predatory animals. Whether territoriality is a human instinct is a subject of continuing debate in the environmental psychology literature. While many scholars agree that humans do exhibit territorial behavior, there are a number of points that distinguish animal and human behavior relative to territorial concerns. For example, animals typically use only one territory, while humans use several (i.e., home, office, school, recreation retreats, etc.).[2]

Deprivation of territory among animals produces severe consequences (e.g., death, starvation), but its impact on humans has not been well researched. Some scholars nevertheless argue that territory gives humans a sense of ownership that is necessary for the development of caretaking and defensive behaviors (Sommer, 1969).

Territory is an important theme in Newman's (1972) concept of "defensible space." Defensible space refers to a variety of design features that provide real and symbolic barriers, strongly defined territories of influence, and improved surveillance opportunities that function to enhance residential control over an environment. Newman (1972:3) defined the role of defensible space in the development of territoriality:

> *Defensible space* is a model for residential environments which inhibit crime by creating physical expression of a social fabric that defends itself. All the different elements which combine to make a defensible space have a common goal—an environment in which latent territoriality and sense of community in the inhabitants can be translated into responsibility for ensuring a safe, productive, and well-maintained living space. The potential criminal perceives such a space as controlled by its residents, leaving him an intruder easily recognized and dealt with.

One study investigating territoriality in correctional settings found that both inmates and correction officers developed feelings of territory and exhibited de-

---

2   Edney (1976:189-205) identifies eight theoretical differences between human and animal territoriality. These are:
   (1)   human territoriality is learned, rather than genetic;
   (2)   the relationship between territoriality and aggression among humans is not as clear-cut as with animals;
   (3)   territories serve the biological needs of animals (e.g., food sources, shelter) while humans use them for a broader range of activities (e.g., recreation);
   (4)   humans maintain several territories simultaneously while animals usually occupy only one;
   (5)   humans share territories with others (e.g., tables at a restaurant) while animals do not;
   (6)   because of the nature of modern weaponry, humans are the only animals that can engage in territorial warfare without themselves entering the territory of another human;
   (7)   widespread invasion of an animal's territory is rare, yet among humans this is typical in times of war;
   (8)   humans are the only organisms that routinely entertain others within their territories.

fensive behavior when their territory was invaded (McReynolds, 1973). Staff claimed as their domain administrative offices within the facility, while inmates' domains included living units, recreational areas, and courtyards. In this facility, territoriality was dysfunctional for the jail organization because inmates reacted defensively to the intrusion of corrections officers in their defined territory.

Other studies in correctional institutions suggest that the establishment of clear territorial boundaries functions to separate conflicting groups and reduce stress and aggression within the institution (Stokols and Marrero, 1976; Sundstrom and Altman, 1974; McReynolds and Palys, 1975). Such territorial boundaries permit inmates to instantly recognize intruders to their areas and to closely observe their activities. It has been suggested as well that this social mechanism serves the important function of reducing thefts of inmate property (Wener and Olsen, 1980).

Although overlooked by many correctional scholars, the architectural design and layout of the traditional, linear jail facility play an important role in weakening institutional control. The physical design obstructs effective staff observation of inmates and prevents detection of exploitive and destructive behavior. It also encourages aberrant inmate behavior by decreasing perceived risks of detection. The architecture further weakens institutional control by creating an unsafe and unprotected environment for both inmates and staff, thus contributing to feelings of defenselessness and heightening fear of victimization.

Absence of Positive Leadership

Given the deficiencies in the linear architectural design and intermittent inmate surveillance style of traditional jail facilities, it is difficult, if not impossible, for correctional officials and staff members to provide consistent and continuous leadership among inmates. The absence of legitimate leadership allows for the development of a system of informal inmate domination, predicated on viciousness and brutality, that undermines the authority and control of the institution.

A form of informal inmate leadership commonly found in jails is that of the "barn bosses." The barn boss system is believed to be a holdover from decades past wherein money was saved by using inmate leaders to supervise the work of convict labor gangs. The Mississippi State Penitentiary relied primarily on inmates to guard other inmates as late as the mid-1970s (McWhorter, 1981:1). Under the Mississippi system, inmate-guards carried keys and guns, chased escapees, and some even assisted local law enforcement agencies in manhunts. Reports of inmate-guard brutality and abuse were widespread. A legislative subcommittee investigation found that "beatings are regularly inflicted and death occurs from a variety of unnatural causes most of which receive little or no attention from the outside world" (quoted in McWhorter, 1981:2).

The barn boss system may also have developed from Kangaroo Courts which were not uncommon in earlier day jails. Kangaroo Courts were organizations of prisoners established to maintain self-discipline and order among prisoners. Kangaroo Courts have been traced back to jails in England in pre-colonial days. They are believed to have thrived in Newgate Prison in 1818 as well as in the Walnut Street Jail in Philadelphia (Barnes and Teeters, 1959).

As a form of inmate self-government, the Court formulated and enforced its own rules. Typically, the purpose of the rules was to maintain a clean and orderly environment (Queen, 1920). Inmates elected their own judges and held mock-trials whereby offending inmates could be fined for disobedience to the rules. Often, the system was condoned by the jailer who may have participated in the system by accepting a portion of the offending inmate's fine. Not surprisingly, the abuses of the Kangaroo Court were extensive. Most states outlawed their existence after a series of inmate murders by Court members received widespread publicity.

Today, "barn bosses" are informal leaders of the tiers or housing units. In some jails, barn bosses are used by jail officials to maintain order among inmates and to act as conduits for communication between jail officials and the inmate population. Although some jails refuse to recognize the leadership of barn bosses, it is generally believed that such leadership still exists. Inmates who accede to barn boss positions are typically the strongest, wiliest or meanest of inmates, and their control is often iron-fisted. Davidson (1968:20) described the reign of barn bosses in the Cook County (Chicago) Jail as one of absolute tyranny.

> They brutalized the prisoners, dictated to the guards and led insurrections. In recent months investigators have found that they sold the jail's food rations, mattresses, blankets, plates and even cells to the inmates in their tiers—for money or for homosexual acquiescence. The going rate for a cell and mattress was $2.50, for a blanket, $3.50, and sheets cost an inmate $2 a week. The barn bosses also sold "protection" to inmates who feared violence from other prisoners. Frequently, the record shows, the barn bosses were the ones who instigated and led the assaults.

Although some scholars, like Clemmer (1940), have claimed that inmate leaders develop irrespective of whether institutional officials recognize their existence, others have suggested that officials play an important role in selecting and maintaining inmate leaders.[3] In his work on social control within prisons, for example, Cloward (1968) examined the formation of inmate subcultures and the role of prison officials in facilitating leadership succession. When prisoners enter the institution they are subjected to a process of status degradation whereby they are stripped of all symbols of status and identity. Through association with the inmate subculture, inmates can secure prestige, deference and status from one another. However, these qualities are in high demand and short supply. Competition between inmates is often bitter and prolonged. Some scholars suggest that institutional violence, both sexual and non-sexual, results from a need to secure dominance over other inmates in order to achieve a relatively positive self-image (for example, see Bowker, 1982a:263-264).

Cloward (1968) argued that subculture leaders perform important social control functions within the correctional organization. As previously discussed, coercion is an ineffective and inefficient means to control inmates. An alternative, though antithetical to official organizational policies and procedures, is for correction officers to control inmate leaders by assisting them in their quest for leadership through the provision of special accommodations. First, officers can ensure that inmate leaders have access to contraband materials. They can either provide the contraband themselves or they can "look the other way" and ignore contraband smuggled into the facility. Second, they can provide information regarding fellow inmates, institutional policies or plans, or other items of interest to the inmate. Finally, officers can provide status by showing deference and respect to the inmate in the presence of other prisoners. By selecting the benefactor of these special accommodations, officers can determine, to some degree, who will accede to inmate leadership positions.

Although such officer involvement generally entails the circumvention of institutional rules and regulations, the corruption is perceived to be counterbalanced by the end goal. Equilibrium within the institution is maintained through officer involvement in inmate leadership succession. Once inmates attain some degree of status they become conservative in the sense that they support the status quo in order to protect their own position (Cloward, 1968:101). The institution benefits from this arrangement in that inmate leaders actively prevent disruption among inmates and promote conformity to institutional rules *by all but themselves.*

> This orientation [among inmate leaders] develops because the inmate
> who wishes to retain his advantageous position finds it in his interest
> to aid in securing custodial objectives. If he cannot effectively coun-

---

[3]   Due to the paucity of research on inmate leaders in jails, the remainder of this section relies solely on research conducted on inmate leaders in prisons. Although caution must be taken in generalizing these works from the prison to jail institution, they at least offer some basis for speculation on the nature of informal inmate leaders in jails.

teract disruptive behavior among his peers, the officials may try to depose him and to elevate potentially more influential leaders (Cloward, 1968:105).

While there are few studies of inmate leadership, even fewer address the relationship between leadership and violence. A number of scholars, however, postulate that as inmates struggle to secure and maintain leadership positions, violence between inmates increases and institutional order is severely threatened. Cloward (1968), for example, concluded that inmate violence is prevalent in the struggle for leadership positions. Still others suggest that the norms held by the inmate subculture and its leaders stimulate aberrant behavior by legitimizing exploitation and destruction.

Schrag's (1970) study on the characteristics of inmate leaders offers support for the notion that the strongest inmates attain leadership positions. In the course of his research, he found that inmate leaders shared the following characteristics: leaders had served more years in prison than non-leader inmates; they had longer terms remaining to be served; they were incarcerated for crimes of violence; and they were repeat offenders (1970:432-433). Significantly more leaders than members of the prison population at large were officially diagnosed as homosexual, psychoneurotic or psychopathic. Finally, leaders had a greater number of serious rule infractions, including escape, attempted escape, fighting and assault (1970:432-433). Schrag concluded that leadership positions were held by criminally mature inmates who were serving lengthy sentences for crimes of violence (1970:433). Although his research goes no further than to identify the characteristics of inmate leaders, the findings lend credence to the popular hypothesis that inmate leaders are among the meanest and most violent inmates.

Physical Confinement and Social Isolation

The nature of incarceration makes the physical confinement and social isolation of prisoners unavoidable. However, both are capable of significantly weakening internal and informal mechanisms that normally control the behavior of individuals in the outside world. Physical confinement and social isolation impact inmates in two ways. First, they negatively alter the emotions and behaviors of inmates. Findings from a growing body of research on the effects of physical confinement and social isolation indicate that both can produce serious effects on human emotions and behavior (for example, see Haythorn, 1973). Excessive or prolonged stress and tension created by confinement and isolation can break down internal control and produce expressive outbursts of violent and destructive behavior, particularly in those individuals predisposed to aggression.

Second, physical confinement and social isolation function to obliterate informal mechanisms that control expression of violent and destructive behavior in the outside world. Inmates, isolated from the outside world, are detached from normal informal social control mechanisms such as family and friends. The addition of other processes within the environment of the jail, such as loss of individuality, establishes a situation wherein impulsive violence and destruction are promoted. Zimbardo (1970) suggested that deindividuation, produced through such institutional practices as status degradation, further reduces or obliterates the mechanisms that normally hold antisocial behaviors in check. Isolation as a consequence of deindividuation holds the potential to incite inmate violence and destruction within the correctional institution. Given the inadequacy of the system of formal control in many jails, expression of aberrant inmate behavior is relatively unrestricted.

Gunderson (1973:170) defined confinement as the "extent to which group members are physically restricted to a fixed space or geographical area by virtue of man-made or natural barriers, territorial boundaries, or hostile surrounds of the environment; within a confining environment, personal space, as a function of group size and of the physically or socially prescribed boundaries limiting movement, can be a most important dimension." Although somewhat tautological given the nature and purpose of the jail, it is nevertheless true that inmates exist in a state of confinement consistent with Gunderson's definition. However, the physical design of most traditional jails unnecessarily maximizes physical constraint. Freedom of movement is restricted by the boundaries of the physical structure of the jail, and, in some cases, by the boundaries of the cell block itself. In all but a few facilities, outdoor or indoor recreation areas, educational or counseling areas, and dining halls are nonexistent. In the absence of these spaces, inmates spend the duration of their incarceration within the limited confines of their cell or dormitory. In many facilities, personal space is also severely limited. In facilities where inmates are housed in multiple-occupancy cells or dormitories, or wherever capacity is exceeded by overcrowding, personal space is minimal at best.

Jail inmates are also subjected to varying degrees of social isolation. Gunderson (1973:170) defined isolation as the:

> extent to which group members are restricted, either by physically or socially prescribed limits, from communication with others outside the immediate group or from receiving information, directly or indirectly, from others outside the immediate group; it is important to differentiate those groups that can send but not receive from those that can receive but not send, and to differentiate those groups from others than can do neither or both.

Both the architectural design and the operating policies invoked by the jail facility influence the degree of social isolation experienced by inmates. In many jails, inmate contact with the outside world is severely limited. The extent of their contact with family and friends on the outside may consist of as little as weekly telephone calls and infrequent personal visits. And even these modest external contacts may be limited in duration by the jail's policies or by the inadequate number of telephones or visiting facilities within the jail. Design features of the physical facility also function to produce feelings of isolation from the outside community. In a number of facilities, for example, windows are conspicuously absent. The effect is to further isolate the inmate from indirect contact and communication with the outside world.

In studying the effects of confinement and social isolation on humans, a range of symptoms and interpersonal dynamics have been noted. Stress and tension were common reactions along with negative emotional symptomatology (Haythorn, Altman and Myers, 1966). Higher levels of stress and emotional symptomatology were noted in pairs of confined individuals who had competitive, noncomplementary and incongruent needs (Haythorn and Altman, 1967). Higher levels of stress and the establishment of clear-cut territorial behavior were also evident between pairs of men with competitive, high dominance needs (Haythorn, 1970). Resentment was commonly directed at others in confinement; although when motivation and discipline were high among those confined, resentment was expressed latently rather than overtly (Haythorn, 1973).

Anecdotal literature reveals that a common source of irritation and boredom for men in confinement is that of the telling and retelling of favorite stories or personal information by companions in confinement (Byrd, 1938; Smith, 1969). Haythorn (1973) concluded that interpersonal stress is a common human reaction to group isolation because people cannot escape from one another. However, he noted that in the research conducted on isolation, direct expressions of aggression were suppressed because group members recognized their interdependence. His conclusion suggests that when interdependence is absent, aggression will be directly expressed.

In sum, the architecture and operations of the jail subject inmates to excessively high levels of physical confinement and social isolation. Research indicates that both can produce stress and anxiety, either of which may diminish internal control over behavior and result in expressive outbursts of violent and destructive behavior.

A second aspect of isolation is its impact on external mechanisms that control antisocial behavior. As noted previously, Zimbardo (1970) suggested that when people become deindividuated and feel anonymous, whether in a society, an organization, or a group, conditions are appropriate for the overt expression of antisocial behavior. He argued that expressions of such behaviors as hostility, destruction, greed, and lust are normally inhibited by a learned concern for how others will react to the behavior. The power of this external behavioral control mechanism, however, can be reduced or even obliterated if a person feels alienated from others, or anonymous and deindividuated.

> When a dehumanized person has become an object, then it may be that the only means he can use to get anyone to take him seriously and respond to him in an individuated way is through violence. A knife at someone's throat forces the victim to acknowledge the power of the attacker and his control. In one sense, violence and destruction transform a passive, controlled object into an active, controlling person. When driven to the wall by forces of deindividuation, the individual must assert his own force or become indistinguishable from the wall. Conditions which foster deindividuation make each of us a potential assassin (Zimbardo, 1970:304).

When inmates enter the jail they are stripped of their individuality and their links to the outside world. The world of the jail is novel and appears unstructured; group cohesion seems to be lacking given the high turnover among inmates, and informal controls over behavior appear to be minimal. In their place is a formal control system dominated by institutional rules and regulations and enforced by the staff of the facility. As demonstrated in previous chapters, these formal control systems are less than adequate. In the traditional, linear jail facility the formal social control agents (guards) may be present only periodically. Consequently, there are few controls over the inmates' behavior.

While Zimbardo (1970) viewed this situation as appropriate for the expression of antisocial behavior, he also argued that "releaser cues" must be present for the behavior to be overtly expressed. Releaser cues are those environmental indicators that suggest that inappropriate behavior will be tolerated or ignored. Evidence of past vandalism, for example, acts as a releaser cue for future vandalism. When one person destroys property and the act is overlooked by correction officers and other inmates, a message is sent to others that destruction will be tolerated. The same is true for exploitation. Past exploitation that was allowed to occur provides a clue for how future exploitation will be dealt with. Again, because of the intermittent supervision received by inmates in traditional, linear jails, the probability is high that acts of vandalism and exploitation will not be detected and dealt with by those in control. These behaviors act as stimuli for future destruction and exploitation.

Although Zimbardo's theory of deindividuation is still in the embryonic stage of development, he nevertheless has provided an interesting approach to understanding inmate violence and destruction in the correctional setting. Whether intentional or not, jail processes induce feelings of anonymity, alienation and deindividuality. Isolated from family and friends and confined in an environment that sends a message that destructive and exploitive behavior will be tolerated, it is reasonable that inmates behave in antisocial ways.

Negative Expectations

Traditional jails are designed and operated with the almost paranoid expectation that inmates will engage in violent and destructive behavior if given the chance. The heavy metal bars, stainless steel accoutrements, bars, grills, razor wire and reinforced concrete; the relentless headcounts, lockdowns, strip searches and shakedowns; the overabundance of rules and regulations that dictate all aspects of the inmate's life; and the exaggerated concern over key, cutlery and narcotic control are evidence of this expectation. However successful these architectural and operational features are in preventing violence and destruction, they may, in fact, foster misbehavior by communicating and reinforcing negative expectations to inmates.

There is a substantial body of literature that demonstrates the influence of expectations on human behavior. Some call this phenomenon the "self-fulfilling prophecy." Merton (1957:423) defined the self-fulfilling prophecy as "...in the beginning, a *false* definition of the situation evoking a new behavior which makes the originally false conception come *true*." Others refer to this process as labeling (Jones, 1977:88-126).

In the first stage of the labeling process, characteristics or behaviors are attributed to a certain category or type of person by others. Once these characteristics or behaviors are attached, recipients are expected to behave in accordance with them. Through verbal and non-verbal communication, expectations are transmitted to the recipient. Proponents of the theory argue that this communication pushes the recipient into responding as anticipated (Jones, 1977:90). By behaving in ways consistent with expectations, the recipient confirms initial stereotypes. The nature of these transactions indicates that expectancies influence the behavior of both the person transmitting and the person receiving the expectations (Jones, 1977:125).

A number of experiments demonstrate the dynamics of the labeling process. The most well known research was conducted by Rosenthal and Jacobson (1968). In the experiment, public school teachers were told that certain students in their classes were fast learners and were expected to do quite well in class. In actuality, the identified students were selected from the class at random. After several months, the researchers measured the I.Q. of the students and compared them to I.Q scores taken prior to the start of the research. The students identified as fast learners showed significantly larger gains in I.Q. than did the other students.[4] Teachers also described these students as happier, more affectionate, more interesting, more appealing, better adjusted and having less need for social approval. The research demonstrated how teachers' expectations of students' scholarly abilities influenced the actual performance of the students and the teachers' evaluations of the qualities and characteristics of the students.

Expectancies can also entail the attribution of negative characteristics to an individual and, as postulated in the self-fulfilling prophecy, force the recipient to respond in ways consistent with these negative expectations. In an experiment conducted by Farina and Ring (1965), participants were assigned to play a simple tilt-game with a partner. In one of the trials, participants were advised that their partners were mentally ill. In a second condition, both were advised that their partners were mentally ill. In the final condition, neither partner was given any information about the other. In conditions where partners were believed to be mentally ill, participants were significantly more likely to say that their partners hindered their performance than were subjects who were not told about their partners. The researchers (1965:50) concluded that "believing an individual to be mentally ill strongly influences the perception of the individual; this is true in spite of the fact that his behavior in no way justified these perceptions." In later research, a more startling impact of expectancies was discovered. In experiments on the effect of negative expectancies, Farina, Allen and Saul (1968:178) found that "if an individual believes he is perceived in an unfavorable way by another person, his behavior in a subsequent interaction is affected independently of the other person's actions in the situation."

Situational factors may also influence the expectations of others. Findings from a series of experiments conducted in mental hospitals indicated that staff members expected patients to be mentally ill *even if nothing in their behavior indicated that they were*. Patients were perceived to be mentally ill simply by virtue of their presence in a mental hospital. In one such experiment, Rosenhan (1973) and seven co-workers gained admission as patients to 12 mental hospitals located in various parts of the United States. The researchers were voluntarily admitted to the hospital by feigning mental illness. They claimed that they were hearing voices saying such things as "empty" and "hollow" to indicate experienced meaningless of life. Although the pseudo-patients behaved normally as soon as they were admitted to the hospital, their daily behavior was interpreted by the staff as indicative of mental illness. According to the notes of one pseudo-patient:

> Once a person is designated abnormal, all of his other behaviors and characteristics are colored by that label...One psychiatrist pointed to a

---

4   Rosenthal and Jacobson's study has been severely criticized for a number of reasons (for example, see Snow, 1969; Thorndike, 1968). The chief criticism has been directed at the I.Q. test that they used. However, the research has been replicated a number of times with similar results.

group of patients who were sitting outside the cafeteria entrance half an hour before lunchtime. To a group of young residents he indicated that such behavior was characteristic of the oral-acquisitive nature of the syndrome (1973:253).

In reality, life in the hospital was so boring and dull that the only thing patients had to look forward to was mealtime.

It was agreed among the researchers that the pseudo-patients would not leave the experiment and the hospital until they convinced the staff that they were sane. The average stay was 19 days; one subject remained in the hospital for 52 days. None of the research participants were able to convince the staff of their sanity. Rosenhan (1973:257) concluded that "the Hospital itself imposes a special environment in which the meanings of behavior can be easily misunderstood."

Rosenhan's research also uncovered a variety of cues given by the staff to communicate their expectations of the mentally ill. Among the behaviors exhibited by the staff were: conducting physical examinations in semi-public rooms, staff discussions about patients held within hearing distance of the person, staff avoidance of eye contact with patients, failure to acknowledge patients' questions, and verbal denigration.[5] Voice intonation, physical distance, and quality and duration of time spent in interpersonal contact were other communication mechanisms found in expectancy research projects (Friedman, 1967; Kleck, 1969).

Although caution must be exercised in generalizing research findings from one setting to another, the studies cited above nevertheless support the assumption that negative expectations communicated through the jail environment, staff and processes influence the behavior of inmates. According to these findings, negative expectations communicated through the architectural and interior design of the facility, through the operations of the jail, and through staff interactions with inmates, will produce negative inmate behavior. If the staff of the jail expect inmates to act like animals, or if the architecture and operations of the jail are designed with the expectation that inmates will engage in violent and destructive behavior, inmates will indeed respond as expected.

Environmental Irritants

Empirical research has demonstrated an interrelationship between environmental conditions and human behavior in a wide range of settings. This research has found that environmental "stressors," such as excessive heat, noise,

---

5   Rosenhan (1973:256) cites the example of a morning attendant waking patients with the expression, "Come on, you m——- f——s, out of bed!"

and crowding, influence physical and mental health, task performance, and social behavior. More importantly, these environmental irritants hold the potential to foment aggressive and destructive behavior, particularly among individuals predisposed to such behavior.

The physical environment of the typical jail includes a number of features or "stressors" that are particularly noxious to inmates and staff. Some of these features, such as excessive noise, lack of privacy, and overcrowding, alter and influence inmate and staff behavior, and under certain circumstances can even produce violent and destructive behavioral responses. Although without immediate external consequences, other features, such as institutionalized furnishings and the lack of sensory stimulation, further intensify stress experienced by inmates and staff.

Environmentally induced stress can produce five different psychological states from which aggression might eventuate (Mueller, 1983). First, the stressor may produce arousal, or a generalized drive for behavior. For those individuals who are predisposed to aggression arousal, environmental stressors may facilitate and provoke its expression. Second, environmental stressors may produce stimulus overload, whereby the individual becomes overwhelmed and incapable of effectively processing incoming information. The typical response to overload is an attempt to adapt; however, for some persons, adaptation may be inappropriate and result in the misinterpretation of signals within the environment. In other words, the individual may respond aggressively when situations do not demand it. Third, the stressor may interfere with ongoing behavior, thereby producing frustration and the perception of loss of control over the environment. Fourth, environmental stressors may produce annoyance, irritability and discomfort. In turn, these negative affects can increase aggression. Studies indicate, however, that the relationship between aggression and the discomfort from environmental stress is curvilinear—taking the shape of an inverted U distribution. Up to a point, the discomfort increases aggression, but beyond that point, individuals become so uncomfortable that they respond in other ways (e.g., withdrawal) that reduce the discomfort (Mueller, 1983:52).

In the jail setting, the relationship between environmental stressors and human behavior is very likely intensified. In contrast to noninstitutional settings, prisoners are neither free to escape from sources of environmental stress nor are they possessed of the means to substantially control the sources of discomfort in their environment. Finally, inmates are deprived of many normal strategies for coping with stress.[6]

---

6   For example, some individuals find that engaging in physical exercise reduces physical or psychological stress. Others may deal with stress through the consumption of excessive amounts o alcohol or drugs. Still others may find that withdrawal to a quiet and isolated location reduce stress. For jail inmates, none of these stress-reducing strategies are readily available. Nor doe the physical environment of the jail provide many legitimate alternatives for coping with stress.

One source of environmental stress within the jail is the lack of privacy. Westin (1970) defined privacy as "the claim of individuals, groups or institutions to determine for themselves when, how, and to what extent information about them is communicated to others." If an individual believes he has this power of determination, he experiences the state of privacy. Westin argued that the function of privacy is four-fold. First, privacy protects and helps maintain an individual's personal autonomy. Autonomy involves both a sense of individuality and of control over one's environment. The ability to have privacy when one wants it is part of such control. Second, privacy serves to facilitate emotional release. People need privacy in order to give vent to emotions caused by tension-creating social and biological factors. Third, privacy allows the individual opportunities for self-evaluation; removal from day-to-day activities is desirable in order to process, reflect on and integrate information. Finally, privacy serves the function of limiting and protecting communication. Privacy fulfills an individual's need to share confidences and intimacies with those he trusts, while it also aids in the establishment of psychological distances when these are desired in interpersonal situations.

The most important aspect of privacy is the ability it affords to control interpersonal communication and contacts. Some evidence is available which suggests that when this freedom is lost, the individual so deprived becomes stressed (Farbstein, Wener and Gomez, 1979; Toch, 1977). Lack of privacy can also evoke irritability, resentment, and excessive criticism and boasting among prisoners (Vischer, 1919).

In the jail setting, multiple-occupancy living units make it difficult for inmates to remove themselves from others. Even in facilities where inmates are assigned to single-occupancy cells, privacy is elusive. Although inmates can seek physical sanctuary in the individual cells, barred walls prevent them from visually and auditorally separating themselves from others. In dormitory living units the situation is even worse. Inmates have very few opportunities to escape from the company of other inmates.

A second source of environmental stress within jail institutions is noise. Exposure to excessive noise levels has been found to lead to a variety of physical and psychological problems, among these are a loss of hearing (Kryter, 1970), high blood pressure (Cohen, et al., 1980), increased stress symptoms and annoyance (Hitchcock and Waterhouse, 1979), and interference with ongoing and subsequent task performance (Glass and Singer, 1972). In addition, other studies suggest that decreased frustration tolerance (Glass and Singer, 1972), decreased ability to attend to relevant physical and social stimuli (Cohen and Lezck, 1977), and decreased helping behavior (Matthews and Canon, 1975; Page, 1977) are all attributable to excessive noise. At certain levels, noise is arousing and can promote aggressive behavior among individuals predisposed to aggression (Kryter, 1970; Poulton, 1978). Aggression can also result when noise is perceived to be unpredictable and uncontrollable (Glass and Singer, 1972).

Little research has been conducted on the effect of noise on individuals in correctional institutions. The extant literature has focused instead on *assessments* of noise levels. These studies tend to indicate that noise in jails generally exceeds levels considered comfortable for humans (Gersten, 1977; Wener and Clark, 1976). High noise levels in correctional institutions are typically the product of metal bars, doors, and furnishings, the absence of adequate sound-absorption materials, and a lack of staff control over the noise created by competing televisions, radios, conversations, arguments, and so forth.

Overcrowding is another source of environmentally induced inmate stress. In addressing the impact of crowding, scholars have differentiated between "density" and "crowding." According to Stokols (1972), density refers to the relationship between the number of people and amount of space. Density is usually defined in terms of number of people per area, or amount of space per person. In contrast, crowding is a *perception* which does not depend on an unvarying, linear relationship with density figures. It is argued that density is a necessary but not sufficient condition to cause perceptions of overcrowding (Farbstein, Wener and Gomez, 1979).

Most research conducted in this area has focused on the effects of spatial and social density. The findings indicate that high social and spatial density can be arousing (Aiello, et al., 1977), can cause stimulus overload and reduce the quality and quantity of social interactions (Baum and Valins, 1977), and, among males, can enhance negative moods including anger (Nogami, 1976), irritability (Sundstrom, 1975), and aggressiveness (Schettino and Borden, 1976). Other studies have found a relationship between social density and discomfort, psychological stress and social withdrawal (Farbstein, Wener and Gomez, 1979).

In the prison setting, high population density has been found to be arousing and to stimulate aggression by individuals who are violence-prone (D'Atri, 1975). High population density also has been found to be positively related to the number of assaults (Nacci, Teitelbaum and Prather, 1977), disciplinary violations (McCain, Cox and Paulus, 1980; Megargee, 1977), illness complaints (McCain, Cox, and Paulus, 1980) and subsequent recidivism (Farrington and Nuttall, 1980). In dormitories where personal space tends to be most limited, inmates reported a higher number of illness complaints than did inmates in one- or two-man cells (McCain, Cox and Paulus, 1976). D'Atri (1975) found that inmates in dormitories had consistently higher blood pressures and pulse rates than did inmates in single or two-man living units.

Institutionalized accoutrements have also been cited as a source of inmate stress. The assumption that inmates are generally destructive and untrustworthy with respect to proper care for the property of the institution is clearly represented in the designs and furnishings of correctional institutions. In accordance with this assumption, jails are usually equipped with durable steel furniture that is resistant to vandalism and destruction. Despite the durability of these furnishings, however, vandalism and destruction are commonplace.

Sommer (1972) suggested that vandal-resistant furnishings may, in fact, incite the vandalism and destruction they are designed to resist. Institutional furnishings tend to be cold, uncomfortable, and unattractive; they tend to be immune to all efforts to personalize them. In addition, they are continuous reminders that inmates are not trusted to be considerate of the institution's property. It is not surprising that inmates feel no compunction about vandalizing and destroying these furnishings.

Sommer argued that if institutions want inmates to care for property, they must provide property inmates can care about. The scant amount of research which exists on this topic provides evidence to support Sommer's argument. Wener and Olsen (1980) and Frazier (1985) found that when soft, comfortable and attractive furnishings and accoutrements were provided to inmates they remained largely free from vandalism and destruction. Furthermore, the evidence suggests that inmates take better care of soft furnishings than of metal ones and that, in consequence of this increased care, they feel more positive about their environment (Whiting and DeJoy, 1976).

Stimuli deprivation is a final source of environment stress. The architecture and interior of correctional facilities are typically designed without consideration of human needs for sensory diversity and stimulation, particularly for visual stimulation. The typical correctional facility is painted a dull and uninspiring color, its interior walls barren—with the exception of the ubiquitous calendar.[7] Living units possess a certain uniformity. Each is identically furnished and all of the furniture is of the same design and material. Visual monotony is further intensified by the lack of windows and natural light. In sum, the environment of most jails is monotonous, boring and devoid of the most vivid and pleasurable types of sensory stimulation.

> As a rule, the scale of architecture in such institutions is inhumanely large, the colors of walls, furniture, clothes, bedding, and other objects are drab and monotonous, the surfaces of any open area are either concrete or sparse grass, windows are small and are made functionally even smaller by bars or shutters. Thus, the visual environment is usually uninteresting. So, too, is the array of auditory inputs, which for the greater part of the day is restricted to the voices of other men, with

---

[7] In many situations, inmates will attempt to brighten the living units by posting pictures on the walls ("centerfolds") or draw their own pictures or murals. In one Washington state jail I visited, an inmate (or group of inmates) had drawn a detailed and remarkably beautiful mural on the full expanse of one wall. The mural represented one of the few sources of color within the living unit.

the occasional radio or television program to break the monotony. Movement is within this same environment day after day, from cell to mess hall to work to recreation, with very little change. Indoor and outdoor surfaces are mostly hard, and do not vary highly. Even in well-funded institutions in wealthy countries, where the food is nutritious and palatable, it is hardly exciting. Thus, the total sensory impact is one of low stimulation at any given time and low levels of change over time. The resultant boredom may reach substantial levels of stressfulness, which may be alleviated by bursts of sometimes violent activity (Suedfeld, 1980:92).

There has been little research on the impact of sensory deprivation among inmates of correctional institutions. The extant literature has focused on the impact of deprivation experienced by prisoners in solitary confinement. However, research conducted in other settings indicate that sensory deprivation can produce "difficulty in thinking, a shortening of time perception, distorted impressions of [an individual's] body, and hallucinations" (Leroy, 1975:46). Some scholars have suggested that lack of sensory stimulation and the resulting boredom and monotony contribute to vandalism within the facility. According to Moyer (1975:56), "with enforced idleness and sensory deprivation predominating...individual expression is suppressed, but not eliminated."

While most correctional scholars agree that inmate violence and destruction are problematic, they disagree as to the causes. The New Generation philosophy maintains that traditional jails are defective institutions designed and operated in such a manner that aberrant inmate behavior is commonplace. Inmate violence and destruction are common human responses to the fear of victimization, the lack of defensible physical territory, the absence of positive leadership, isolation from the outside world, the negative expectations of the staff and institution, and the stressful physical environment. The architecture and inmate management style advocated by the New Generation philosophy are designed to overcome the obstacles to institutional control of inmate behavior. In tandem, they function to reduce inmate and staff fear of victimization, promote among inmates and staff the perception of protected and protectable space, replace inmate power with staff authority, break down the isolation of the inmates from the outside world, promote a climate of positive expectations where just and humane interaction are the norm, and create a less stressful and irritating physical environment for inmates. The following chapter addresses how the architecture and inmate management style are implemented to achieve an incarceration environment that is free of violence and destruction.

Chapter Six

Implementation of the New Generation Philosophy

The New Generation philosophy is predicated on the belief that inmates are rational human beings who will conform to the rules and expectations of the facility as long as compliance fulfills their needs.

> Just as most inmates have the capacity for negative behavior in order to achieve their ends, they also have the capacity to conform their behavior to the desires of the administration if that will serve to meet their needs. Many "street wise" inmates learn at an early age to manipulate their environment to their best advantage. In the traditional jail or prison environment, violent and destructive behavior is one of the means usually employed by inmates to effectively achieve their needs (Nelson and O'Toole, 1983:7).

The architecture and inmate management style shapes the environment is such a way that critical inmate needs for safety, privacy, personal space, activity, familial contact, social relations, and so forth, can only be achieved through compliant behavior. Inmates who attempt to fight the control imposed by the institution or to manipulate it for their own benefit will not only meet with frustration but will lose the privileges and advantages they were initially granted by the institution.

It is important to note that the architecture and inmate management style do not miraculously transform inmates into compliant and obedient individuals. As in traditional institutions, inmates in the New Generation facilities will attempt to manipulate their environment to their best advantage. The difference between the two facilities is that the New Generation jail structures the environment in such a way that these attempts will be readily detected and dealt with by staff. Therefore, the architecture and inmate management style function to minimize the power of inmates while maximizing control by the institution.

The Architectural and Interior Design of Podular Facilities

The architecture and interior design of New Generation facilities is guided by a substantial body of literature on the effects of the environment on human behavior. Both the architecture and interior structure the inmate's physical environment to allow for the fulfillment of legitimate needs while simultaneously reducing opportunities for fulfillment of illegitimate needs.

The exterior of the podular/direct supervision jail in Spokane County, Washington. The jail (to the right) opened in July 1986 and has a capacity of 483 inmates. An elevated walkway connects the jail to the Spokane County Courthouse (to the left). Barely discernible on the facade of the jail are the open mesh windows of the modules' outdoor exercise areas. (Photograph courtesy of Don Manning.)

A basic principle of the design requires inmates to be grouped in manageable units and housed in a space (typically called a "module" or "pod") which facilitates continuous and direct staff observation and supervision. Each module houses between 16 to 46 inmates.[1] By dividing inmates into smaller groups custodial personnel are better able to manage and supervise inmate activities. In addition, limiting the number of inmates in a living unit reduces perceptions of overcrowding.

An advantage of the module system is the flexibility it provides in the classification of prisoners. Members of conflicting groups or gangs can effectively be separated and housed in different units where they will have little or no contact during their period of incarceration. Inmates with special needs can be assigned to specific modules. For example, in several New Generation facilities, separate modules are maintained for mentally ill or handicapped inmates.

In most facilities, modules have two floors. On the main floor level, individual inmate rooms are situated around a common, multi-purpose activity area. Additional inmate rooms are located on the mezzanine level which is accessible by a staircase. Each inmate room is furnished with a bed, desk and chair. In some facilities these are made of molded plastic rather than the steel and metal found in traditional jails. Not only does the use of plastic cell furniture reduce noise, but such furniture cannot be as easily dissembled to create weapons.

Each inmate room contains a toilet and sink made of porcelain rather than the heavy-duty metal typically used in traditional facilities. Porcelain toilets and sinks are less expensive to purchase and they reduce feelings of institutionalization usually associated with the excessive use of metal furnishings. The rooms also include a narrow window facing the exterior of the building. Windows are included in the design of the rooms in order to reduce feelings of isolation from the outside world and to ensure adequate levels of natural light within the modules.

---

[1]   There is some disagreement over the optimal capacities of the modules. Nelson and O'Toole (1983) argue that the experience of podular/direct supervision facilities over the last eight years indicates that 50 inmates per module is the maximum number for effective supervision by one corrections officer. Module capacities of 12 to 16 may be fiscally prohibitive, particularly to staff each module. In several podular/direct supervision facilities, overcrowding has become a serious problem. Some have been forced to double-bunk the modules, meaning that the population of the module is doubled. In order to supervise so many inmates, facility officials found it necessary to staff the modules with two corrections officers rather than one. There are serious questions as to the impact of overcrowding in the podular/direct supervision of facility. A strong argument can be made that the benefits of the philosophy's architecture and inmate management style are reduced in overcrowded conditions. For example, double-bunking deprives the inmate of the privacy provided by the individual cell. In addition, the resources of the facility are severely strained during periods of overcrowding. Nevertheless, administrators of overcrowded podular/direct supervision facilities report that even with double-bunking, the incidence of inmate misconduct is lower than in overcrowded traditional facilities.

In contrast to traditional facilities where entrance to inmate cells is through a set of bars, doors give access to inmate rooms in the podular/direct supervision facility. The absence of bars minimizes noise and helps promote the feeling of a noninstitutional environment within the module.

A podular/direct supervision design features multi-purpose dayrooms which provide open and unrestricted space that allow the inmates freedom of movement. These dayrooms are designed to reduce the cage-like and confined circumstances of the living environment within traditional facilities. In most of the podular facilities examined, the dual level communal dayrooms are carpeted and furnished with moveable tables and chairs for inmate dining, games and card playing. In addition to normalizing the environment, carpeting provides further soundproofing within the modules.

Spaces designed for small group activities such as television viewing, reading, and exercise are found in the corners of the dayroom and mezzanine areas. Most of these areas are furnished with couches, chairs, tables and televisions. In contrast to traditional facilities where the furniture is made of hard, indestructible metal that is often bolted to the floor to prevent it from being moved, the furniture within the podular/direct supervision modules is constructed of soft, padded materials, and can be moved to facilitate inmate conversations or television viewing. As with carpeting, the soft and comfortable furniture is provided to absorb noxious and stress-producing noise. It is also expected that inmates will take greater care of soft and attractive furniture than they will cold and impersonal metal furniture. Other areas in the dayrooms contain exercise equipment such as weightlifting apparatus. All of the modules have several televisions in order to reduce fights over their use, and multiple telephones to ensure that inmates have ample opportunity to communicate with family and friends.

The architectural design permits varying levels of privacy for inmates. Individual rooms allow inmates total privacy in that they can physically, visually and auditorially remove themselves from others. The television and exercise areas located in the corners of the dayroom and mezzanine provide inmates with the option of semi-privacy where they can interact with small groups of other inmates yet still be under the observation of custodial personnel. Finally, inmates can congregate in larger groups in the multi-purpose dayrooms.

In addition to providing inmates with areas in which privacy can be achieved, the operating policies of the facilities provide inmates with the ability to control privacy need fulfillment. In most of the facilities, inmates are free during the day to move between their rooms, the dayroom, television or exercise areas and outdoor recreation areas. As in most traditional jails, inmates are locked in their individual rooms at night. Correctional staff can also lock inmates in their rooms for disciplinary purposes or in the case of an emergency.

Territorial needs are also considered in the design of podular/direct supervision modules. First, individual rooms allow for the development of a sense of ownership and caretaking behaviors among inmates. In most facilities, this feeling is further fostered by a prohibition against inmates entering the rooms of others. Second, the inclusion of semi-private spaces for small group interaction provides for territorial needs at a group level.[2]

The design of the module also fulfills inmate safety needs. Inmates who feel threatened or fearful can withdraw to the safety of their individual rooms. Shower facilities, a common site for victimization in traditional jails, contain individual, rather than communal, stalls. In most facilities, shower stalls have partial doors that ensure inmate privacy and security yet permit correctional personnel to easily monitor them. The dayrooms are laid out in such a way that "blind spots" are virtually eliminated, thus enhancing the ability of the corrections officer to observe all areas of the module from most locations and reducing opportunities for inmates to engage in misconduct without detection by staff.[3]

The layout of the module also facilitates a sense of territory among the corrections officers. In most of the facilities, offices are not provided for corrections officers, although some provide desks at which they can do their paperwork. The purpose is to ensure that officers move about the modules and interact with inmates rather than "hide" within offices. It is expected that exclusion of an office will encourage officers to look upon the entire module as their "territory" and facilitate officer "ownership" of the module. This sense of territory is vital to ensure that officers, rather than inmates, exert control and leadership in the module.

Many of the "symbols of incarceration" commonly found in correctional institutions are noticeably absent in the interior design of these facilities. By eliminating bars, grates, grills, metal and steel furnishings, the cage-like feeling typically associated with incarcerative environments is reduced. It is expected that not only will inmates be less inclined to act like animals in the "normalized" environment but that staff will be less inclined to treat them as such.

---

2   In a user assessment of the Chicago Metropolitan Correctional Center, Wener and Olsen (1980:490) found that these areas became the meeting place for group activity based on television taste, ethnicity and language. They concluded that the "regular association of groups within these spaces served to foster group membership and cohesion" and helped to reduce theft because of their proximity to and easy observation of inmates' rooms.

3   In several of the facilities, there are areas within the module that are not easily observable by the corrections officer. There is debate over these designs. Some administrators argue that inclusion of unobservable areas makes it more difficult for officers to supervise inmates and provides inmates with enhanced opportunities to victimize other inmates. Other administrators, however, argue that these areas force corrections officers to move about the module instead of situating themselves in one location, such as behind a desk. Such movement about the module forces officers to interact with inmates.

A module dayroom in the Spokane County Detention Center. Ten self-contained housing modules each house 46 inmates. Inmate cells open onto the dayroom. The walls and fixtures of the modules are painted a variety of colors, including teal, peach, rose and white. The carpeting in the dayroom aids in absorbing excess noise. (Photograph courtesy of Don Manning.)

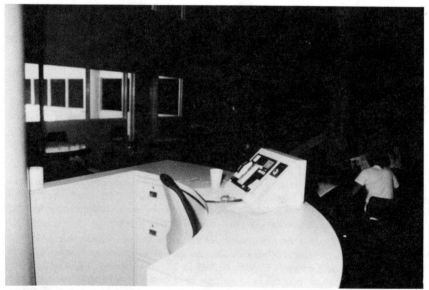

Corrections officer work station located in the modules of the Spokane County Detention Center. The modified control panel allows officers to maintain audio contact with other parts of the jail. The windows on the left permit officers to monitor inmate activities in the outdoor recreation area. (Photograph courtesy of Don Manning).

An outdoor recreation area in the module. Open mesh windows allow natural light and fresh air to enter the area. The area is equipped with an exercise bicycle and a basketball hoop. Inmates are permitted to enter the area any time during the day and early evening. (Photograph courtesy of Don Manning.)

Each module of the Spokane County Detention Center contains four television viewing areas. The area is furnished with commercial wood furniture, padded seating and carpeting. The wood and padded furniture aid in reducing noise levels, are less expensive than traditional metal furniture, and are less likely to be vandalized by inmates. (Photograph courtesy of Don Manning.)

Many of the facilities make use of a variety of colors and textures within the interiors of the modules to further lessen the institutional "feel" of the environment and to enhance the perception of openness while simultaneously reducing the perception of crowding and confinement. In one facility, module interiors were painted in shades of rose, teal, gray and peach—colors that subdue rather than arouse human emotions. In a number of facilities, brightly colored posters and paintings decorate the walls of the modules. Use of attractive wall paints, colorful posters, and patterned and textured furniture provide inmates with visual stimulation and diminish the institutional ambience of the units.

The modules are designed to be self-contained in order to reduce inmate movement in the facility and potential breeches to security. With the exception of appearances in court or visits to the medical unit, all inmate activities, including meals, programming, visitation and recreation, are conducted within the modules. In several facilities, areas for outdoor recreation, visitation and programming (e.g., educational, vocational, counseling) are contiguous to each module. At the most modern high-rise facilities, each module contains a semi-outdoor recreation area. The area is separated from the module by floor-to-ceiling windows so corrections officers can observe the area. The ceiling, floor and two walls of the recreation area are made of cement. The fourth wall, however, consists of open mesh material that permits natural light and fresh air to enter from the outside. While the area is physically secure, it gives the "feeling" of being outdoors. The recreation areas are equipped with basketball hoops to provide activities for inmates. The inclusion of the outdoor recreation area within the modules fulfills a number of inmate needs. First, it provides a much needed physical outlet for inmate stress and anxiety. Second, it reduces inmate idleness. During the day, inmates are free to enter the recreation area whenever they desire.

In contrast to traditional facilities where inmates are transported to a centrally located area away from the living units in order to visit friends and family or to consult with attorneys, the podular/direct supervision facility provides space for visitation at the module. In a number of such facilities, a separate, public-only elevator transports visitors to the desired module. At the module, visitors enter booths in which they communicate with the inmate. Like traditional facilities, most podular/direct supervision facilities do not allow contact visitation.[4] Instead, visits are conducted through a plexiglass window, or, in some cases, over connecting telephones.

Programming areas for educational, counseling, and vocational classes are located in the modules at several of the facilities examined for this study. These

---

[4]   Contact visits are permitted at one of the facilities in this study. The administrator of the facility believed that contact visits were the primary cause of an inordinate amount of contraband within the facility.

areas are usually partitioned off from the rest of the module and resemble a room within a room. In many cases the programming rooms are furnished with tables and moveable chairs.

Each module is also equipped with multiple telephones to reduce inmate competition over their use and to ensure that inmates have adequate opportunity to maintain contact with family. All calls made from the phones are collect. Profits from these calls are used to purchase inmate supplies and recreational equipment such as basketballs. (Photograph courtesy of Don Manning.)

Spaces for outdoor recreation, visitation and programming are included in the modules to reduce idleness and feelings of isolation from friends and family outside of the jail. In traditional facilities, opportunities for outdoor recreation, visitation and programming are usually restricted because the jails lack the necessary space and personnel for these activities. For example, the number and duration of weekly visits permitted to inmates may be limited because the facility has only a small number of visiting booths. Overcrowding places additional demands on these facilities and further reduces opportunities for visitation. Visitation, outdoor recreation and programming also require personnel to transport inmates from the living units to the site of the activities and to supervise them. When facilities are understaffed, these programs may be severely curtailed. In podular/direct supervision facilities, the lack of activity space and personnel are not problems. Most modules are designed to provide adequate space for outdoor recreation, visitation and inmate programs. Because these activities are conducted within the module, additional personnel for transportation and supervision are not needed.

A major obstacle to public acceptance of the New Generation concept is the perception that inmates are provided physical accommodations far more comfortable and luxurious than many law-abiding citizens can afford. Carpeting, multiple televisions, and individual rooms are all criticized as too extravagant for people who are believed to be criminals. Proponents of the New Generation philosophy counter with the argument that the architecture and interior are designed to maximize inmate control and minimize inmate freedom. Inmate comfort is a secondary, but not necessarily intended, consequence.

Proponents also argue that New Generation jails are cheaper to build than are traditional jails. Nelson (1988a) compared construction costs of New Generation and traditional jails and estimated a potential cost savings of $20,580 for a typical 48-inmate housing unit in a New Generation facility. Most of these savings were attributed to the use of commercial grade furnishings and accoutrements in place of more expensive metal and stainless steel furnishings. For example, porcelain toilet fixtures are used in place of more expensive stainless steel fixtures; commercial grade lighting fixtures are used in place of more costly vandal-proof fixtures; wood and plastic tables and chairs are used in place of more expensive stainless steel tables with attached seating; and hollow block interior walls are used in place of more costly metal and concrete reinforced walls. It is assumed that the intensive supervision by staff will deter inmates from vandalizing these more fragile furnishings.

According to administrators and staff at the facilities, all but a few inmates adapt as expected to the environment in the modules. Those inmates who cannot function within the living units are housed in a maximum security unit. All podular/direct supervision facilities have at least one maximum security living unit. The design of the unit is very similar to a living unit in a traditional jail. The accoutrements in this module are institutional (e.g., stainless steel toilets and sinks, immovable metal furniture, etc.), and while inmates have individual cells, they are locked within their cells 23 hours a day. One hour of recreation is provided per day, which inmates take alone. The maximum security unit is used not only for inmates who cannot function in the general population but also for protective custody and disciplinary purposes.

In summary, the architecture and interior design of podular/direct supervision facilities function to reduce or eliminate irritating and stress-inducing features of the environment and to enable to custodial staff to observe inmate activities and maintain control of the modules at all times. While the architecture alone is incapable of controlling inmate behavior or fulfilling critical inmate needs, it provides a context in which a particular philosophy and style of inmate management can be implemented.

Direct Inmate Supervision

The second, and most critical, component of the New Generation philosophy is the inmate management style—how inmates are supervised by custodial staff. Like the architecture, the inmate management style is designed to reduce inmate stress associated with incarceration and to increase institutional control over inmate behavior. Unlike its treatment of architectural design, the literature on the New Generation lacks an explanation of how direct inmate supervision is operationalized. Nelson and O'Toole (1983) and Gettinger (1984) identified six objectives of direct inmate supervision:

(1) staff, rather than inmates, will control the facility and inmates' behavior;

(2) inmates will be directly and continuously supervised and custodial staff, rather than inmates, will direct and control the behavior of all inmates;

(3) rewards and punishments will be structured to ensure compliant inmate behavior;

(4) open communication will be maintained between the custodial staff and inmates, and between staff members;

(5) inmates will be advised of the expectations and rules of the facility; and,

(6) inmates will be treated in a manner consistent with "constitutional standards and other applicable codes and court decisions," and will be treated equitably and fairly regardless of their personal characteristics or the reasons for which they are in jail.

Although these broad and rather ambiguous objectives are helpful in understanding the *goals* of direct supervision, they reveal little about how the management style is practiced by custodial staff in the modules.

To understand how direct supervision is implemented, corrections officers and first-line supervisors in two established, podular/direct supervision facilities were interviewed about the critical behaviors required for effective inmate management.[5] Three themes were emphasized throughout the interviews. The first was the relationship between an officer's behavior and the interpersonal climate of the module. Officers are effective when they produce an environment free

---

5   For a description of the interview methodology, see Appendix.

from conflict among inmates and between inmates and staff. Ineffective module officers are those who engage in behaviors that give rise to verbal or physical confrontations, or produce tension, anger and resentment which either directly or indirectly fosters inmate rebellion or misbehavior.

Because officers are in direct physical contact with inmates, they cannot depend on architectural features such as bars and steel doors to protect themselves or other inmates from victimization. Nor can they rely on physical strength and defense techniques to control inmates without inciting violence among other inmates in the module. Instead, they must rely almost exclusively on more sophisticated management and leadership skills to maintain order within the modules.[6] The officers expressed a strong belief that they can produce an environment within the modules that is safe for both themselves and for inmates without the protection of bars to separate them from inmates and without resorting to the use of physical coercion to force inmate compliance.

The second theme focused on the need for officers to protect themselves from manipulation by inmates within the modules. Direct supervision places officers in a vulnerable position. In contrast to traditional facilities, contact between officers and inmates in the podular/direct supervision facility is frequent and quite direct. Officers spend an eight-hour shift in continuous contact with inmates. In addition, because of the module system, officers are isolated from co-workers and work alone largely without the assistance or direct support of their peers. Under these circumstances it is natural for friendships with inmates to develop. While in most cases these friendships are not problematic, there are situations where relationships are developed between inmates and officers wherein inmates seek to manipulate or exploit the guards. These attempts to maneuver officers into violating minor facility rules out of friendship are referred to as "con games" by inmates (Allen and Bosta, 1981). Such violations often become progressively more serious. Sometimes by the time officers realize their mistakes, inmates have enough evidence of prior duplicity that officers dare not refuse new demands for fear of exposure of their rule violations to their superiors. At this point inmates exercise considerable influence, even to the point of making demands that threaten the security of the facility and the safety of staff and other inmates. Effective module officers are those who can protect themselves from this type of subtle inmate manipulation.

---

6   This is not to imply that officers are completely unprotected. In most facilities, a number of sophisticated alarm systems and operational policies have been implemented to protect officers working within the modules. In one particular facility, module officers are equipped with body alarms which automatically signal for assistance should the officer lay prone. In addition, the officers are provided walkie-talkies which have "panic buttons" in case of emergency. Furthermore, sound alarms are located in the modules. If noise within the module increases above a certain level, an alarm automatically sounds. Finally, officers are assigned as "rovers" to patrol between the modules and to quickly respond to calls of assistance from the module officers.

The third theme was the need for officers to be ever-vigilant and to promptly deal with every and all rule violations, arguments, or peculiar behaviors, no matter how trivial or seemingly unimportant. Minor rules are enforced as if they are of major consequence; petty disagreements are resolved as if they were serious disputes; unusual behaviors are investigated as if they are life threatening. While to many observers, this hyper-attentiveness to the minor and trivial may appear to be excessively rigid, or even repressive, it was believed to be vital in maintaining order within the modules. When ignored, minor rule violations act as stimuli for more major rule violations. When ignored, petty disagreements escalate to major disturbances between inmates. When ignored, unusual behaviors can result in the death of a suicidal or ailing inmate. In essence, the concept of "total inmate control" requires officers to attend to all inmate behaviors and activities, not just those that have immediate and obvious consequences.

The following seven dimensions summarize the most important behaviors officers cited as necessary for effective supervision and control of inmates in the modules. While the behaviors may be innovative when applied to inmate management, many are clearly reminiscent of more general principles of effective personnel supervision or even, as several officers pointed out, of effective parenting.[7]

Dimension One: Resolving Inmate Problems and Conflicts

Within the close confines of any detention facility, conflicts and disputes will arise among inmates as well as between inmates and the correctional staff. The officers recognized the potential for escalation of these minor daily conflicts to large scale disruptive events that could threaten the security of the module and the entire facility. They argued that the effective officer was proactive and dealt with conflicts at the first sign of disharmony. In contrast, the ineffective officer allowed disputes to continue until they erupted into full blown fights. One officer recounted a situation involving inappropriate officer behavior:

> Inmates are not assigned specific chairs (for dinner, etc.). However, as a courtesy from one inmate to another, the inmates who have been in the pod for a while usually have favorite seats. Most new inmates are aware of this and usually concede to this. A new inmate had his dinner and in looking for a place to sit down moved the tray of an

---

[7] In the analysis of the interview data, the writings of the correctional personnel are presented as transmitted to the researchers. Orthography and grammatical constructions may have been altered.

older inmate to another place. When the new inmate was confronted by the old inmate, the new inmate began to yell and throw food, thus leading to a food fight that further led to a chair fight and ultimately a fist fight. The corrections officer on duty during the above incident did not make an attempt to defuse the problem until it had developed into a full blown chair fight. Without agreeing to the pre-selected seating arrangements, it could have been possible to terminate the fight at the initial confrontation stage. Sometimes a simple act such as asking the question "What's the problem?" can talk a person out of fighting.

The behaviors described under this dimension focused on officers' conflict management and problem-solving abilities. Respondents pointed out that the effective officer separated inmates in a dispute by sending them to their rooms to calm down, gathered information about the causes of disputes, and offered alternatives for resolution of the problems. Several officers indicated that when dealing with angry inmates the most effective approach was to ask them to go to their rooms. This allowed time for both inmates and officers to calm down. After a sufficient period of time, the officer could initiate a calm discussion with the inmate about his/her behavior.

The officers argued that by investigating the causes of disputes, inmate misunderstandings producing tension and unrest could be resolved. An officer provided the following example:

A lot of times inmates will say things about other inmates which are not true but all of a sudden every inmate in the pod hears and believes it is true. This happens a lot in regards to theft, charges against inmates, homosexuality, etc. An inmate was accused of being a thief. No inmate had actually seen him take anything that was missing and he did not have any of the stolen items on his person or in his room. The inmates in the pod demanded the thief be removed from the pod. Sometimes before drastic measures a little investigative work can help a lot. Talking with inmates is very important in a direct supervision facility. The C.O. on duty did not believe the inmate to be a thief and talked to almost all of the inmates. Upon talking to the inmates [the officer] discovered no inmate had witnessed any theft or knew of any incident but were merely going along with other inmates. Upon questioning the inmate who made the initial accusation, he had not seen the inmate steal anything but only thought the man to be a thief on the street. The inmate was not moved and had no further problems. The officer got a lot done by just talking.

The officers also underlined the importance of a patient and calm demeanor when discussing problems with inmates to prevent further agitation of the inmates. An officer related an incident where the officer's nonthreatening body language and low tone of voice were able to subdue an aggravated inmate:

> An inmate was on the phone in the pod when apparently the inmate became agitated with the person with whom he was speaking. The inmate slammed the phone down and proceeded to push furniture and curse. Note: This inmate had a history of violent behavior toward other people, especially corrections officers. At this time the officer approached the inmate and in a low voice began to talk to the inmate, telling him that if he did not calm down he would have to return to his room. The inmate was becoming incoherent and continued to curse in a loud voice. The inmate turned from the officer and violently kicked a chair. The officer at this time ordered the inmate to his room at once. The inmate began to crumble, but he went to his room without assistance which was very unusual for the inmate. The officer was able to maintain control of the pod and also control of the inmate without resorting to physical force.

The officers agreed that, except in emergency situations when the physical restraint of an inmate is absolutely necessary, officers should never shove, grab, hit or physically touch an inmate. Shoving, grabbing or hitting inmates will most likely provoke them to retaliate against the officer in a like manner and may even incite other inmates to revenge the officer's abusive treatment of another. Physical contact with inmates also exposes the officer to allegations of abuse and excessive force. The general consensus among the interview subjects was that officers who resort to physical force are no longer in control of inmates and are unfit to work in the modules. Touching an inmate, even if it is meant to be nonthreatening, violates the individual's personal buffer zone and is most often interpreted as an act of aggression. In response, the inmate may instinctively engage in defensive and possibly assaultive behavior.

The officers pointed out the importance of formulating innovative and creative solutions to deal with inmate problems and disputes. Several examples were provided of the use of such solutions in resolving inmate problems:

> Inmates in the module had been misusing the phone; not letting a certain few use it. Three C.O.s that had talked about this misuse gathered up a system that was believed to work. The phone list was made up by the module officer. These inmates did not like the system since they felt they were being treated like children. Within three days everyone was getting equal time on the phone and there have been few disputes over it since.

And in another example:

> New clothing comes into the pod every Tuesday and Friday. The pod officer is in to make sure everyone gets their clothes and that the old, dirty ones are returned. In pod 2D, in the past, inmates could be trusted to come up and get their own clothing rolls from the cart, but now have been opening up other inmates' clothing to trade clothing if they don't like the colors they got. The clothing is left in a mess with some articles missing. Who is doing this is unknown. The officer left the inmates on lockdown rather than let them out after count, and took the clothing to each inmate in his room. This kept the inmates locked down approximately 10 minutes into their dayroom time. When inmates asked why, the officer informed them that there are inmates in the pod that are ripping off others' clothing, so he was delivering it. This way peer pressure gets involved because all are locked down, every one gets their clothing and the officer has control. Two to three weeks later inmates can be trusted again because nobody wanted [to be] locked down. The officer has held control with little effort.

In another situation recounted by an officer, inmates were arguing over the use of the telephone. Several inmates needed to make "life-threatening" telephone calls at the same time. An argument ensued. To deal with the potentially volatile situation, the officer arranged a row of chairs by the telephone. Inmates were instructed to take a seat and, when the telephone was available (each call was limited to 10 minutes), move forward one place. Although the solution appeared simplistic, the droll manner in which the officer announced it broke the tension and ended the argument. Thus, the officer was prompt and innovative in his actions and resolved a situation that was certain to erupt into a major confrontation between inmates.

During the interviews the corrections officers provided many examples of inmate disputes and conflicts that arose over seemingly insignificant acts. It is not unusual for inmates to react aggressively or violently over something as inconsequential as someone sitting in their favorite chair or receiving the smallest portion of dessert. The relative deprivation that inmates experience, even within New Generation facilities, makes it inevitable that meager comforts and luxuries, such as a favored chair or the quantity of dessert, take on critical importance to inmates. The officers agreed that these disputes seriously threaten order within the module. Not only do they hold the potential for escalation, but they often erupt suddenly and without warning. Therefore, it is critical that officers be alert to these minor sources of conflict and deal with them before they intensify to major inmate altercations.

Dimension Two: Building Positive Rapport and Personal Credibility With Inmates

The officer, as the formal leader in the module, is expected to take responsibility for setting a positive tone for interaction between inmates and staff. If officers dehumanize, belittle or degrade inmates, or are unable to control their own emotions, they communicate the message that negative, antisocial and uncivil behavior is an acceptable norm. Inmate compliance and cooperation with staff thus become problematic. If the officer's behavior exhibits a mature, polite and civil demeanor, the message that incivility is intolerable is communicated and reinforced.

The need to create an environment of mutual respect in the module is accomplished by demonstrating consistency in day-to-day interactions with inmates, maintaining a courteous demeanor, using polite phrases such as "please" and "thank you," and remaining emotionally controlled in contacts with inmates regardless of the situation or circumstances. Officers described several incidents in which co-workers were defamed and insulted by inmates. It was generally agreed that abuse by inmates was an occupational hazard and, while officers should never ignore verbal abuse by inmates, they should never react with violence and physical force. One officer related the following incident:

> [A] white male drunk is verbally abusive—mildly combative but being controlled by officers. Male inmate tells the black CO that he is a "fucking nigger." The CO in question snatches up the inmate, slaps him a couple of times in the face, hits his head on the wall for good measure, then throws the inmate onto the toilet, resulting in the inmate having to be sent out to the hospital for stitches and concussion. This was excessive force which was covered up. The officer could not handle getting called a "fucking nigger." In the job—I don't care who you are or what color you are—you had better be able to put up with it. If name-calling bothers someone then they are not fit for the job. As the inmate was already being controlled there was no need for the violence that was shown on the part of the officer.

In a similar case, an inmate infuriated an officer by whistling the theme song from the Andy Griffith television show. (The officer looked like "Opie," Griffith's television son.) The officer responded by locking the inmate in his room and charging him with disrespectful and aggressive behavior toward staff. The inmate was angry for what he perceived to be unfair treatment and other inmates in the module learned how to "get under the officer's skin." Soon, everyone was whistling the tune. Retaliation against inmates by calling them names or by taking excessive disciplinary action in an emotional fashion only serves to provoke further inmate hostility and misbehavior.

Another example of counterproductive staff behavior was given by one officer who related the story of a co-worker who regularly swore at inmates. When they responded in kind, he took disciplinary action against them. Such "double standard" conduct was defined as ineffective behavior in that it was clearly unfair to inmates and, therefore, ensured hostility and resentment on their part.

To a large extent, the ability of the officers to effectively manage the modules depends on their reputations among inmates. Officers stated that inmates must be treated fairly to build credibility among them and to establish a positive reputation. An officer's reputation for fairness was considered important for ensuring inmate compliance and cooperation.

One way by which officers can establish a reputation for fairness is to treat all inmates the same. Equal treatment is necessary to avoid the appearance of favoritism and the loss of officer credibility. It is also vital for preventing the rise of inmate leaders. Respondents described several situations which demonstrated how favoritism could be avoided. For instance, in one facility only 12 of the 50 inmates in the module could eat at one time. To forestall a sense of rank or favor at each meal, the officer rotated which 12 would be served first. Even in a situation as seemingly trivial as this, the perception that select inmates are receiving preferential treatment can produce resentment among other inmates and seriously threaten module order.

Equal treatment also requires officers to put aside any prejudices they might hold toward certain types of inmates. Examples were provided by the interview subjects of officers who treated certain inmates poorly because of their repugnance for the nature of the offense for which they were in jail. Unknowingly, these officers subtly communicated their dislike to other inmates. In turn, inmates took it upon themselves to harass and victimize the pariah.

Another way for officers to develop a positive reputation is by treating inmates with dignity. Officers who demean and belittle inmates often face serious opposition from inmates who feel no obligation to cooperate with the officer. Furthermore, officers who degrade inmates in the presence of others may, in fact, incite inmate misbehavior, for those who have been publicly humiliated will often publicly challenge the officers or other inmates in order to regain their pride.

Dimension Three: Maintaining Effective Administrative and Staff Relations

In traditional jails, staff-administrative relations are often mistakenly assumed to affect only the dynamics of the organization and the job satisfaction of individual employees. In the course of interviewing at New Generation jails, however, it became clear that these relations are important in the achievement of an orderly module and secure facility. In contrast to officers in traditional jails, whose contributions to the organization are often overlooked, the module officer is considered the most important organizational member in the podular/direct supervision facility.

The officers emphasized the need to maintain effective relationships among staff and between staff and administrators. A common method of inmate manipulation is to drive a psychological wedge between an officer and other staff members by making the officer dependent on inmates for friendships. This is done by inmates in a number of ways, including giving the impression to the intended "mark" that other staff members have expressed dislike for him or that they think he's incompetent. A related technique is to sympathize or agree with the officer when he complains about another staff member. To avoid inmate manipulation, it is critical for officers to present a "united front."

Staff unity of this sort can be achieved in a number of ways. Refraining from expressing criticism of other officers while in the presence of inmates and supporting the appropriate actions of other officers in dealing with inmates are perhaps the most important in this regard. One officer told of an incident in which a colleague released an inmate from a 24-hour lockdown after only eight hours because of disagreement with the disciplinary officer's actions. The officers surveyed agreed that, unless the actions violate facility policies or the law, an officer should not interfere with or counteract the decisions of co-workers in regard to inmates. It was believed that inmates will use conflicts between officers for their own benefit to play officers off against each other.

The need for consistency between officers in dealing with inmates was also critical to the maintenance of effective co-worker relations and for control over inmates. In particular, respondents stressed the need for consistency in approaches to inmate management on the part of module officers who work different shifts in the same module. The rules enforced on one shift must be the same rules enforced on other shifts. Several practices were cited as examples of the effective maintenance of consistency between officers, including holding regular but informal meetings with all shift officers coming on duty,[8] and verifying inmate claims with the appropriate staff.

Inconsistency between officers provides opportunities for inmates to manipulate staff members. For example, in one situation an inmate claimed to

---

8   Many of the facilities have instituted overlapping shifts to ensure communication between officers in the modules and to facilitate staff cohesion. Typically, the first fifteen minutes of the shift are spent in roll call, where supervisors pass on important information to all oncoming officers. Following roll call, officers have fifteen minutes for debriefing by the officers they are replacing. During this debriefing period, the officers exchange information about problems in the module, inmate conflicts, special inmate requests and so forth.

have been given permission to attend an Alcoholics Anonymous meeting. Although the officer could not find the required paper work, he allowed the inmate to attend a meeting the inmate had not been given permission to attend. In reality the inmate wanted to talk with his "partner in crime" who had also conned his corrections officer into believing that his attendance had been authorized previously.[9] Without the appropriate paper work or verification, the consensus among corrections officers was that the officer should not have allowed the inmate to attend the meeting.

Inconsistency in rule enforcement by some officers also makes it more difficult for others to enforce the rules. This example was provided by one officer:

> Pod officer allows inmates to watch movies that are given as incentive to achieve 100% in weekly [sanitation] inspections yet this pod received only 91%. This is ineffective control in that the previous shift's officer had informed inmates that they would not be given "special movies" due to low score on inspection. This attitude by the lenient officer makes the C.O. that follows the guidelines look like a "bad" C.O. because he didn't give them the movies. The second C.O. failed to keep informed of policies and procedures, thus making the other shift's C.O.'s job more difficult by being able to work around them to the "lenient" C.O.

Providing appropriate information to the facility administration in a timely manner is also vital for the protection of the officer. One officer recounted a situation in which an inmate confessed to an experienced officer that he had committed a homicide. The officer, believing this story to be a "tall tale" (the inmate was in jail on lesser charges), did not relate the information to his supervisor. Several months later, the inmate asked the prosecuting attorney why he had not been charged with the murder. An investigation determined that the inmate had indeed killed someone. Not surprisingly, the officer faced disciplinary action for his failure to report the confession to his supervisor. This example further illustrates that open channels of communication between officers and supervisors and among fellow officers are vitally important for module order, facility security and protection of individual officers.

The officer's knowledge of and adherence to facility policies and procedures were mentioned by officers as a vital component of effective staff-administrative relations. Officers argued that the policy and procedures manual should be, in effect, "the Bible."[10] By behaving in ways consistent with policies

---

[9]   The two inmates had been purposefully housed in separate living units because of the security and safety risks they posed when together.

[10]   In moving from a traditional to a New Generation facility, many jails totally revised their policies and procedures to conform to the unique architecture and inmate management style.

and procedures, officers could avoid inmate manipulation and promote consistent module management.

In contrast to corrections officers in traditional jails who allow inmates to bend or break rules in exchange for at least a modicum of compliance and cooperation, officers in New Generation facilities are expected to enforce all jail rules, no matter how minor or inconsequential. Although the officers acknowledged that it was not always easy to enforce all facility rules, they agreed that consistent enforcement was necessary to prevent module disruption. One officer provided the following situation as an example of what occurs when rules are "bent":

> Upon initially entering a pod, inmates are assigned a room. Most pods have tried to adopt a policy that unless a medical problem or mechanical problem occurs the inmate will remain in the room he was initially assigned. This can cut down on inmates constantly wanting to move from one room to another and also prevents racial groupings in areas of the pod. It can also give the pod officer the advantage of spreading inmates out or grouping them as the officer sees fit. The new C.O., wanting to be a nice guy, neglected the pod rule of "no moves" and moved the three inmates all to rooms side by side. Almost immediately the three began to cause problems and eventually homemade liquor was found on several occasions. Sometimes it is hard not to bend a little; however, sometimes even a small bend can cause large problems. Once inmates know that with enough push they can make you reconsider, they will try to push everything to the limit. The new C.O. lost a lot of respect and credibility with other officers.

Dimension Four: Managing the Living Unit to Assure a Safe and Humane Environment

The continuous and active observation of all inmates and their activities is a critical component of the style of inmate management advocated by the New Generation philosophy. Active observation is necessary for officers to gather information about what is occurring in the module, to gauge sources of conflict or tension, and above all, to identify and react to situations before they escalate into serious problems. According to one officer, effective observation in the New Generation jail facility is achieved by "mingling":

> While in a module, no matter how large or small, the officer should mingle through his people. This gives the officer a better feel for his people and the inmates an understanding of their officer. One cannot

sit in his office and expect to run a smooth module. You have to mingle. This doesn't mean to be intimate, it means to be able to go among your people and speak with them, not issue orders.

Effective observation requires officers to move among inmates within the module, engage them in casual conversation, observe their actions, ask questions, and listen attentively. Ignoring inmates, sitting behind one's desk reading a book or newspaper, and otherwise isolating oneself from the activities of the inmates were described as ineffective behaviors which often result in inmate problems. Effective observation also entails investigating situations or behaviors which appear out of the ordinary. For example, one officer described the following situation as an example of ineffective observation:

> An officer was making rounds and interrupted what appeared to be a card game of chance. The officer suspected that gambling was taking place because the score was being kept with pieces of paper rather [than] on a piece of paper as usual. The officer also noticed that in the past three days many inmates had been giving away their [dinner] trays. Rather than investigate this and take action he did nothing including no documentation on the incident. Two days later another officer had the same incident and wrote up charges on the inmates. The charges were dropped because the hearings officer felt that the inmates were under the impression that their action was allowed since the first officer observed the same thing and did nothing about it even though it was clearly against the rules.

Another officer provided an example of a situation where the officer's attentiveness to subtle inmate cues diverted serious problems:

> While making security rounds on the upper tier of the pod, an officer observed an inmate sitting in the corner of his room and crying. Being aware that this is not normal for this inmate, the officer entered the room and began to gather information. It was learned by the officer that the inmate was being threatened by other inmates because they had learned that he was a police informant. The officer assessed the information and felt that the inmate's life was possibly in danger. He notified his sergeant and had the inmate moved to protective custody due to threats on his life. The quick thinking and investigation by the officer prevented the possible injury of an inmate.

In another case, by being particularly observant during a routine search of a module, an officer diverted a possible escape:

This situation took place during the shakedown of a housing unit. One inmate had a great deal of legal paper work which the officer doing the shakedown examined very closely, finding a complete floor plan of the floor this inmate was housed on. This officer was effective because he did take a close look at the inmate's paper work instead of just flipping through it. Many officers while on a shakedown look only for the obvious (i.e., weapons, dope, etc.).

As in most jails, the two facilities at which these interviews were conducted routinely detain inmates who have special medical, mental and emotional problems. For these inmates, close observation by staff members is vital. Several officers related that extra attention must be provided to such inmates because of the unpredictable course of their conditions:

This situation took place in the medical unit. One of the inmate/patients was having a heart attack and had lost the will to live because his case was going bad. This inmate had a nurse's call button by his bed and did not use it. If the officer on duty had not been checking the rooms of those inmates not out on free time, this inmate may have died. This officer was effective because he was keeping track of all the inmates in his charge, even the ones that did not come out of these rooms for free time in the dayroom.

And in another example:

An inmate that was housed in this facility [is] in very feeble condition. Inmate also had a heart condition and had seizures from time to time. During shift change it was learned that [the] inmate's condition was getting worse and that [the] inmate had fallen earlier during the day. Inmate had received a deep gash above right eye during fall that required stitches. Upon learning of this, C.O. then decided to move inmate to a cell that was closer to module office and closer to table and chairs out in the dayroom, so that inmate would not have to walk as far to his room. This action enabled C.O. to keep a closer watch on inmate and was effective in getting to inmate if an emergency should occur.

Dimension Five: Responding to Inmate Requests

In the direct supervision facility, the module officer is the most immediate contact the inmate has with the facility's administration, with other components of the criminal justice system, and with the outside world. In consequence, officers face a daily barrage of questions, complaints, and requests for information from inmates. The manner in which an officer deals with these questions and requests directly influences the degree of isolation inmates experience and indirectly affects their levels of anxiety and hostility.

Several salient behavioral themes were apparent in the interviews. The first was the need to acknowledge and respond to every inmate request, even when the response was to deny the request. As previously discussed, initial entry into the jail is a stressful experience. For many, separation from family who may depend on the inmate is a source of anxiety. Through appropriate action, officers can assist in alleviating inmate anxiety. One officer provided this example of appropriate officer behavior.

> An inmate was very disturbed because his mother was a bedridden invalid. She did not have a phone or any way to call for assistance, and the inmate was the only person helping her when he was arrested. If she didn't have help, she would starve to death. When the corrections officer heard about the inmate's difficulty, he contacted a correction specialist [jail counselor] who called a charitable organization in the community. They were able to help the inmate's mother and report back to the inmate via the correction specialist.

Several officers with experience in traditional jails underscored the importance of acknowledging and responding to inmate requests. They recounted how officers in traditional facilities, because of their intermittent contact with inmates, develop strategies to deal with inmate requests which include lying about what they intend to do in response to requests or by simply ignoring them. These survival strategies promote further inmate isolation and hostility, lead to increased tension and disorderliness within the facility, and result in a tendency for officers to avoid those inmates to whom promises were made and not kept. Several officers related that some co-workers responded to inmate questions by telling inmates to ask someone else instead of taking the time to deal with the questions themselves. "Palming off" the question to others causes undue inmate frustration, and, in some cases, may impel inmates to expressions of anger and aggression. One officer provided the following example:

> Inmate kept asking an officer about her release date. Officer kept telling inmate to put a kite (memo) to records. Inmate insisted she should have been released the previous date. Officer's behavior was ineffective because all the officer had to do was take the time and call records. Inmate became irate and ended up in lockdown. Had the officer called records, she would have found out the inmate in fact

should have been released the day before. The inmate would not have been irate.

On the other hand, officers must be able to say "no" to inappropriate inmate requests. Several officers related stories about co-workers who granted inmate requests out of fear, a desire to be friends with inmates, or because it was easier to give in to inmate demands than to firmly say "no." Such behavior places officers in a precarious position. Once they have succumbed to inappropriate requests, particularly those that violate the rules of the facility, they are vulnerable to future inmate manipulation. Inmates can use the officer's initial transgression as material for overt or implied blackmail to ensure compliance with more serious requests.

A second theme concerns the need for officers to provide inmates with accurate information. If an inmate asks a question to which an officer does not know the answer, the officer is responsible for investigating the question and reporting back to the inmate. Providing inmates with answers one "thinks" are correct can lead to problems. For example, if an officer misinterprets a facility rule and the inmate is later penalized for the officer's error, the inmate is certain to feel betrayed and angry with the officer. In some cases, misinformation is purposefully provided by officers to "cool out" anxious or upset inmates. One officer gave the example of a co-worker who, in order to calm an inmate anxious about upcoming court proceedings, told the inmate not to worry because the judge would let him out of jail. According to the interviewee, "all hell broke loose" when the inmate was not released.

Another theme which recurred in the officers' remarks focuses on the need to respond to inmate requests in a polite and courteous manner. Several officers provided examples of ineffective responses to inmate requests. In one case, an officer's response to a request for a supply item provided by the jail to all indigent prisoners was to remind the inmate that he was in jail and did not deserve air to breathe. In another case, when inmates complained that the graveyard officer's radio kept them awake, the officer responded, "My heart's pissing for you!" In both cases, the requests or complaints of inmates were legitimate, but the responses were inappropriate, exacerbating tension rather than reducing it. The offending officers faced not only the hostility of the inmates who made the request or complaint, but that of all inmates in the module when word of this behavior was circulated.

Other critical behaviors include treating all requests with equal consideration and fulfilling all promises made to inmates. According to the officers, reneging on promises can pose a serious threat to an officer's reputation. When word passes among inmates that certain officers are unreliable and cannot be trusted, they typically find it more difficult to control inmates in the future.

Dimension Six: Handling Inmate Discipline

The jail organization presents a classical example of the Weberian rational-legal authority system. Whether in a traditional or New Generation jail, formal institutional rules and regulations abound. There are few activities or situations involving inmates which are not covered by an institutional rule or regulation. Corrections officers, whose primary responsibility is to control inmates, are also governed by an exhaustive list of rules that prescribe expected behavior in all situations. In contrast to corrections officers in traditional jails who often avoid excessive rule enforcement to pacify supervisors as well as inmates, officers in New Generation facilities are actively encouraged by supervisors and administrators to enforce the rules. Rigorous rule enforcement as evidenced in activity and disciplinary reports is viewed by superiors as a sign that the officer is effectively performing the job.

Given the emphasis on rule enforcement, the process of disciplining inmate violations is of great importance within the direct supervision facility. The purpose of discipline is the maintenance of an orderly environment rather than the punishment of any particular inmate. Discipline consists of a complex structuring of a range of penalties designed to achieve the overriding goal of an orderly module and compliant inmate behavior. Unlike officers in traditional jails, New Generation corrections officers are granted the authority to unilaterally administer informal discipline to inmates who violate minor rules.

The process through which the officer disciplines an inmate for violation of facility rules was repeatedly illustrated in the interviews. Two major behavioral themes emerged:

(1) the use of progressive discipline, and
(2) the application of fair and consistent disciplinary measures.

Progressive discipline requires officers to make distinctions between minor and serious rule violations and between occasional and repeated violations, and to take disciplinary action based on these judgments. The mode of discipline officers can administer without taking formal action against the inmate includes counseling or relaxed discussion with the offending inmate (discussing the rule violated by the inmate, the reason for the rule, determining why the rule was violated and explaining the consequences of repeated rule violations), a verbal warning or reprimand, and/or locking the inmate in his/her room for a short period of time. Informal discipline is viewed as effective in dealing with rule violations too minor to require official disciplinary action. The purpose of informal discipline is to put a stop to misbehavior without removing the inmate from the module or officially charging them with a violation which would necessitate a formal disciplinary hearing. The effectiveness of informal discipline depends on the officer's willingness to follow through on warnings (or promises) regarding further discipline for continued misbehavior. Formal disciplinary options available to officers include extended lockdown of the inmate within his/her room or transfer of the offender to a segregation unit. However, these forms of discipline are only administered after the inmate has received an in-house disciplinary hearing.

A second theme emphasized by officers is the fair and consistent application of discipline. Officers described situations in which inmate perceptions about inconsistent and unfair disciplinary action led to unrest and hostility, a breakdown of order in the module, stimulation of further inmate behavior, disruption of staff/inmate relations and the arousal of tensions among staff members. Officers defined a number of critical behaviors associated with the concept of fair and consistent discipline. First, discipline must only be applied to the offending inmate(s) rather than to all inmates in the module. Several negative examples were provided of "mass punishment." In one case, two inmates sitting at two different televisions engaged in a contest over the volume. One of the inmates would turn up the television, and the other inmate would turn his up even louder. The officer's response was to turn off both televisions. While this action punished the two offending inmates, it also unjustly punished all other inmates who were watching the televisions but were not involved in the contest. In another case, two inmates held a heated debate over use of the telephone. In response, the officer disconnected the telephone and told the inmates, "Now you don't have anything to yell about, assholes." Not only were all inmates unfairly punished for the behavior of a few, but it was believed that inmates would retaliate against the offending inmates at a later time, thereby threatening order within the module.

Another critical behavior concerns disciplining inmates in private rather than in the presence of others. By disciplining inmates in private, the officer can avoid embarrassing them and thereby forcing them into face-saving and potentially disruptive actions. An officer provided this example to illustrate the point:

> Inmates were being served lunch. One new inmate had sat down in a chair that an older inmate had been sitting in for months. The older inmate began arguing with the newer inmate over the chair. The C.O. intervened between the two inmates before the situation could develop into a fight. The C.O. explained to both inmates that there was no assigned seating in the pod and that seating was at random. When the older inmate continued to argue with the C.O., she sent the inmate to his room to cool off. After a short while, she again approached the older inmate and talked with him about the seating arrangements. The older inmate, now away from the inmates in the dayroom, agreed with the pod officer and apologized for creating a scene. The officer rec-

ognized the situation before it could turn into a major incident and corrected the problem. By getting the inmate away from the other inmates, she stopped the inmate from putting on a show for the other inmates.

Fair and consistent discipline also requires officers to explain the reason for the disciplinary action to the inmate, and in particular, to identify the rule violated by the inmate and provide an opportunity for the inmate to explain the circumstances of his/her behavior. By talking with the inmate prior to taking disciplinary action, officers can determine the presence of extenuating circumstances for the violation. This example was provided by an officer:

> Inmates in [the] general population pod have a weekly sanitation inspection. Each inmate is assigned a specific duty to finish. The pod is then graded and if a high enough grade is achieved rewards are given (first run movies shown, popcorn and soda). On inspection day a Spanish-speaking inmate would not clean up. His personal appearance was bad, his room was a mess, and he did not want to work. The inmate could have received a facility in-house charge as a disciplinary action. Inmates are required to keep themselves clean and their rooms clean and also participate in the cleaning of common areas. Before charging the inmate and locking him down the officer had another inmate who spoke Spanish talk with the inmate. Upon talking to the inmate it was found out he did not have a rule book to explain to him the rules and due to his not speaking English was not given the individual pod rules. The inmate was explained the rules in Spanish and was no further problem. The majority of the problems encountered can be resolved by simply talking.

Finally, officers expressed the importance of discussing rule violations with inmates in order to ensure that discipline was warranted. An officer told of an incident where one inmate assaulted another. One inmate had been the instigator while the other had attempted to flee from the assault. The officer locked down both inmates without investigating the situation. In consequence, the victim was unfairly disciplined.

In contrast to the discipline process in a direct supervision facility, the linear architecture and intermittent inmate supervision style of traditional facilities precludes fair and consistent disciplinary action. As a result of the recurrent presence and absence of the officer, discipline for rule infractions is differentially distributed and results from either an officer's chance observation of misbehavior or from inmate "snitches." Furthermore, unless inmates are engaged in flagrant misbehavior, the officer patrolling the corridors of the traditional linear jail may not observe inmates long enough to discern more subtle forms of misbehavior such as extortion and gambling. Thus, in a traditional detention facility an officer's ability to control inmate behavior is structurally compromised and his/her authority is highly subject to manipulation by inmate groups.

Dimension Seven: Supervising in a Clear, Well-Organized and Attention-Getting Manner

The principles of effective supervision, irrespective of organizational settings, require specific skills and abilities. Effective supervision of inmates in New Generation facilities entails an especially broad range of such behaviors. Several themes were commonly addressed by corrections officers and supervisory staff in the interviews conducted. First, effective supervision of inmate task performance depends on the ability of the officer to:

(1) clearly communicate orders, requests and the requirements of a task;

(2) equitably assign tasks which are consistent with inmate abilities;

(3) motivate inmate compliance through praise and constructive criticism;

(4) make certain that inmates are able to comply with orders;

(5) provide continual feedback to inmates on their performance; and

(6) follow up on inmate compliance.

Several interview subjects underlined the need for officers to be decisive when issuing orders. One officer recounted an incident in which the inability of the officer to make a decision about a situation and issue an order posed serious threats to order within the module. Several inmates were throwing dice, while others slept or watched television. The inmates watching television complained to the officer that the dice playing inmates were too noisy and were making it difficult to hear their programs.

> The officer approaches the two inmates playing dice and asks them if they could maybe stop playing until the movie was over. The two inmates claim they have just as much right to play dice as they do to watch the movie. The officer then tells the inmates to turn the T.V. up a little bit, so they can hear it. As time goes along, those watching the baseball game turn their T.V. up also because they can't hear it clearly over the movie on the other set. Now, we have inmates yelling "Turn it down!" from their rooms because they can't sleep because the T.V.s are too loud. Now what?

In addition to issuing orders, it is necessary for officers to ensure that inmates comply with the orders. Two examples were given in which inmates ignored officers' orders. In one situation, instead of making certain that the inmate complied, the officer gave the same order to another inmate, hoping that this inmate would obey the command. In a similar situation, the officer himself performed the task that had been assigned to the inmate. These behaviors were ineffective because they demonstrated the officers' inability to exercise authority. It was predicted that both officers would be confronted with greater inmate disobedience in the future.

Effective supervision requires more than the ability to issue an order. It also involves the ability to motivate inmates with techniques other than threats of punishment. One officer related the following incident as an example of effective inmate supervision:

> A corrections officer was assigned a pod where they had been receiving low scores on the pod inspection. This officer found that the inmates had no desire to score 100, because a lack of interest in the former C.O.'s attitude. This new officer decided to show a positive attitude and take it very seriously. This officer made out all the assignments and had a pod meeting right after dinner, informing the inmates of their assignments. When each inmate completed his assignment he told the C.O. who then inspected each area and gave encouragement when the job was done well and constructive criticism when needed. Within two weeks the pod scored a 100 and took pride in pod inspection. The C.O.s that worked that pod knew how to supervise and communicate. They received a 100, seven weeks in a row.

Although officers have the authority to issue orders and discipline inmates who fail to comply, the consensus among corrections staff interviewed was that positive reinforcement was most effective in gaining consistent compliance and maintaining good relations with inmates. One officer recounted the following story to demonstrate positive rule enforcement techniques:

> An inmate was booked into the facility on some minor charges. From his appearance and odor it was obvious that the inmate had not bathed for quite some time. After the inmate officer had searched the inmate, he asked him if he wanted to take a shower. The inmate answered "no, but I would like a smoke." The officer told the inmate that he didn't have any cigarettes but if he took a shower and got cleaned up he would try to get him one. The inmate thought about it for a second and decided it was worth it, and he took a shower. This was a good example of effective behavior because the officer was able to manipulate the inmate with the promise of a cigarette which he was autho-

rized to give to the inmate. This behavior was also effective in that it enabled the intake officer and other officers that this inmate came in contact with not to be overcome by the inmate's horrendous body odor.

A second group of behaviors emphasized by officers as necessary for daily module management focus on the need to communicate official facility rules and policies to inmates, and to explain their own personal expectations. Rules and expectations are effectively communicated in a number of ways, ranging from a showing of a video tape upon an inmate's arrival at the facility to a meeting with inmates upon their arrival to the module. Similarly, by holding daily meetings with inmates and casually discussing relevant issues when the inmates gather at meal time, the occasions for clear communication of rules and expectations are enhanced. Officers view these behaviors as effective because they reinforce facility rules, alert inmates to officer expectations, and explicitly define the bounds of acceptable behavior. Failure to communicate rules and expectations is seen by nearly all corrections personnel interviewed as an invitation to inmate misbehavior and is believed to result in inmate hostility and tension concerning disciplinary action.

A final group of behaviors that were defined as crucial to the daily operation of the module concern the vigilant guarding of officers' authority to prevent encroachment by inmates. The direct supervision philosophy of inmate management is predicated on the belief that the officer can be the only leader in the module (Nelson and O'Toole, 1983). This condition of staff leadership among inmates is in direct contrast to the practice in most traditional jails described earlier; in general, traditional jails operate in such a way as to tolerate inmate leaders whose leadership is used to maintain a semblance of order among inmates. Authority, when granted to or usurped by an inmate, can become a coercive weapon used to manipulate others, including the officer.

Officers described several incidents in which an inmate assumed duties that should have been the sole responsibility of the officer. In one situation an officer assigned an inmate to supervise the clean-up duties of other inmates. The inmate was free to manipulate the situation for his own benefit and other inmates viewed the action as a case of "playing favorites." As a result of the officer's error in judgment, hostility and tension consequently developed between the supervising inmate and other inmates. The situation deteriorated to the point of threatened violence against the supervising inmate and disruption of the module.

Officers also agreed among themselves that inmate challenges to their authority must be dealt with quickly. Several examples were provided of situations wherein inmates openly defied the orders of officers or the rules of the facility. The officers agreed that swift and certain responses were necessary to quell these challenges and to reinforce the notion that officers, rather than inmates, are in charge of the modules. An officer provided the following example:

> Several inmates staged a group demonstration by way of a refusal to do standard pre-inspection clean-up work on the midnight shift prior to inspection day. Their reason for refusing to work was because an officer denied them the privilege to make coffee during clean-up that evening. This was because the officer was substituting in that pod for that night only and was uncertain if the regular officer assigned to that pod allowed this privilege or not, and, after searching for documentation addressing the subject and finding none, denied the inmates that privilege. The next day, an inmate who was a constant source of disruption, as well as the voice of leadership for inmates, was "rolled-up" and moved to the disciplinary pod, following more disruptive behavior, as well as verbal abuse and a threat on the officer on dayshift...This was effective because it served as a reminder to enforce the idea that the pod officer is to be the only authority in the pod. Authority is not to be shared with inmates. The pod became quieter, more respectful, and control was restored.

While many of the behaviors relating to the seven dimensions described above may be practiced in traditional jails, the architectural design of these facilities limits their full and effective use. The fundamental element for the success of direct supervision is immediate and continuous contact between officers and inmates. The linear design of traditional jails makes it structurally and fiscally impossible for this type of contact, while intermittent surveillance cannot provide the degree of interaction between inmates and officers that is necessary for effective control of inmate behavior and maintenance of institutional order. Without the direct supervision of inmates, proactive rule enforcement, communication, progressive discipline, consistency, rigorous observation and the other principles described above are virtually impossible. And without the appropriate inmate supervision style, the podular facility suffers problems similar to those of traditional jails. In order to achieve the difficult goals of humane and safe incarceration, both architecture and inmate management style must conform to the dictates of the New Generation philosophy.

Conclusions

Despite the growing popularity of the New Generation design concept and the increasing number of jurisdictions throughout the country that are investing millions of dollars in the construction of these facilities, a comprehensive and rigorous evaluation of the effectiveness of the design and operations in reducing inmate violence and destruction has yet to be completed. However, early observations by direct supervision jail administrators and representatives of the National Institute of Corrections indicate that: "New Generation jails [are] at least as secure as traditional linear jails and provid[e] a higher level of safety for both staff and inmates" (Nelson and O'Toole, 1983:1). Staff and administrators at the facilities that were visited in the course of this research claim that the move from a traditional to direct supervision facility produced a dramatic reduction in the number of assaults among inmates and between inmates and staff, the amount of vandalism and property destruction, the number of inmate suicides, and the number of civil lawsuits filed by prisoners.[11] Wener, et al. (1987) report that violent incidents in federal metropolitan correctional centers and other direct supervision facilities were reduced by 30% to 90% and homosexuality virtually disappeared after the move to the new architecture and operations. Officials at other New Generation facilities report similar reductions. Bucks County (Pennsylvania) jail, for example, experienced a 50% decline in the frequency of inmate fights and a 30% decrease in the use of disciplinary segregation after the move from a traditional to a New Generation facility (Nelson, 1988a). And in the first 18 months of operation, Middlesex County (New Jersey) experienced no incidents of violence between inmates or between inmates and correctional staff (Nelson, 1988a).

In addition to the testimonials of New Generation jail administrators and representatives of the National Institute of Corrections, there exist several studies that either focus on a specific facility or attempt to compare a limited number of New Generation facilities with traditional jails. Although these studies can be faulted for a number of methodological problems, they nevertheless provide limited evidence to suggest that podular/direct supervision facilities are safer for inmates and staff.

In one of the few controlled studies of inmate misconduct in New Generation facilities, researchers at the National Institute of Corrections (Nelson and O'Toole, 1983) compared incidents of aggravated assaults (among inmates and between inmates and staff), homicides, suicides, escapes and escape attempts in five podular/direct supervision facilities and six traditional linear facilities of

---

[11] All of the studies cited in this section use official reports filed by corrections officers to assess the frequency of inmate misconduct. Because direct supervision corrections officers have greater opportunities to observe inmate activities and to detect incidents of misconduct, we would expect *more reports* of inmate misconduct in the New Generation jails than in traditional jails. It is interesting to note that, in study after study, the findings indicate that there are *fewer reports* of inmate misconduct in New Generation facilities than in traditional jails. Researchers and administrators at these facilities interpret these findings to mean that New Generation jail inmates are less likely to engage in violence than inmates in traditional jails. However, this interpretation may not be accurate. An alternative explanation is that corrections officers in New Generation facilities are *less likely* to report incidents of inmate misconduct than officers in traditional jails.

comparable size.[12] A perusal of the findings indicates that there are important differences between both types of facilities regarding the number of inmate incidents (see Tables 6.1, 6.2, and 6.3). The differences in numbers of aggravated assaults are the most dramatic. The podular/direct supervision facilities averaged 10.4 assaults in 1981 and 8.7 in 1982. In contrast, traditional facilities averaged 154.3 assaults in 1981 and 141.5 in 1982.[13]

Table 6.1. New Generation Jail Survey: Comparative Data from 1981 and 1982 on (Aggravated) Assaults

	1981		1982	
	Inmate to Inmate	Inmate to Staff	Inmate to Inmate	Inmate to Staff
PODULAR/DIRECT SUPERVISION FACILITIES				
Chicago MCC	3	0	1	0
San Diego MCC	2	6	4	8
New York MCC	2	1	1	1
Tucson MCC	N/A	N/A	0	0
Contra Costa	64	5	67	5
COMPARATIVE TRADITIONAL FACILITIES				
County A	57	11	43	15
County B	220*	—	71*	—
County C	772	94	735	74
County D	354	90	290	86
County E	7	7	36	22
County F	180	60	182	144

* Not broken down.

Source: Nelson, W.R. and M. O'Toole (1983) *New Generation Jails*. Boulder, Colorado: Library Information Specialists, Inc.

---

[12] Four of the five direct supervision facilities were federal Metropolitan Correctional Centers; the fifth was county jail located in Contra Costa, California. The traditional facilities were located in "urban counties felt to be roughly comparable to the MCCs and Contra Costa and all [were] considering 'new generation' concepts for their new jails" (Nelson and O'Toole, 1983:31).

[13] There are a number of methodological problems with this study that make the findings less than reliable. One methodological problem concerns the representativeness of the sampled New Generation and traditional jail facilities to jails in general. Some correctional experts would question the validity of comparing inmates in federal jails to inmates in county jails due to possible differences in the characteristics of the inmates. A more serious methodological problem concerns the failure on the part of the researchers to control for the inmate classification systems of the facilities. In the transition from a traditional to direct supervision design, many facilities implement more sophisticated systems of inmate classification. The differences in the number of inmate incidents between the two jail types may actually reflect differences in the classification systems rather than the architecture and inmate management styles of each.

**Table 6.2. New Generation Jail Survey:
Comparative Data from 1981 and 1982 on Homicides and Suicides**

	1981		1982	
	Homicides	Suicides	Homicides	Suicides
PODULAR/DIRECT SUPERVISION FACILITIES				
Chicago MCC	0	0	0	0
San Diego MCC	0	0	0	1
New York MCC	0	0	0	1
Tucson MCC	N/A	N/A	0	0
Contra Costa	0	1	0	3
COMPARATIVE TRADITIONAL FACILITIES				
County A	0	0	0	0
County B	0	2	0	0
County C	0	0	0	2
County D	0	0	0	2
County E	1	1	0	0
County F	0	2	0	2

Source: Nelson, W.R. and M. O'Toole (1983) *New Generation Jails.* Boulder, Colorado: Library Information Specialists, Inc.

**Table 6.3. New Generation Jail Survey:
Comparative Data from 1981 and 1982 on Escapes**

	1981		1982	
	Number of Events	Number of Escapes	Number of Events	Number of Escapes
PODULAR/DIRECT SUPERVISION FACILITIES				
Chicago MCC	0	0	0	0
San Diego MCC	4	7	2	3
New York MCC	2	2	0	0
Tucson MCC	N/A	N/A	0	0
Contra Costa	1	4	0	0
COMPARATIVE TRADITIONAL FACILITIES				
County A	0	0	0	0
County B	1	1	1	1
County C	15	15	1	11
County D	1	1	4	1
County E	3	3	1	1
County F	4	4	8	10

Source: Nelson, W.R. and M. O'Toole (1983) *New Generation Jails.* Boulder, Colorado: Library Information Specialists, Inc.

Herbert R. Sigurdson, a private jail consultant, conducted evaluation studies of New Generation jails in New York City, Pima County, Arizona, and Larimer County, Colorado for the National Institute of Corrections. In the Manhattan House of Detention he found that in the first full year of operation there were no homicides, sexual assaults, aggravated assaults, suicides, inmate disturbances, escapes, lawsuits or adverse judgments (Sigurdson, 1985). In addition, there were only four reports of contraband weapons (fashioned from plastic razor blades). In his assessment of the Pima County Detention Facility, Sigurdson (1987a) found that no homicides, suicides, sexual assaults, aggravated assaults, disturbances, or court-ordered judgments occurred in two and a half years. During this period, only one contraband item (a broken mop handle) was reported being found in the possession of inmates. In his study of the Larimer County Jail, Sigurdson (1987b) found similar results. In a three-and-a-half-year period, there were no inmate homicides, suicides, sexual assaults, disturbances or court-ordered judgments against the jail. There were, however, four incidents of aggravated assaults and five contraband weapons found (two fashioned from broken mop handles and three from small plastic utensils).[14]

New Generation jail administrators also report that the incidence of inmate destruction and vandalism to jail property is also reduced. In one facility, the number of damaged mattresses dropped from 150 per year in the traditional jail to none during the first two years of occupancy in a direct supervision facility; television repairs dropped from two per week to two in two years; the number of destroyed sets of inmate clothes dropped from approximately 99 sets per week to 15 sets in two years (Wener, Frazier and Farbstein, 1987:42). Administrators in several New Generation facilities also report a decrease in the amount of vandalism to the building after the transition from a traditional facility (Nelson, 1988a). In particular, inmates broke fewer windows and lighting fixtures, and started fewer fires within their rooms and the modules. There was also a reported decrease in the number of plumbing and painting repairs (Nelson, 1988a). The most dramatic reports concern the amount of graffiti in these facilities. New Generation jail officials claim that graffiti is less prevalent in the housing modules, and in some facilities, almost nonexistent except in court holding cells which are traditional in design and supervision (Nelson, 1988a). Although cigarette burns in the carpet are commonplace in several New Generation facilities, officials attribute these burns to an insufficient number of ash-

---

14   Like the National Institute of Correction's study, the reliability of Sigurdson's research is questionable. The most serious problem with his studies is that he fails to provide comparison data on suicides, assaults, homicides, escapes and so forth *before* the transition from traditional to podular/direct supervision operations or from comparable traditional facilities. Without this comparison data, it is impossible to conclude whether the transition from traditional to New Generation operations decreased, increased, or even affected the frequency of inmate misconduct.

trays in the modules, rather than to malicious inmate behavior. Some facilities have dealt with this potential fire hazard by limiting smoking to individual rooms which are not carpeted.

In addition to reducing inmate violence and destruction, proponents of the New Generation philosophy claim that the innovative architecture and inmate management style create a more humane environment for inmates and staff. The following two chapters address the impact of the new architecture and operations on the quality of life experienced by inmates and staff in these facilities.

Chapter Seven

Staff Evaluations
of Direct Supervision Facilities

The architecture and inmate management style advocated by the New Generation philosophy introduce significant change into the work life of corrections officers. Implementation of the new philosophy produces two potentially beneficial, yet originally unplanned, changes for these employees. First, it significantly alters the physical environment in which the job is performed; secondly, the new philosophy redefines the job tasks and responsibilities of corrections officers.

Corrections officers, like inmates, are captives within the physical structure of the jail facility, albeit only for the duration of their shifts. Nevertheless, officers are susceptible to the same environmental irritants that produce stress among inmates. In the traditional jail facility, officers work in a stress-inducing physical environment. The work setting is excessively noisy and overcrowded; it lacks windows and natural light, and is furnished with hard metal accoutrements and painted in dull and unattractive colors. As with inmates, these physical characteristics of the environment can negatively affect the mental and physical health, task performance and perceptions of staff. Features of the New Generation architecture and interior originally designed to fulfill the needs and alleviate the stress of inmates serve the dual function of providing staff with a pleasant physical workplace and reducing environmental sources of staff stress.

The job performed by direct supervision corrections officers possesses a number of characteristics that make it "enriched." Hackman, et al. (1981) argued that people are motivated by and find satisfaction in jobs that are perceived as meaningful, that provide employees with responsibility for the outcome of their efforts, and that provide feedback about the success or failure of their performance. In accordance with the theory of job enrichment, work is redesigned to provide optimal opportunities for workers to experience these conditions. Job enrichment is a strategy of job redesign which:

> involves a deliberate attempt to increase the amount of responsibility and challenge in work. The job must be expanded vertically as well as horizontally. Thus responsibilities and controls that formerly were reserved for management are given to the employees. This inevitably leads to greater worker autonomy. Workers are granted control over such job components as resource allocation and utilization, performance measures, and problem solving. Consequently, the workers' feelings of personal responsibility and accountability are heightened. In an enriched job, the employee is given an opportunity to demonstrate what he or she can do and to apply his or her creative talents freely (Hays and Reeves, 1984:273).

Hackman, et al. (1981), in developing a conceptual basis for measuring job enrichment, argued that the design of the job influences three critical work-related psychological states: experienced meaningfulness of work, experienced responsibility, and knowledge of results. In turn, the presence or absence of these psychological states influences personal and work outcomes such as motivation, satisfaction, productivity, turnover, and absenteeism. Hackman and his fellow researchers proposed that enriched jobs possess characteristics that induce the three critical psychological states. These characteristics include: skill variety (the extent to which a job requires a number of different skills and talents); task identity (the extent to which a job requires completion of a whole, identifiable piece of work); task significance (the impact of the job on the lives and work of others); autonomy (the extent of freedom, independence, and discretion in setting work standards); and feedback (the extent to which work activities provide direct and clear information about effective performance). It is hypothesized that optimal levels of each of these five characteristics in a job will induce the critical psychological states, and will in turn produce positive personal and work outcomes.

Analysis of the job performed by direct supervision corrections officers suggests that it possesses a number of these enriching characteristics. The job requires officers to observe, investigate and resolve inmate problems, providing officers with the opportunity to use a variety of skills and abilities. It requires officers to resolve problems and manage difficult situations within the modules, thereby allowing them to complete a job from beginning to end. Officers in these facilities must assess the impact of their own management skills on module order, hence they experience direct and immediate feedback on their performance. Furthermore, they must make most decisions within the module single-handedly, thereby enhancing their sense of responsibility and autonomy. Finally, officers are required to maintain order and exercise leadership within the modules largely by the use of their wits—a difficult task of evident importance to society.

Given these changes in the corrections officers' job and in the environment in which it is performed, we would expect that implementation of the New Generation philosophy would enhance the quality of work life experienced by custodial staff. More specifically, we would expect direct supervision officers to evaluate their job as more enriched, experience greater job satisfaction, and experience less stress than officers in traditional, linear jail facilities.

Data were collected from corrections officers at four podular/direct supervision jails and from three traditional, linear facilities.[1] All officers within the facilities were asked to participate in the research. Of the 378 corrections officers in podular/direct supervision facilities, 217 (57.4%) returned usable questionnaires. Seventy-five out of 146 (51.4%) corrections officers in the traditional facilities returned usable questionnaires.

While administering the surveys at the sampled jails, it became apparent that one of the New Generation facilities was atypical. Although the architecture and accoutrements in this facility were identical to those found in other podular/direct supervision facilities, the style of inmate management was different—due primarily to the paucity and type of training provided to the correctional staff. The officers were given only two weeks of training—compared to the six or eight weeks of training received by officers in other podular/direct supervision facilities—and the training was more appropriate to work in traditional jails (e.g., emphasis on physical control rather than inmate control through interpersonal skills). In addition, the inmate management practices in this facility differed from those of the other podular/direct supervision facilities. For example, inmates were locked in their cells without supervision while officers took lunch and coffee breaks away from the module. The consequence of these and other facility-specific factors (e.g., pronounced labor-management tensions) were reflected in the number and severity of problems the facility was experiencing with inmates and staff. One week prior to the researchers' visit to the facility, a counselor was taken hostage by an inmate in a module. On the day of the research visit, a corrections officer was seriously assaulted. Absenteeism among corrections officers was also so high as to allow one officer, eager for overtime, to double his annual salary. For these reasons, the responses of offi-

---

1 At the time the research was conducted, there were only four podular/direct supervision county jails in operation in the western United States. These facilities were chosen for this research because of their proximity. The traditional jails used in this research represent three of the six largest jails in Washington state that granted permission for the research to be conducted.

cers in this facility were analyzed separately from officer responses in both traditional and podular/direct supervision facilities.[2]

The officers from podular/direct supervision, traditional facilities, and Facility C who returned usable questionnaires are fairly similar in regard to important demographic characteristics (see Table 7.1). The typical respondent in these facilities was a white male, between 35 and 37 years of age, with some college education, who had been employed at the jail for between two and five years. Characteristics of the sampled corrections officers in Facility C appear to differ from the samples from both the podular/direct supervision and traditional facilities. Males, American Indians, and baccalaureates were more prevalent in the sample from Facility C than from the other two types of facilities. In addition, while the distribution for length of employment was fairly normal in the samples from other direct supervision and traditional facilities, the distribution for Facility C was tri-modal, with a larger percentage of officers having been employed at the facility for either less than one year, 2 to 5 years, or over 10 years.

Job Enrichment

The job analysis conducted with corrections officers in podular/direct supervision jails suggested that the job performed by these officers possessed a number of enriching characteristics. If this observation is correct, we would expect that officers in direct supervision facilities would report higher levels of enrichment in their job than would officers in traditional facilities.

The Job Diagnostic Survey, developed by Hackman and Oldham (1974) was used to measure the "motivating potential" or self-assessed enrichment levels of the corrections officers' job. This instrument assesses the degree to which enriching characteristics are present within a job and is designed to solicit descriptions of the job rather than affective reactions to it. The instrument measures five characteristics of a job: skill variety, task identity, task significance, autonomy, and feedback. The scale scores for each of these characteristics range from 1 to 7. In addition to a score for each characteristic, a single "motivating potential" score is created by combining job characteristic scores that have been weighted to reflect the importance of the particular dimension. Motivating potential scores range from 0 to 360, with 0 signifying a total absence and 360 signifying total presence of motivating potential in the job.

Contrary to expectation, there were no significant differences on any of the enriching job characteristics or in the overall motivating potential score between officers in podular/direct supervision and traditional jails (see Table 7.2). Although officers in New Generation facilities described their job as providing

---

2   For the remainder of this work, the facility will be referred to as "Facility C."

higher levels in four of the five job characteristics and in motivating potential, these differences were not statistically significant. When the responses of officers in traditional and podular/direct supervision facilities were compared with those of officers in Facility C, only one significant difference was found. Officers in Facility C described the existence of significantly less task identification with their job than officers in either traditional or podular/direct supervision facilities.

**Table 7.1. Distribution
of Corrections Officer Characteristics**

	Direct Supervision	Traditional	Facility C
NUMBER OF CASES	173	75	44
SEX:			
Male	77.1%	72.0	90.7
Female	22.9	28.0	9.3
RACE:			
Black	7.8%	4.2	2.4
White	77.8	87.3	82.9
Hispanic	5.4	1.4	0.0
Native American	4.8	2.8	12.2
Other	4.2	4.2	2.4
EDUCATION:			
High School or Less	17.4%	30.7	0.00
Some College	54.1	46.7	43.2
AA Degree	14.0	9.3	13.6
BA or Higher	14.5	13.3	43.2
LENGTH OF EMPLOYMENT:			
Less Than 1 Year	9.8%	4.0	13.6
1 to 2 Years	23.7	30.7	6.8
2 to 5 Years	42.2	45.3	52.3
6 to 10 Years	17.3	10.7	9.1
Over 10 Years	6.9	9.3	18.2
AGE:			
Mean	34.7	37.4	34.5
Standard Deviation	10.0	9.5	8.1

Table 7.2. Comparison of Job Diagnostic Survey Scores Between Corrections Officers

	Direct Supervision	Traditional	Facility C
NUMBER OF CASES	168	72	44
SKILL VARIETY			
Mean	4.4	4.2	4.1
SD	1.3	1.3	1.1
TASK IDENTIFICATION			
Mean	4.1	4.2[a]	3.5[b]
SD	1.4	1.4	1.4
TASK SIGNIFICANCE			
Mean	5.6	5.5	5.3
SD	1.0	1.2	1.1
AUTONOMY			
Mean	4.9	4.7	4.8
SD	1.1	1.1	1.2
FEEDBACK FROM THE JOB			
Mean	4.7	4.5	4.7
SD	1.2	1.3	1.2
MOTIVATING POTENTIAL			
Mean	113.3	103.5	106.4
SD	58.6	53.6	54.6

a =   Significant difference (at .05 level) between officers in Traditional Facilities and in Facility C using a one-tailed test.
b =   Significant difference (at .05 level) between officers in Direct Supervision Facilities and in Facility C using a one-tailed test.

NOTE: The higher the mean the more the characteristic is present in the job.

These findings indicate that the job performed by officers in New Generation jails was not perceived as any more or less enriched than the job performed by officers in traditional facilities. This equivalence contradicts the results of the job analysis, which suggested that the job performed by corrections officers in direct supervision jails possesses a number of enriching characteristics.

Job Satisfaction

If the podular/direct supervision design improves the work performed by corrections officers as well as the organizational and physical environment in which it is performed, we would expect officers in these facilities to be significantly more satisfied with their job than are officers in traditional jails. Corrections officer job satisfaction was assessed by the use of the Job Descriptive Index developed by Smith, Kendall, and Hulin (1969). This instrument measures employee satisfaction in five job-related domains (character of work, level of pay, opportunity for promotion, quality of supervision, and people on the job). The five indexes contain from 8 to 18 items and the range for index scores varies depending on the weights assigned to each item and the number of items. An overall satisfaction measure is created by summing the five index scores. A low index score indicates low job satisfaction while a high score indicates a higher level of job satisfaction.

Table 7.3 presents comparisons on the job satisfaction measures between officers in the three jail types. Corrections officers in New Generation jails were significantly more satisfied than were officers in traditional facilities as to their level of pay and opportunities for promotion; however, officers in traditional facilities were significantly more satisfied with the character of their work and quality of the supervision they receive. The finding that traditional officers were more satisfied with the character of their work is surprising given the fact that, based on the findings from the job analysis, the work of officers in direct supervision facilities was believed to possess the characteristics of an enriched job. The finding that traditional officers were more satisfied with the supervision they received than were direct supervision officers is not surprising. Corrections officers in podular/direct supervision facilities have assumed many tasks that are the primary responsibility of first- line supervisors in traditional facilities. In visits to podular/direct supervision facilities, administrators and corrections officers repeatedly commented that the responsibilities of the first-line supervisors have yet to be adequately defined by facility administrators. In the view of officers, supervisors often interfered with or usurped the responsibilities of corrections officers, thereby angering them. Another complaint from the officers was that their supervisors had never worked in the modules and were therefore unqualified to advise or direct them on how to perform the job. Because of the ambiguity in the supervisors' role, it was expected that officers in the direct supervision facilities would be somewhat negative about the supervision they received.

Officers in Facility C were systematically less satisfied than were officers in other podular/direct supervision and in traditional jails. These officers were significantly less satisfied than were officers in traditional jails on all job satisfaction scales, with the exception of the people on the job dimension. Officers in Facility C were also significantly less satisfied than were officers in podular/direct supervision facilities with character of work, level of pay, opportunities for promotion, and on the overall satisfaction scale. These findings are not surprising given the problems at Facility C, particularly the intense management-labor tensions.

Table 7.3. Comparison of Job Descriptive Index Scores Between Corrections officers

	Direct Supervision	Traditional	Facility C
NUMBER OF CASES	173	75	44
CHARACTER OF WORK			
Mean	25.6[a]	28.0[b]	21.1[c]
SD	10.1	10.1	10.5
LEVEL OF PAY			
Mean	29.6[a]	18.2[b]	14.2[c]
SD	14.3	12.1	11.4
OPPORTUNITY FOR PROMOTION			
Mean	23.0[a]	18.2[b]	12.4[c]
SD	13.2	10.3	8.1
QUALITY OF SUPERVISION			
Mean	31.2	36.3[b]	29.9
SD	14.8	13.8	15.4
PEOPLE ON THE JOB			
Mean	34.8	37.1	34.5
SD	13.5	12.9	13.5
OVERALL SATISFACTION			
Mean	144.2	137.7[b]	112.1[c]
SD	47.5	37.6	42.5

a =   Significant difference (at .05 level) between officers in Direct Supervision and in Traditional Facilities using a one-tailed test.

b =   Significant difference (at .05 level) between officers in Traditional Facilities and in Facility C using a one-tailed test.

c =   Significant difference (at .05 level) between officers in Direct Supervision Facilities and Facility C using a one-tailed test.

NOTE: Higher means indicate higher levels of job satisfaction.

Overall, the findings on job satisfaction measures failed to support the hypothesis that employees in New Generation jails are more satisfied with their work than officers in traditional jails. Although podular/direct supervision officers were more satisfied than traditional officers on two of the five satisfaction dimensions, they were significantly less satisfied on another two of the dimensions. Even more revealing was the amount of dissatisfaction among officers in Facility C. When compared to officers in traditional and direct supervision jails, officers in Facility C were dissatisfied with most dimensions of the job. Only in regard to their attitudes toward their colleagues were the officers in Facility C similar to their counterparts in traditional and direct supervision jails.

Stress

In many regards, the podular/direct supervision facility provides an organizational and physical environment that is less stressful than that of traditional facilities. For example, the goals of the organization are clear-cut and well-defined, reducing ambiguity about the purpose of one's performance. Officers in podular facilities also receive more extensive training in the skills necessary for direct supervision, thereby better preparing them to work in the jail. Finally, the physical environment of the facility is designed to reduce stressful irritants such as noise. However, the direct supervision philosophy is more stress-inducing with regard to the amount and type of interaction it requires between officers and inmates. In traditional jail facilities, officers control the amount of contact they have with inmates. If tensions caused by inmates rise too high, an officer can retreat to more isolated areas of the jail. In podular/direct supervision facilities, officers are locked in modules in direct and continuous contact with inmates. They do not have the ability to isolate themselves from inmates or from the tensions generated by inmates. Furthermore, officers are isolated from co-workers for the majority of their work day. Because of these factors, we would expect corrections officers in podular/direct supervision facilities to experience neither more nor less stress than their counterparts in traditional jails.

Psychological and physical stress experienced by corrections officers was measured through the use of a symptom checklist developed by Gurin, Veroff and Feld (1960). The ten-item checklist was used to assess psychological anxiety, physical health, immobilization and physical anxiety experienced by corrections officers. For each item, respondents were asked whether they experience a given symptom, and if so, with what frequency. Additive scales were created for each of the four dimensions. The ranges of the scores differed for each of the four scales. Low scores indicate lower levels of stress; high scores indicate higher levels of stress.

**Table 7.4. Comparison of Stress Scores
Between Corrections Officers**

	Direct Supervision	Traditional	Facility C
NUMBER OF CASES	173	73	44
PSYCHOLOGICAL ANXIETY			
Mean	11.4[a]	10.9	10.9
SD	1.9	2.0	2.4
PHYSICAL HEALTH SYMPTOMS			
Mean	3.8	3.8	3.8
SD	.4	.5	.5
IMMOBILIZATION			
Mean	6.5	6.5	6.3
SD	1.2	1.1	1.3
PHYSICAL ANXIETY			
Mean	6.7	6.3	6.6
SD	1.6	1.6	1.5

a = Significant difference (at .05 level) between officers in Direct Supervision and in Traditional Facilities using a one-tailed test.

NOTE: Low means indicate high levels of stress; high means indicate low levels of stress.

The hypothesis that New Generation corrections officers would experience neither more nor less stress than officers in traditional facilities is supported in comparisons between officers in the three jail types on the stress scales (see Table 7.4). Only on the psychological anxiety scale did officers in New Generation facilities differ significantly from officers in traditional facilities. Overall, officers in all three facilities reported similar levels of experienced stress.

In summary, the data reported here fail to confirm initial expectations concerning the impact of the New Generation architecture and operations on custodial staff. These findings reveal that corrections officers in the sampled podular/direct supervision facilities do not perceive the job as more enriched, are not more satisfied with their job, and do not experience less stress than do their counterparts in traditional facilities. These findings are further confirmed by the fact that officers in Facility C were systematically more negative on all measures than were officers in either traditional jails or in other New Generation facilities. This finding is surprising given the fact that Facility C has implemented the podular architectural design and direct inmate supervision style.

Before concluding that the New Generation philosophy has no (or a negative) effect on the attitudes and perceptions of corrections officers, it is first necessary to examine other possible reasons for these findings. First, the findings may reflect differences between the jurisdictions in which the podular/direct supervision and the traditional jails were located. Unlike the states in which the direct supervision facilities are located, Washington—where the sampled traditional jails are located—has imposed stringent mandatory standards for the administration of local jail facilities. The Washington State Corrections Standards Board conducts annual inspections of all local facilities and has the power to close facilities that are in violation of the state's standards. In addition, Washington is one of the few states that requires jail corrections officers to complete a two-week basic training academy within one year of their employment, and which provides continuing in-service training to officers. Because the traditional jails in this sample are more rigidly controlled by the state than are the sampled podular/direct supervision facilities, and because this factor was not controlled for in the selection of both types of facilities, the findings may be biased.[3]

A second possible explanation concerns the appropriateness of using cross-sectional data to analyze the impact of changes within the institutions. Although the podular/direct supervision corrections officers in this survey fare no better than do their traditional jail counterparts, their perceptions and attitudes may have been significantly more positive than they were prior to the move to the New Generation facility. Hence, it may be an issue of relativity. Direct supervision officers may be more positive after the transition from a traditional, linear facility than they were prior to the move.

Zupan and Menke (1988) conducted a longitudinal study of the work-related perceptions of corrections officers at one transitional jail facility located in the western United States. Six months prior to and six months after the move from a traditional linear jail to a podular/direct supervision facility, levels of corrections officer job satisfaction and job enrichment were measured along with officer evaluations of the organization's climate. Although officers perceived a more positive organizational climate, expressed more overall job satis-

---

3   As suggested above, there may be many factors, including organizational ones, that account for the finding of no difference between corrections officers in traditional and New Generation facilities. For example, it may be that these findings are the result of aggregating officer responses for each jail type. Aggregation of the responses by jail type may mask important facility-specific response patterns. While under ideal circumstances an institution-by-institution analysis would be preferable, the small number of cases from some of the facilities in this study precludes this type of analysis.

faction and evaluated the job as more enriched after the move to the podular/direct supervision facility, only modest changes were noted.

Aside from problems with research design, a number of intriguing explanations can be offered as to why differences between corrections officers in New Generation and traditional jails, and between corrections officers before and after a move to the podular/direct supervision facility, were not more robust. Although the following are offered as possible explanations for the findings, they also represent an agenda for future research on podular/direct supervision facilities.

The first possible explanation concerns the level of social distance between inmates and staff. Direct supervision significantly reduces the degree of social distance between these two groups. In contrast to traditional, linear facilities where inmate supervision is intermittent and officers interact infrequently with inmates, officers in podular/direct supervision facilities are in direct and personal contact with inmates. While inmates may benefit from this type of contact because it is less dehumanizing and alienating, staff may be negatively affected by it. Some scholars suggest that social distance acts as an emotional buffer between the staff and inmates. It is a survival mechanism that allows workers to deal with truly needy people without becoming overwhelmed by their situations and problems.

Direct inmate supervision also makes it difficult for officers to withdraw from contact with inmates. Compulsory interaction, combined with the continuous and intimate contact with inmates, makes officers susceptible to cooptation and manipulation by inmates. Gilmartin and Davis (1986) suggest that, because of the degree of contact with inmates, corrections officers in podular/direct supervision facilities are much more likely than officers in traditional facilities to suffer from the Stockholm Syndrome wherein their primary loyalty is transferred from the organization to the inmate. Once this transference occurs, officers are more likely to commit acts of omission (e.g., ignoring inmate violations of the rules) and commission (e.g., providing contraband to inmates), and, consequently, endanger their own safety and the security of the facility.

A second possible explanation concerns status inconsistency experienced by the officers. At several podular/direct supervision facilities visited for this research, management emphasized that corrections officers were the most integral part of the organization. They were responsible for the complex implementation of direct supervision and, to a large extent, the success or failure of the facility depended on their performance. However, in several of the facilities the officers were not compensated at a rate commensurate with their responsibilities (e.g., comparable to their patrol counterparts within the sheriff's office) or with the status management claimed they possessed.

This status inconsistency also applied to the degree of discretion and control officers were provided by management. The officers were told that they were managers of people and, at most of the facilities, they received extensive training in leadership and managerial skills. However, the manner by which most were supervised and managed was inconsistent with the role that had been assigned to them. Rigid, bureaucratic control designed to structure the activities of staff to the highest degree did not provide the discretion and autonomy necessary for those who must continuously deal with people. Furthermore, this style of managerial control clearly communicated the message that officers could not be trusted to appropriately exercise discretion or autonomy.

A final possible explanation may involve managerial and administrative approaches adopted within direct supervision facilities. While direct supervision promises to provide an enriched job for the custodial staff, the managerial style of the organization may prevent employees from experiencing the benefits of job enrichment. The design of the corrections officer's job in the direct supervision facility provides a potential for enrichment, but without appropriate managerial commitment the organizational and employee benefits associated with enriched work will not be actualized. Adherence to traditional bureaucratic, hierarchical, command-obey styles of management, for example, may confound the link between the enriched job characteristics and the critical triad of experienced meaningfulness of work, experienced responsibility and knowledge of results. Instead, management must revise its approach to take into account at least three factors necessary for full implementation of job enrichment. These factors include developing a sense of job "ownership" among employees, vesting employees with responsibility for planning, coordinating and conducting the work (vertical loading), and open feedback channels between supervisors and line personnel (Hackman, et al., 1981:238-243).

The concept of job ownership is realized when employees are given full responsibility for an identifiable, meaningful and coherent body of work. Hence, job ownership implies a movement away from over-reliance on fragmented specialization and external control of employees. Job ownership, however, has been avoided by correctional institutions in particular and by criminal justice organizations in general. The reasons for this are many and include the following widely shared perceptions and schemas: management styles emphasize bureaucratization as the key to efficiency; quasi-military models of organization are based on a belief in the untrustworthy nature of human beings; less than adequate personnel standards and training are accepted as normative; and a desire to protect the organization from a litigious society promotes secrecy and insularity.

The direct supervision operating principles dictate that there is "only room for one leader" in each module and that employees must maintain control over the entire module. Given the degree of control that officers wield within the module and the level of discretion they possess in task performance, territoriality and job ownership among employees are inevitable. Ownership is facilitated not only by the design of the job and the architecture of the workplace but by managerial response to the employees. Through training, performance appraisal, and daily supervision, management can demonstrate its trust in the ability of employees to exercise responsible discretion and thereby reinforce the employees' sense of ownership. In the words of one direct supervision corrections officer, "Supervisors must recognize that this is my module. When things go well, I'll take the credit. When things go poorly, I'll take the responsibility."

Work in jails is generally characterized by the separation of planning and coordination functions from the actual performance of the job. While line personnel are responsible for performance, supervisors control the planning and coordination of the work. Vertical loading refers to the process of moving some measure of responsibility and control, specifically planning and coordinating functions, from management to line employees. In direct supervision facilities this process can be achieved by allowing corrections officers more discretion in deciding work methods, by using them to train less experienced officers, and by requiring them to assess the quality of their own work. In addition, corrections officers can be granted greater authority and responsibility for time management, troubleshooting and crisis management (Hackman, et al., 1981:241).

Team building is another means by which vertical loading can be accomplished. The design of the direct supervision facility requires that module officers from three different shifts develop a consistent and coherent strategy among themselves for inmate management. This requires two commitments from management: first, a demonstrable trust in the accumulated wisdom of officers, and second, a more mundane recognition that shift scheduling must promote interaction between staff members. Through such strategies as overlapping shifts and meetings between module officers, administrators can facilitate the exchange of information vital to the consistent management of the module.

While management's response to matters such as changes in schedule is easily accomplished, changes in traditional management perceptions about the competence of employees are more difficult to achieve. The critical factor, however, remains the extent of management's trust in its employees' ability to wield discretion.

The final consideration for management of enriched jobs concerns the provision of a forum for open and continuous feedback to employees about job performance. There are several sources from which employees receive information about their performance. These sources include management and direct supervisors, co-workers, clients and the work itself. Traditionally, corrections officers receive feedback from clients on an irregular basis (since officers are not in direct and continuous contact with inmates in traditional jails), from management on an occasional basis (as a regularly scheduled performance appraisal, or often only in reaction to malperformance) and from co-workers (who tend to support subculture values rather than the formal values of the organization).

By the nature of the design of their jobs, direct supervision corrections officers receive immediate feedback from inmates as to the success or failure of their management styles. This learning can be direct and immediate. It is important that the supervision of corrections officers move from a command-obey style of management with only occasional performance appraisal to a method of continuous coaching and counseling that takes advantage of this feedback source. Through coaching and counseling, supervisors can assist officers in interpreting daily events and experiences in a manner consistent with the direct supervision philosophy.

Analysis of the core dimensions of the corrections officer's role indicates that it requires skills (managerial and leadership) usually possessed by individuals at higher levels of management. This fact presents at least two dilemmas (or challenges, depending on one's point of view). First, most organizations promote people to positions of responsibility after extensive preparation (academic or organizational). Employees are typically promoted after they have been exposed to traditions and norms of long standing. Their cognitive map of the organization and its various work roles have been molded by both formal and informal experience. In contrast, the direct supervision facility recruits people with little or no experience in requisite leadership and management skills. Thus, forging consensus about the corrections officers' role becomes crucial and problematic and requires a thorough reexamination of traditional personnel and human resource development programs. It is critical, then, that antiquated systems for employee recruitment and selection, socialization and orientation, basic and in-service training, daily supervision and regular performance appraisal, and compensation and rewards, be revised to fulfill the personnel needs of the unique New Generation jail organization.

Second, direct supervision inmate management, with its explicit link between philosophy, operations and architectural design, represents a major innovation in institutional corrections experience. There is a change in the architecture, a change in the mission of the organization, a change in the operating principles and a change in the nature of the corrections officers' job. The direct supervision style of inmate management mandates careful coordination of the physical surroundings, the orienting philosophy and work performance. This coordination, in turn, requires reevaluation and change from traditional management orientations. More specifically, it demands a move away from an organizational culture based on bureaucratic necessities and expediencies to one predicated upon mutual trust and support between management and corrections officers.

Comments made by corrections officers involved in podular/direct supervision suggest that the orientations of managers and supervisors have not dramatically changed in the transition from traditional to direct supervision. Some officers complained that they were denied authority in their modules, which made it difficult to control inmate behavior:[4]

> C.O.s do not have authority in their pods.   Inmates always want to talk to a sergeant if they are not happy with the C.O.'s decision. There have been times when a sergeant will overrule a C.O.'s decision and that is not right. To the inmates it doesn't look like the C.O. has much authority. C.O.s should rule the pods, not the sergeant. It's very frustrating when sergeants, lieutenants and the major dictate how to run a pod when they have not idea what it entails. All management should work a pod first then change what's needed.

A number of the New Generation facilities studied in this research had been in operation for less than two years. As a consequence, many supervisors in these facilities had no experience working in the modules. These supervisors also received little reorienting training before transition to the New Generation operations. During informal discussions and in the survey, a number of corrections officers complained that supervisors were incompetent to provide the necessary support and counseling because they lacked experience and training.

Other officers complained about the lack of communication between administration and the line officers:

> The thing that I have observed as one of the biggest problems is the lack of communication between administration, and I mean upper administration, and the C.O on the decks. This is the most frustrating part of the job. Sometimes it seems that they are so out of touch with the officers doing the work. This is a job where your officers' lives are always on the line. Please do not forget this when writing S.O.P.s [standard operating procedures] concerning inmate activities, wants and grievances.

Several other officers complained about the lack of input they had in administrative policies that directly affect them:

> Employees are asked for their opinions on major changes but management does it their way regardless, i.e., mandatory shift change. Almost nobody wanted it, but it is still enforced.

---

[4] The surveys administered to corrections officers in New Generation jails provided a space for respondents to write open-ended comments. The comments showed overwhelming concern about the styles and abilities of supervisors and administrators. Officer comments are presented as transmitted to the researchers. Orthography and grammatical constructions may have been altered.

As stated by another employee:

> There are constant rule changes without any regard to the working officer's direct knowledge of his/her post and continuous threats of disciplinary [action] and/or termination of officers in general whenever one, two, or maybe three officers act in bad judgment.

Another complaint of officers was the lack of trust demonstrated by supervisors and administrators and the degree of control they exerted over the officers:

> Your sergeants and lieutenants should be there to back the officers or fire them—or hunt for things—nickpicking—bullshit. Stick to important matters that concern the safety of the facility and its officers. Show the officers that they can be trusted to carry on their duties and that they are trained professionals. If you have a bad apple, counsel them—and if that doesn't work get rid of them. But the same should go for the administration and sergeants and lieutenants. If the administration is not willing to talk to its line officers and listen to what they have to say and apply it to their jobs, then the administration isn't worth a flying fuck. The line officer will either make or break a facility. If you have good work relations between personnel, sergeants, lieutenants and administrators you will have a better run department. Treat your people as people. They will learn from you and you will also learn from them.

Finally, officers complained about administrative reliance on coercion rather than positive reinforcement to ensure corrections officer compliance:

> When a policy or decision is made, the people it concerns most have no choice, except to quit, if they don't like it. Positive reinforcement is a must in any job and a lack of it makes for low morale and hostilities. The lack of pay raises means employees tend to give less of themselves. The lack of positive rewards for term of employment means that staff turnover is greater.

And, according to another officer:

> If and when your new jail opens, please make sure that your officers are treated the same as you would treat inmates. We do not believe in mass punishment for inmates, but our administration seems to believe

in it for their officers. And make sure your administrators are open minded enough to listen to the line staff, since they are the core of the system. And they deal with the inmates more often than not. And be willing to tell the line staff about "atta boys" just as much as you would "the aw shits." Your morale will be a lot better and things will run a lot smoother.

Although these comments are not proof that the orientations of supervisors and administrators confound the link between job enrichment and positive work outcomes, they nevertheless suggest a direction for future research to follow in seeking an explanation for the lack of substantial differences between the work-related attitudes and perceptions of officers in podular/direct supervision and in traditional jail facilities.

Chapter Eight

Inmate Evaluations
of Direct Supervision Facilities

A major assumption underlying the New Generation philosophy is that inmates will tend to engage in undesirable behavior designed to manipulate and control their environment in circumstances of confinement which fail to provide for their *critical human needs*.[1] Proponents of the philosophy argue that when appropriate architecture and inmate management practices provide for these inmate needs—safety, privacy, personal space, activity, familial contact, social relations, and dignity—the need for inmates to manipulate and control their environment will be minimized. In the podular/direct supervision facility, the architectural design and style of inmate management consciously provide for critical inmate needs while concurrently reducing opportunities for inmates to exercise inappropriate control over staff, other inmates and the jail's physical environment.

While proponents of the New Generation philosophy assert that the architecture and inmate management style they advocate provide safer and more humane incarceration for inmates, the costs to inmates are great in terms of opportunities to exert control and power. In exchange for a more pleasant and less stressful environment, inmates forfeit the power and control they characteristically share with custodial staff in traditional facilities.

---

[1] Parts of this chapter originally appeared in "Doing Time in the New Generation Jail: Inmate Perceptions of Gains and Losses," *Policy Studies Review*, 1988 Vol. 7, pp. 626-640, co-authored with Mary K. Stohr-Gillmore and adapted and reprinted by permission of the Policy Studies Organization.

To understand how inmates respond to incarceration in the podular/direct supervision facility, inmates in four New Generation facilities in the western United States and three traditional linear jails in the state of Washington were questioned about the quality of life within their respective facilities.[2] To control for jurisdictional differences, longitudinal data were collected from inmates at one facility six months before and six months after the move from a traditional to podular/direct supervision facility.

Self-administered questionnaires were distributed to all inmates within a sample of randomly selected medium security and female housing units.[3] Of the 195 male and female inmates surveyed in traditional medium-security jails, 115 (59%) returned complete and usable questionnaires. In the podular/direct supervision facilities, 218 of 412 inmates (53%) completed usable questionnaires.

Table 8.1 reports the distribution of sampled inmate characteristics within the three jail types.[4] Although there are differences in the distribution of characteristics among facility types, these differences are slight. The samples are fairly similar with the exceptions of the following groups: Black, Hispanic and female inmates; inmates charged with minor traffic/criminal offenses; and inmates with no prior jail experience. The samples also differ in the average length of inmate incarceration in each type of facility. The affect of these differences will be noted in discussion of the findings.

The first important question concerns whether inmates in traditional and in podular/direct supervision facilities differ in their perceptions of the facilities' social climate. If, as proponents claim, the environment and operations of the podular/direct supervision facility fulfills critical inmate needs for safety, privacy, activity, familial contact, and so forth, the perceptions of inmates in these facilities should be more positive. Wright (1985:258) defined social climate as "a set of organizational properties or conditions that are perceived by its members and are assumed to exert a major influence on behavior." Climate evolves from shared impressions of life within the institution which are formed from experiences of events and conditions within the institution.

---

[2] These are the same facilities at which corrections officers were surveyed. For a discussion of how the podular/direct supervision and traditional facilities were selected, see Chapter 7.

[3] Minimum security (trustee) and maximum security (protective or close custody) were not included in the sampling frame because there are few differences between traditional and podular/direct supervision facilities as to how minimum and maximum security inmates are housed and supervised. As a result, we would expect few differences in inmate responses.

[4] As in the analysis of staff data, Facility C (a podular/direct supervision facility) is analyzed separately because of a number of factors that distinguish it from other podular/direct supervision jails. For a discussion of these factors, see Chapter 7.

Table 8.1. Distribution of Inmate Characteristics

	Direct Supervision	Traditional	Facility C
NUMBER OF CASES:	220	115	61
SEX:			
Male	75.7%	82.5	62.3
Female	24.3	17.5	37.7
RACE:			
White	56.5%	50.9	49.1
Black	19.6	4.7	21.1
Hispanic	8.6	15.1	5.3
Other	15.3	29.2	24.6
OFFENSE:			
Minor Traffic/Criminal	10.2%	19.8	6.8
Property Crimes	33.7	30.7	45.8
Crimes Against Persons	25.9	17.8	22.0
Other	30.2	31.7	25.4
PRIOR JAIL EXPERIENCE:			
Never	11.6%	14.4	10.0
1 time	14.0	10.8	21.7
2 or more times	74.4	74.8	68.3
AGE:			
Mean	30.1	29.5	28.7
(Standard Deviation)	(7.4)	(10.4)	(6.7)
DAYS INMATE HAS BEEN IN JAIL:			
Mean	90.7	75.4	73.4
(Standard Deviation)	(81.3)	(117.1)	(80.2)

A modified version of Wright's (1985) Prison Environment Inventory was used to measure inmate perceptions of the jails' social climate. In developing the instrument, Wright drew heavily from Toch's (1977) work on transactions between inmates and the prison environment. In the course of his work, Toch conducted over 900 interviews with inmates in prisons to determine which conditions within the correctional environment were considered "valuable" and which were "noxious" to inmates. A content analysis of the interview data yielded eight central environmental concerns. According to Toch, these dimensions represent the most significant elements of the prison environment as experienced by inmates. The eight dimensions and their definitions are:

PRIVACY:

A concern about social and physical overstimulation; a preference for isolation, peace and quiet, absence of environmental irritants such as noise and crowding.

SAFETY:

A concern about one's physical safety; a preference for social and physical settings that provide protection and that minimize the chances for being attacked.

STRUCTURE:

A concern about environmental stability and predictability; a preference for consistency, clear-cut rules, orderly and scheduled events and impingements.

SUPPORT:

A concern about reliable, tangible assistance from persons and settings, and about services that facilitate self-advancement and self-improvement.

EMOTIONAL FEEDBACK:

A concern about being loved, appreciated and cared for; a desire for intimate relationships that provide emotional sustenance and empathy.

SOCIAL STIMULATION:

A concern with congeniality, and a preference for settings that provide an opportunity for social interaction, companionship, and gregariousness.

ACTIVITY:

A concern about understimulation; a need for maximizing the opportunity to be occupied and to fill time; a need for distraction.

FREEDOM:

A concern about circumscription of one's autonomy; a need for minimal restriction and for maximum opportunity to govern one's own conduct (Toch, 1977:16-17).

Wright's inventory consists of 48 items. For each of the items, inmates were asked to assess frequency of occurrence on a four-point scale ranging from "never happens" to "always happens." When necessary, the wording of the items was modified to reflect a jail, rather than a prison, environment. For each of the eight dimensions, an index was constructed with multiple items from the inventory. For example, the safety index consisted of the following items: "An inmate is sexually attacked on this unit," "Inmates fight with other inmates," "Someone's cell is robbed on this unit," "A weaker inmate is physically attacked," "Weaker inmates are sexually attacked," and "An inmate's cell is robbed."

Responses to Wright's Prison Environment Inventory indicate that, with the exception of the Freedom dimension, inmates in podular/direct supervision facilities are significantly more positive in their evaluations of the facilities' climate than are inmates in traditional jails (see Table 8.2). Although the differences on the Freedom dimension are in the appropriate direction (inmates in New Generation facilities report more freedom than did inmates in traditional facilities), a lack of a statistically significant difference is not surprising given the degree of custodial staff supervision received by inmates in podular/direct supervision facilities.

A comparison of Facility C and podular/direct supervision facilities indicate that there are important and significant differences between the perceptions of inmates in both of these types of facilities. Inmates in Facility C are significantly less positive in their evaluations of the Freedom, Activity, Emotional Feedback, Social Stimulation, and Support dimensions than are inmates in podular/direct supervision facilities (see Table 8.2). Yet when Facility C and traditional facility inmates are compared, inmates in Facility C are significantly more positive in their evaluations of the Safe, Structure, Activity, and Privacy dimensions. This leads to the tentative conclusion that the environment of Facility C is not as positive as in other podular/direct supervision facility but not as negative as in traditional jails. In part, this may be due to the architecture. Inmates in Facility C may be responding positively to the physical environment which is more pleasant and comfortable than a traditional jails' physical environment, yet responding negatively to the inmate management style of the facility. This conclusion, however, is speculative. Further research must be conducted to separate the influence of physical environment from the influence of the inmate management style on inmate evaluations.

An analysis of the longitudinal data indicates that inmates, after the move from a traditional to a podular/direct supervision facility, are significantly more positive in their evaluations of the climate on the Freedom, Safety, Activity, Social Stimulation and Privacy dimensions (see Table 8.3). Inmates are also more positive on the Structure and Emotional Feedback dimensions after the move than they are before the move; however, the differences are not significant. Any conclusions drawn from these data must be tentative. The recentness of the transition and the time required to implement such far-reaching organizational changes may be influencing the data.

Table 8.2. Comparison of Prison Environment Inventory Scores for Inmates in Direct Supervision Facilities, Traditional Facilities and Facility C

	Direct Supervision	Traditional	Facility C
NUMBER OF CASES	220	115	61
FREEDOM			
Mean	2.8	2.7	2.6[d]
SD	.57	.55	.54
SAFETY[a]			
Mean	1.7[b]	1.9[c]	1.4[d]
SD	.49	.61	.35
STRUCTURE			
Mean	3.4[b]	3.1[c]	3.3
SD	.53	.56	.51
ACTIVITY			
Mean	2.5[b]	2.0[c]	2.2[d]
SD	.56	.59	.65
EMOTIONAL FEEDBACK			
Mean	2.6[b]	2.3	2.3[d]
SD	.52	.44	.52
SOCIAL STIMULATION			
Mean	2.9[b]	2.4	2.6[d]
SD	.52	.65	.59
SUPPORT			
Mean	2.0[b]	1.7	1.7[d]
SD	.62	.62	.57
PRIVACY			
Mean	3.0[b]	2.5[c]	2.9
SD	.56	.53	.59

a = Reverse Scoring - Higher scores represent negative evaluations.
b = Significant difference (at .05 level) between inmates in Direct Supervision and Traditional Facilities.
c = Significant difference (at .05 level) between inmates in Traditional Facilities and Facility C.
d = Significant difference (at .05 level) between inmates in Direct Supervision Facilities and Facility C.

Table 8.3. Comparison of Prison Environment Inventory Scores for Inmates Before and After the Move to a Direct Supervision Facility

	Before the Move	After the Move
NUMBER OF CASES	39	63
FREEDOM		
Mean	2.8	2.9[b]
SD	.48	.49
SAFETY[a]		
Mean	1.9	1.7[b]
SD	.57	.32
STRUCTURE		
Mean	3.1	3.3
SD	.56	.55
ACTIVITY		
Mean	1.9	2.2[b]
SD	.64	.49
EMOTIONAL FEEDBACK		
Mean	2.4	2.6
SD	.41	.49
SOCIAL STIMULATION		
Mean	2.6	3.0[b]
SD	.60	.43
SUPPORT		
Mean	1.7	1.7
SD	.56	.45
PRIVACY		
Mean	2.3	3.2[b]
SD	.58	.45

a =   Reverse Scoring - High scores represent negative evaluations.
b =   Significant difference at the .05 level.

Another concern is the level of stress experienced by inmates.   If podular/direct supervision facilities are safer and more humane we would expect inmates in these facilities to report less stress than inmates in traditional jails. Psychological and physical stress experienced by inmates was measured through the use of a symptom checklist developed by Gurin, Veroff and Feld (1960). The ten-item checklist assessed psychological anxiety, physical health, immobilization and physical anxiety. For each item, inmates were asked if they experience the symptom and to report the frequency with which they experience it. Additive scales were created for each of the four dimensions of stress. Low scores indicate high levels of experienced stress; high scores indicate low levels of stress.

**Table 8.4. Comparison of Evaluation
and Stress Scores for Inmates in Direct Supervision Facilities,
Traditional Facilities and Facility C**

	Direct Supervision	Traditional	Facility C
NUMBER OF CASES	220	115	61
JAIL EVALUATION[a]			
Mean	3.0[c]	4.1	4.0[d]
SD	1.2	1.3	1.2
CORRECTIONAL STAFF EVALUATION[a]			
Mean	3.3[c]	4.1	4.2[d]
SD	1.2	1.4	1.1
INMATE EVALUATION[a]			
Mean	3.9	3.9	3.9
SD	1.1	1.3	.94
PSYCHOLOGICAL ANXIETY[b]			
Mean	9.5[c]	8.5	8.1[d]
SD	2.2	2.4	2.5
PHYSICAL HEALTH SYMPTOMS[b]			
Mean	3.6[c]	3.3	3.4
SD	6.2	.75	.75
IMMOBILIZATION[b]			
Mean	5.9	5.6	5.6
SD	1.4	1.5	1.5
PHYSICAL ANXIETY[b]			
Mean	5.7[c]	5.2	5.2[d]
SD	1.7	1.7	1.7

a = Index items scored 1 (very positive) to 7 (very negative).
b = Index items scored so low scores indicate high stress and high scores indicate low stress.
c = Significant difference (at the .05 level) between inmates in Direct Supervision and Traditional Facilities.
d = Significant difference (at the .05 level) between inmates in Direct Supervision Facilities and Facility C.

NOTE: There were no significant differences between inmates in Traditional Facilities and Facility C.

**Table 8.5. Comparison of Evaluation
and Stress Scores for Inmates Before and After the
Move to a Direct Supervision Facility**

	Before the Move	After the Move
NUMBER OF CASES	40	63
JAIL EVALUATION[a]		
Mean	4.1	3.0[c]
SD	1.3	1.0
CORRECTIONAL STAFF EVALUATION[a]		
Mean	3.8	3.3
SD	1.1	1.1
INMATE EVALUATION[a]		
Mean	4.2	4.0
SD	1.2	.93
PSYCHOLOGICAL ANXIETY[b]		
Mean	8.6	9.3
SD	2.3	2.1
PHYSICAL HEALTH SYMPTOMS[b]		
Mean	3.2	3.8[c]
SD	1.5	1.3
IMMOBILIZATION[b]		
Mean	5.7	5.6
SD	1.5	1.3
PHYSICAL ANXIETY[b]		
Mean	5.3	5.7
SD	1.5	1.6

a = Index items scored 1 (very positive) to 7 (very negative).
b = Index items scored so that low scores indicate high stress and high scores indicate low stress.
c = Significant difference at the .05 level.

Analysis of the four stress scales indicates that inmates in podular/direct supervision facilities experience significantly less psychological anxiety, physical health symptoms of stress, and physical anxiety than do inmates in traditional jails (see Table 8.4). Although inmates in podular/direct supervision facilities experience lower levels of immobilization than do inmates in traditional jails, the difference is not significant.

There are no significant differences in the levels of stress experienced by inmates in Facility C and traditional jails. However, inmates in Facility C experience significantly higher levels of psychological and physical anxiety than do inmates in other podular/direct supervision facilities. Again, this suggests that the situation for inmates in Facility C is more similar to traditional jails than to other podular/direct supervision facilities. The stress scales from the longitudinal data reveal that after the move to a podular/direct supervision facility, inmates experience significantly lower levels of immobilization and slightly lower (not significant) levels of psychological and physical anxiety than inmates prior to the move (see Table 8.5).

A final concern is general inmate evaluations of the facility, the custodial staff, and other inmates. Because of the nature of the architecture and furnishings of the podular/direct supervision facility, the opportunities for interaction and increased familiarity with staff, and the degree of protection offered to inmates in the New Generation facilities, we would expect inmates in these facilities to be more positive in their evaluations of all three.

Inmate evaluations of the facility, the correctional staff and other inmates were measured by the use of semantic differential word pairs. The semantic differential word pairs were selected on the basis of their evaluative quality and strength. A traditional seven-point semantic differential continuum allowed for directional assessment of the respondents' evaluations. For example, inmates were asked to evaluate the jail on the dimension of "clean-dirty" and evaluations were scored from 1 (positive evaluation) to 7 (negative evaluation). Six word pairs were used to assess the jail, 13 to assess evaluations of the custodial staff, and 12 to assess evaluations of other inmates. In addition to separately analyzing the word pairs, three indices were created for an overall evaluation of the facility, custodial staff and other inmates. The alpha coefficients for each index were .9, .93, and .91, respectively.

Table 8.4 shows that inmates in podular/direct supervision facilities are, indeed, significantly more positive in their evaluations of the facility and the staff. However, there is no significant difference between the inmates in their evaluations of other inmates. Evaluations of other inmates are unique in that the means are almost identical for inmates in podular/direct supervision and those in traditional facilities. Regardless of the type of facility, inmates evaluate other inmates similarly.

Comparisons of the evaluation indices for inmates in Facility C and traditional jails reveal no significant differences between inmate responses (see Table 8.4). However, comparisons between inmates in Facility C and podular/direct supervision facilities show that inmates in Facility C are significantly more negative in their evaluations of the facility and the staff than are inmates in other podular/direct supervision facilities. Again, this provides evidence to suggest that Facility C is different from other podular/direct supervision facilities and more similar to traditional jails.

An analysis of the longitudinal data reveals that after the move to a podular/direct supervision facility, inmates are more positive in their evaluations of the facility but are only slightly (not significantly) more positive in their evaluations of the staff and other inmates (see Table 8.5).

In summary, inmates in New Generation jails are systematically more positive in their evaluations of the facility's climate, the staff and the facility than are inmates in traditional jails.[5] They also report fewer symptoms of stress than did their traditional jail counterparts. In comparing inmates in Facility C to inmates in other podular/direct supervision and traditional facilities, the patterns that emerge are most similar to those of inmates in traditional facilities. This finding supports the perceptions that the inmate management style implemented in Facility C is different from the style implemented in the other podular/direct supervision facilities in this research. The fact that inmates in Facility C are more positive on some variables than inmates in traditional facilities may be the result of the podular architectural design rather than the direct style of inmate supervision.

Analysis of the longitudinal data gathered at one facility reveals emerging patterns similar to those found between inmates in podular/direct supervision and traditional facilities. However, the dramatic changes undertaken by the facility during transition from one style of architecture and inmate management to another, and the relatively short time elapsing before the second inmate survey was administered, may have muted the differences between inmates before and after the move.

---

5   Analysis of individual inmate characteristics indicate that, with a few notable exceptions, race, gender, and prior jail experience have little influence on inmate evaluations. Male inmates were more strongly influenced by the jail environment than were female inmates. They were more negative about the traditional jail and more positive about the direct supervision jail than were females. The evaluations of white and non-white inmates in both types of facilities were very similar—both were more positive in the direct supervision facility. However, non-white inmates in direct supervision facilities reported significantly less stress than did their white counterparts. Inmates with prior jail experience were more positive in their evaluations of direct supervision than were experienced inmates in traditional jail facilities. Surprisingly, inexperienced inmates in direct supervision facilities were less positive in their evaluations and reported slightly higher levels of stress than did inexperienced inmates in traditional jails.

Two final points concerning the data is this research need to be discussed. First, the traditional facilities at which inmates were surveyed are atypical of traditional facilities in general. The state of Washington, in which the traditional facilities are located, has imposed fairly rigid and exacting standards of inmate care, supervision and housing onto local detention facilities. Hence, the traditional jails used in this study may not be representative of jails in other states. However, this factor would, if anything, mute differences between podular/direct supervision and traditional facilities. The systematic and significant differences found between inmates in podular/direct supervision and traditional facilities are even more surprising given the high standard of inmate care found in traditional jails in Washington.

The second issue concerns the influence of organizational change on inmate perceptions and evaluations. The podular/direct supervision facility provides a unique incarcerative environment for inmates, particularly for inmates who have experienced incarceration in traditional jail facilities. The newness of the building and its furnishings, the enthusiasm of the staff, etc., may create short-term positive evaluations by inmates that will erode as the newness wears off, enthusiasm dies away, and inmates gain experience in their new surroundings. Only through future research will we be able to determine if the differences between inmates in podular/direct supervision and traditional facilities are transitory.

Conclusions

Through the interaction of an innovative architectural design and style of inmate management, the podular/direct supervision jail provides an environment where it is hypothesized that the critical needs of inmates are met, safety of inmates and staff are promoted, and the security of the institution is maintained. The benefits for inmates are not without their costs. While the podular/direct supervision facility is better able to provide for physical and socioemotional needs, the philosophy and operations require inmates to sacrifice the illegitimate power and control they wield in traditional jail facilities. How do inmates react to the apparent benefits offered by the podular/direct supervision facility and the concurrent reduction of illegitimate power and control? The data in this study suggest that, regardless of lost power and control, inmates in podular/direct supervision facilities are systematically more positive in their evaluations of the environment, the jails' climate, the staff and the jail itself, and report less psychological and physical stress than do inmates in traditional jail facilities. The overall finding is that when the physical and sociopsychological environments of the jail are altered, inmates respond in predictable ways. Inmates in podular/direct supervision facilities respond positively to a physical and organizational environment in which their needs are legitimately fulfilled.

Chapter Nine
Conclusions

The New Generation, podular/direct supervision philosophy represents a radical departure from the traditional architecture and past custodial practices of local jails. Moreover, the innovative new philosophy profoundly challenges the contention of many correctional and organizational scholars that the creation of a safe and humane incarcerative environment is difficult, if not impossible, given inherent defects in the organization of coercive, total institutions (Cloward, 1968; Blau and Scott, 1962; Etzioni, 1961; Goffman, 1961; Schrag, 1961; Sykes, 1958).

A principal tenet of the New Generation philosophy is that reduction of inmate and staff fear is critical for production of an orderly module environment. Yet fear and perceived orderliness of an environment are inexorably related. Fear develops from contact with an environment perceived as disorderly. Human responses to fear contribute even greater disorderliness to the environment. This relationship is supported by empirical research concerning the relationship between public fear and the perceived level of community orderliness. Many studies have demonstrated that citizen fear of crime is more directly associated with their perceptions of the incivility of their neighborhoods than with actual crime rates (Biderman, et al., 1979; Lewis and Maxfield, 1980; Wilson and Kelling, 1983). It is not only criminal activities that create fear, but also an environment perceived as uncontrolled and uncontrollable. Community fear develops within an environment where it is perceived that both informal and authoritative control of misbehavior is absent. Graffiti and vandalism are two environmental indicators of the absence of control. When it is believed by the community that even those with authority lack the ability to control these types of behavior, other situations—such as a group of young people loitering at a particular corner—appear particularly menacing and dangerous.

163

This explanation of the development of fear of the environment is clearly reminiscent of the fear found in traditional detention facilities. Inmates quickly learn upon their arrival that the staff lacks control over inmate activities. Although officers periodically patrol the living areas, inmates are left unsupervised for most of the time. Away from the view of staff, violence and destruction occur as inmates vie for power and dominance or give expression to pent-up anxieties and frustrations. A new inmate soon learns that correctional staff share power with inmates and that survival depends, in large measure, on the ability to strike bargains with other inmates or to meet the threat of violence with violence.

Staff members grudgingly accept the fact that they must share power with inmates. Their fear grows from having to deal with a population which appears out of control. The bars that separate them from inmates cannot protect them from inmate taunts and threats as they patrol the catwalks and hallways. Soon surveillance becomes even less frequent and the primary concern of officers is to ensure their own safety rather than the safety of inmates. Out of this situation develops what Sykes (1958) referred to as the "corruption of authority." Officers find it more expedient and safer to allow inmates to bend or break rules in exchange for at least the appearance of cooperation. By allowing the usurpation of authority, officers demonstrate to inmates the powerlessness and inefficacy of their authority.

In the community, when informal neighborhood social control breaks down and when formal agencies of control seem to be separated from or absent to community members, the sentiment of fear escalates. Human responses to fear have been well documented (for example, see Lorenz, 1963). They range from apathy (learned helplessness) to the formation of dominance hierarchies whose rule by strength rests upon predation.

As with the community, separation of staff (formal control) from inmates robs the corrections officers of the ability to wield authority effectively and contributes to the fear that no one is in control. For effective use of authority, officers must have knowledge about what is occurring between inmates. When separated from inmates, they are prevented from using the most important tool of information-gathering—their own senses. Without knowledge about what is occurring between inmates, the officers cannot prevent or control misbehavior. Without the abilities to control inmate behavior, officers can control neither their own fears nor the fears of inmates.

The architecture and operations of the direct supervision facility attempt to break this cyclic relationship between fear and disorder by seizing power from the inmates and vesting it with its legitimate agents, the corrections officers. One of the guiding principles of the direct supervision philosophy maintains that ensuring inmate safety reduces the need for and struggle over power, and the accompanying predation between inmates. Only when power resides with those in authority and when officers are in control of inmate behavior can the facility provide a safe and humane environment.

The direct supervision facility deals with the interrelationship between fear, disorder and predation by imposing an architectural design that functions to reduce environmental sources of stress that stimulate inmate violence and allows corrections officers to control a specifically-defined territory in order to prevent opportunities for violence. Once the appropriate architecture is in place, the success or failure of direct supervision rests on the corrections officer's ability to reduce inmate fear of victimization, promote the perception of protected space, prevent the rise of inmate leaders, reinforce inmate links with the outside world, and create a climate of positive expectations where just and humane interaction is the norm.

Although the New Generation philosophy is the most thoroughgoing innovation in institutional corrections in decades, it is by no means a "cure-all" for the many and varied problems that continue to plague modern jails. Like many traditional jails, direct supervision facilities are faced with the problems of less than adequate funding, public and political apathy, mismanagement, misuse of the facility, and most importantly, burgeoning inmate populations. At one direct supervision facility visited during the course of this research, overcrowding had reached critical proportions. The official capacity of the facility was 323 inmates; the facility was housing 813 inmates at the time of my visit. At first, the overflow population was housed in areas of the jail other than the living units. As the inmate population grew, administrators were forced to assign two inmates to each cell, thus violating an important tenet of the New Generation philosophy—that is, the provision of single cells to all inmates. Inmate populations in the living units increased from a capacity of 24 inmates to a population of 48 inmates. Because the possibility of overcrowding was not considered in the original design of the facility, cells and dayroom floor spaces were woefully inadequate for the number of inmates housed in the overcrowded modules. To ensure rigorous supervision, two officers, rather than one, were assigned to above-capacity housing modules. Visitation and recreation hours were extended and additional programs added to ensure that all inmates had access to them.

At another direct supervision facility, the inmate population exceeded the capacity by approximately 20%. Administrators at this facility had yet to double-bunk inmates in the living units. The overflow population was housed in other parts of the facility and, in a few modules, bunk beds were set up in programming rooms. In designing the facility, planners and architects ensured that the facility design was sufficiently flexible to handle overcrowding. For example, individual inmate rooms were designed with enough floor space to hold two inmates if double-bunking were necessary and yet still meet the American Corrections Association space requirements. Module dayrooms were also designed with enough floor space to handle inmate populations double their official capacity. Although the facility was operating with above-capacity inmate populations, the flexibility in the architectural design forestalled the need to double-bunk single-occupancy rooms or to significantly increase the populations in the living modules. While administrators at these and other direct supervision facilities report that incidents of inmate misconduct increased with inmate populations, they steadfastly maintain that even when overcrowded, the direct supervision facility is safer for inmates and staff than an overcrowded traditional facility.

Another critical problem facing administrators of direct supervision facilities concerns deficiencies in personnel systems. Since the success of direct supervision depends in large measure on the complex and sophisticated management skills of line-level corrections officers, personnel processes such as selection, training, compensation and retention take on critical importance to the jail organization. Antiquated personnel systems developed to meet the staffing needs of the traditional jail are inappropriate in the New Generation facility, and may even be dangerously dysfunctional.

An example of the grave consequences of obsolete personnel systems was found at one of the direct supervision facilities visited in the course of this project. At many direct supervision facilities, corrections officers receive from six to eight weeks of extensive training in requisite direct supervision skills. Among the subjects covered in this training are interpersonal communications, conflict resolution, problem-solving, and principles of leadership and supervision. The training is usually provided in-house and is designed specifically for work in direct supervision facilities. At one particular facility, the training received by corrections officers did not adequately prepare them to work in a direct supervision environment. The officers received only four weeks of training which was provided free of charge by the state. The training was "generic," meaning that it was designed for jail and prison corrections officers in traditional, intermittent or remote surveillance facilities. The content of the training focused on skills and abilities necessary for work in a traditional jail. For example, primary emphasis was placed on physical restraint techniques, while human relations skills were covered in just a day-and-a-half. Consequently, the officers in this facility were relatively untrained in the necessary skills required for effective inmate supervision and ill-prepared to assume leadership roles in the modules. From all indications, this facility was experiencing serious problems, particularly with regard to inmate control. Soon after the transition from traditional to direct supervision operations, an inmate hostage situation occurred. Another hostage situation occurred less than a year later. According to the officers at the facility, inmate assaults against staff were not uncommon. A number of officers expressed dissatisfaction with the type of training they received and believed that it was a major contributor to violence and unrest in the institution. More importantly, officers did not feel confident working in the modules or dealing with inmates without the protection of traditional bars to separate them from their charges. This insecurity may have been communicated to inmates. Although as yet unsubstantiated, it appears that when direct inmate supervision is not appropriately practiced, the direct supervision facility poses greater threats to the safety of staff and inmates than a traditional linear facility.

Agenda for Future Research

The research presented herein is not intended to be the final, or even the definitive, word on the New Generation philosophy. Instead, it serves as an introduction to and a guide for further research. While the extant research points to the success of the New Generation model, the data indicate that caution is required. What is most critically needed at this point is a comprehensive and rigorous evaluation that compares direct supervision facilities with traditional jails. Not only must this evaluation address the link between architecture, supervision styles and inmate behavior, but it must also consider variations in architectural designs, classification systems, inmate treatment and education programs implemented in different direct supervision facilities, the impact of overcrowding, and the long-term effectiveness of direct supervision. On a more theoretical level, the research agenda offers the opportunity to investigate more thoroughly the link between human behavior and architecture, the brutalization hypothesis with released inmates, and the effects of a more personal, consistent, safe and humane incarceration upon inmate attitudes and behaviors.

Finally, additional research is required in determining the suitability of the podular/direct supervision design in institutions such as prisons. Some have suggested that application of the New Generation model to the prison setting may enhance the delivery of programs, even rehabilitation, to long-term prisoners. It may be that the effectiveness of institutional programs is dependent on ensuring inmate and officer safety through the creation of order within the institution. While there are prisons that use some of the principles of the New Generation philosophy, its application to long-term confinement remains an intriguing, yet unanswered, question.

A final question—one that cannot be easily answered through scientific means—concerns the ethics of the New Generation philosophy. While some scholars and practitioners applaud the philosophy for providing the means to restore order within correctional institutions, others deplore the overtly and covertly repressive means by which order is attained. The ethical questions raised by the New Generation philosophy are certainly important and will continue to be debated in the foreseeable future as more jurisdictions opt to build direct supervision facilities and as further research is conducted on the effectiveness of the new model.

Appendix

Research Methodology

Analysis of Architectural and Interior Design

Observations of architecture and interior design were conducted at five podular/direct supervision facilities located in the western United States and three in the eastern United States. Although all of the facilities were designed in the podular style, each differed slightly in both their exterior and interior designs. The facilities varied in size as measured by official inmate capacity. The smallest facility had an official capacity of 300 inmates, while the largest had a capacity of 856 inmates. Five of the facilities were high-rise structures, two had a sprawling, ranch-style design, and one was located in temporary, trailer-like modules.

Two of the facilities had been originally designed as traditional jails, but were modified during construction to produce podular/direct supervision facilities. Both facilities reflected features of traditional and podular designs. For example, in one of the facilities, the modules were staffed with correctional officers but control centers were included on each floor for the remote supervision of inmates. Such control centers were not present in the other podular/direct supervision facilities.

In addition to on-site observation of the facilities, informal interviews with staff and administrators at each facility provided information about specific aspects of the design. Finally, related data were gathered from user-based assessments of the federal Metropolitan Correctional Centers (Wener and Olsen, 1978; Wener and Clark, 1976). These reports were helpful in contrasting the designs

169

of federal detention facilities with those of local podular jails. Although each of the facilities visited differed slightly in its architectural and interior design, it was possible to prepare a composite using the characteristics common to most of the institutions.

Analysis of Direct Inmate Supervision

Direct inmate supervision was analyzed by interviewing correction officers and first line supervisors in two podular/direct supervision detention facilities located in the western United States about the critical behaviors required for effective correction officer job performance. The interviews were conducted by the author and a colleague in August, 1985. The first facility was located in a major metropolitan area (1980 population: 463,087). The facility was built to fulfill a federal court consent decree. It opened in September, 1984. The facility's capacity is 858 inmates, yet at the time the interviews were conducted the average daily inmate population was 915. The facility employs 227 correction officers, 31 sergeants, 5 lieutenants, 2 captains and 1 administrator. The second facility was located in another metropolitan area (1980 population: 531,443). The facility opened in June, 1984. With an inmate capacity of 468, the average daily inmate population in 1984 was 400. This and an ancillary facility employ 168 correction officers, 5 corporals, 19 sergeants, 8 lieutenants, 4 captains and 1 major.

The critical incident technique, a method of job analysis developed by Flanagan (1954) and commonly used in personnel-related research (Latham, et al., 1980; Latham and Wexley, 1981), was used to identify correction officer behaviors required for the effective implementation of direct inmate supervision. Each interview subject was asked to describe actual incidents of both effective and ineffective correction officer job performance observed within the past 6 to 12 months. They were asked to describe, in detail:

(1) the situation, circumstances or background of the incident;

(2) the effective or ineffective behavior exhibited by the officer; and

(3) the outcome of the incident or why the behavior was an example of effective or ineffective behavior.

The advantage of the critical incident technique over other methods of job analysis is that it provides behavioral-based information about what correction officers are actually doing and focuses on the behaviors associated with successful or unsuccessful task performance. At each facility subjects were selected from the following groups:

(1) correction officers with more than one year of experience in a podular/direct supervision facility;

(2) officers identified by a majority of supervisors as particularly effective in performing their job ("waterwalkers"); and

(3) first line supervisors.

Eighteen interviews (with 12 officers, 3 waterwalkers, 3 supervisors) were conducted at one facility while ten (6 with officers, 2 waterwalkers, 2 supervisors) were conducted at the second. In addition to the interviews, a group of officers from each facility was given detailed instructions and asked to provide examples of critical incidents and behaviors in writing. Twenty-three officers in one facility, and 28 in the other, provided written incidents and behaviors. A total of 346 incidents were collected, with 177 resulting from the interviews and 169 being self-reported in the survey context.

After all the incidents were collected, those that were similar were subsumed under one item and ambiguous incidents were eliminated. The wording of the incidents was edited to form brief statements of effective correction officer behavior. In this stage, the incidents were translated into 70 behavioral statements. The statements were then categorized according to the similarities in the effective and ineffective behavior. The analysis yielded seven descriptive categories or dimensions of critical correction officer behavior, each associated with 6 to 15 behavioral items. Content validity of the items and dimensions was assessed by withholding 10% of the incidents prior to the editing stage (Latham and Wexley, 1981). These incidents were examined after development of the dimensions and were found to describe behaviors already represented in the established items and dimensions.

In addition to the structured critical incident interviews, informal discussion were held with correction officers, supervisors and administrators from six podular/direct supervision facilities and one facility which was in the process of moving from traditional to a direct supervision design. These discussions provided contextual information to aid in understanding the dynamics of direct inmate supervision.

References

Advisory Commission on Intergovernmental Relations (1984). *Jails: Intergovernmental Dimensions of a Local Problem, A Commission Report.* Washington, DC: U.S. Government Printing Office.

Aiello, J.R., D.T. DeRisi, Y.M. Epstein and R.A. Karlin (1977). "Crowding and the Role of Interpersonal Distance Preference." *Sociometry.* 40:271-282.

Allen, B. and D. Bosta (1981). *Games Criminals Play.* Susanville, California: Rae John Publishers.

Allinson, R. (1982). "Crisis in the Jails: Overcrowding Is Now a National Epidemic." *Corrections Magazine.* April:18-40.

American Correctional Association (1985). *Jails in America: An Overview of Issues.* College Park, Maryland: American Correctional Association.

American Correctional Association (1983). *Design Guides for Secure Adult Facilities.* College Park, Maryland: American Correctional Association.

American Correctional Association (1981). *Standards for Adult Local Detention Facilities.* College Park, Maryland: American Correctional Association.

American Correctional Association (1966). *Manual of Correctional Standards.* Washington, DC: American Correctional Association.

American Medical Association (1973). *Medical Care in U.S. Jails: Report of the 1972 AMA Medical Survey of the U.S. Jail System.* Chicago: American Medical Association.

Ardrey, P. (1966). *The Territorial Imperative.* New York: Athenium.

173

Atlas, R. (1986). "Crime Site Selection for Assaults in Four Florida Prisons." A paper presented at the annual meeting of the Academy of Criminal Justice Sciences, in Orlando, Florida, March, 1986.

Babington, A. (1971). *The English Bastille: A History of Newgate Gaol and Prison Conditions in Britain 1188-1902*. London: McDonald and Company (Publishers). Ltd.

Barnes, H.E. and N.K. Teeters (1959). *New Horizons in Criminology*. Englewood Cliffs, New Jersey: Prentice-Hall, Inc.

Barnes, H.E. (1927). *The Evolution of Penology in Pennsylvania: A Study in American Social History*. Montclair, New Jersey: Patterson Smith Publishing Corporation.

Baum, A. and S. Valins (1977). *The Social Psychology of Crowding: Studies on the Effects of Residential Group Size*. Hillsdale, New Jersey: Erlbaum.

Bell v Wolfish, 441 U.S. 520 (1979).

Benton, F.W., E.D. Rosen and J.L. Peters (1982). "National Survey of Correctional Institution Employee Attrition." New York: National Center for Public Productivity.

Bevis, C. and J. Nutter (1977). *Changing Street Layouts to Reduce Residential Burglary*. St. Paul, Minnesota: Governor's Commission on Crime Prevention and Control.

Biderman, A.D., L.A. Johnson, J. McIntyre and A.W. Weir (1967). *Report on a Pilot Study in the District of Columbia on Victimization and Attitudes Toward Laww Enforcement*. Washington, DC: U.S. Government Printing Office.

Bishop, G.W. (1964). "Four and a Half Days in Atlanta's Jails." *Atlantic Monthly*. July:68-70.

Blau, P.M. and W.R. Scott (1962). *Formal Organizations*. San Francisco: Chandler Publishing Company.

Bowker, L.H. (1982a). *Corrections: The Science and the Art*. New York: Macmillan Publishing Co., Inc.

Brantingham, P. and P. Brantingham (1978). *Theoretical Model of Crime Site Selection*. Dallas: American Society of Criminology.

Brief, A.P., J. Munro and R.J. Aldag (1976). "Correctional Employees' Reaction to Job Characteristics: A Data Based Argument for Job Enrichment." *Journal of Criminal Justice*. 4:223-230.

Brill, W. (1979). *Assessing the Social Environment*. Washington, DC: U.S. Government Printing Office.

Brower, S.N. (1965). "The Signs We Learn to Read." *Landscape*. 15:9-12.

Burns, H. (1975). *Corrections: Organization and Administration*. St. Paul, Minnesota: West Publishing Co.

Byrd, R.E. (1938). *Alone*. New York: Putnam.

Cahn, W. (1973). "Report on the Nassau County Jail." *Crime and Delinquency*. 19:1-14.

Call, J.E. (1983). "Recent Case Law on Overcrowded Conditions of Confinement." *Federal Probation*. 47:23-32.

Carney, R. (1982). "New Jersey: Overcrowding Is Blamed on the State." *Corrections Magazine*. April:24-27.

Chesney-Lind, M. (1988). "Girls in Jail." *Crime and Delinquency*. 34:150-168.

Children's Defense Fund (1976). *Children in Adult Jails*. Washington, DC: Children's Defense Fund.

Clear, T.D. and G.F. Cole (1986). *American Corrections*. Monterey, California: Brooks/Cole Publishing Company.

Clemmer, D. (1940). *The Prison Community*. Boston: The Christopher Publishing House.

Cloward, R.A. (1968). "Social Control in the Prison." In L. Hazelrigg (ed.). *Prison Within Society*. Garden City, New York: Doubleday and Company, Inc.

Cohen, S., G.W. Evans, D.S. Krantz and D. Stokols (1980). "Physiological, Motivational and Cognitive Effects of Aircraft Noise on Children: Moving from the Laboratory to the Field." *American Psychologist*. 35:231-243.

Cohen, S. and A. Lezak (1977). "Noise and Inattentiveness to Social Cues." *Environment and Behavior*. 9:559-572.

Cooper v. Pate, 378 U.S. 546 (1964).

Corrections Compendium (1987). "Survey: COs In Demand in Many States."

Cressey, D.R. (1968). "Contradictory Directives in Complex Organizations: The Case of the Prison." In L.E. Hazelrigg (ed.) *Prison Within Society*. Springfield, Illinois: Charles C Thomas.

Criminal Justice Newsletter (1987). "OJJDP to Award Some Funds to States for Jail Removal Efforts." 18:17.

Cullen, F.T., B.G. Frank, N.T. Wolfe, and J. Frank (1985). "The Social Dimensions of Correctional Officer Stress." *Justice Quarterly*. 2:505-533.

Danto, D. (1973). "Suicide at the Wayne County Jail: 1967-70." In L. Danto (ed.) *Jail House Blues*. Orchard Lake, Michigan: Epic.

D'Arti, D.A. (1975). "Psychophysiological Responses to Crowding." *Environment and Behavior*. 7:237.

Davidson, B. (1968). "The Worst Jail I've Ever Seen." *Saturday Evening Post*. (October 13):17-22.

Davis, A.J. (1968). "Sexual Assaults in the Philadelphia Prison System and Sheriff's Van." *Transaction*. 6:8-16.

de Beaumont, G. and A. de Tocqueville (1964). *On the Penitentiary System in the United States*. Carbondale, Illinois: Southern Illinois University Press.

Deming, B. (1972). "Prisoners Don't Exist." In D.M. Petersen and M. Truzzi (eds.) *Criminal Life: Views From the Inside*. Englewood Cliffs, New Jersey: Prentice-Hall, Inc.

Edney, J.J. (1976). "Human Territoriality." In H.M. Proshansky, W.H. Ittelson, and L.G. Rivlin (eds.) *Environmental Psychology: People and Their Physical Settings*. New York: Holt, Rinehart and Winston.

Esparza, R. (1973). "Attempted and Committed Suicides in County Jails." In L. Danto (ed.) *Jail House Blues*. Orchard Lake, Michigan: Epic.

Estelle v. Gamble, 429 U.S. 97 (1976).

Etzioni, A. (1961). *A Comparative Analysis of Complex Organizations*. New York: The Free Press.

Farbstein, J., R. Wener and P. Gomez (1979). *Evaluations of Correctional Environments: Instrument Development*. Washington, DC: National Institute of Corrections.

Farina, A., J.G. Allen and B.B. Saul (1968). "The Role of the Stigmatized Person in Affecting Social Relationships." *Journal of Personality.* 36:169-182.

Farina, A. and K. Ring (1965). "The Influence of Perceived Mental Illness on Inter-personal Relations." *Journal of Abnormal Psychology.* 70:47-51.

Farmer, R.E. (1977). "Cynicism: A Factor in Corrections Work." *Journal of Criminal Justice.* 5:237-246.

Farrington, D. and C. Nuttall (1980). "Prison Size, Overcrowding, Prison Violence, and Recidivism." *Journal of Criminal Justice.* 8:221-231.

Federal Bureau of Investigation (1987). *Crime in the United States: Uniform Crime Reports—1986.* Washington, DC: U.S. Government Printing Office.

Fishman, J.F. (1922). "The American Jail: Pages from the Diary of a Prison Inspector." *Atlantic Monthly.* 130:792-805.

Fishman, J.F. (1923). *Crucibles of Crime: The Shocking Story of the American Jail.* Montclair, New Jersey: Patterson Smith.

Flanagan, J.C. (1954). "The Critical Incident Technique." *Psychological Bulletin.* 7:327-355.

Flynn, E.E. (1973). "Jails and Criminal Justice." In L.E. Ohlin (ed.) *Prisoners in America.* Englewood Cliffs, New Jersey: Prentice-Hall, Inc.

Fogel, D. quoted in "The Scandalous U.S. Jails." *Newsweek.* August 18, 1980, p. 74.

Fowler, F., M.E. McCalla and T. Mangione (1979). *The Hartford Residential Crime Prevention Program.* Washington, DC: U.S. Government Printing Office.

Frazier, F.W. (1985). *A Post Occupancy Evaluation of Contra Costa County's Main Detention Facility.* Dissertation: Golden Gate University, San Francisco, California.

Friedman, N. (1967). *The Social Nature of Psychological Research: The Psychological Experiment as a Social Interaction.* New York: Basic Books.

Gettinger, S.H. (1984). *New Generation Jails: An Innovative Approach to an Age-Old Problem.* Washington, DC: National Institute of Corrections.

Gersten, R. (1977). *Noise in Jails: A Constitutional Issue.* Washington, DC: National Clearinghouse for Criminal Justice Planning and Architecture.

Gibbs, J. (1987). "Symptoms of Psychopathology Among Jail Prisoners." *Criminal Justice and Behavior*. 14:288-310.

Gibbs, J. (1982). "The First Cut is the Deepest: Psychological Breakdown and Survival in the Detention Setting." In R. Johnson and H. Toch (eds.) *The Pains of Imprisonment*. Beverly Hills: Sage Publications, Inc.

Gibbs, J. (1983). "Problems and Priorities: Perceptions of Jail Custodians and Social Service Providers." *Journal of Criminal Justice*. 11:327-338.

Gilmartin, K.M. and R.M. Davis (1986). "The Correctional Officer Stockholm Syndrome: Management Implications." In J. Farbstein and R. Wener (eds.) *Proceedings of the First Annual Symposium on New Generation Jails*. Boulder, Colorado: National Institute of Corrections.

Glass, D.C. and J.E. Singer (1972). *Urban Stress*. New York: Academic Press.

Goffman, E. (1961). *Asylums*. Garden City, New York: Anchor Books.

Goldfarb, R. (1966). "No Room in the Jail." *The New Republic*. 154:12-14.

Goleman, D. (1981). "The New Competency Tests: Matching the Right People to the Right Jobs." *Psychology Today*. January:34-36.

Gross v. Tazewell County Jail, 31 Cr. L. 2061 (W.D. V. 1982).

Gunderson, E.K.E. (1973). "Individual Behavior in Confined or Isolated Groups." In J.E. Rasmussen (ed.) *Man in Isolation and Confinement*. Chicago: Aldine Publishing Company.

Gurin, G., J. Veroff and S. Feld (1960). "Symptom Patterns." *Americans View Their Mental Health*. New York: Basic Books, Inc.

Guy, E., J.J. Platt, I. Zwerling, and S. Bullock (1985). "Mental Health Status of Prisoners in an Urban Jail." *Criminal Justice and Behavior*. 12:29-53.

Hackman, J.R. and G.R. Oldham (1974). *The Job Diagnostic Survey: An Instrument for the Diagnosis of Jobs and the Evaluation of Job Redesign Projects*. Technical Report No. 4., Department of Administrative Sciences. Yale University.

Hackman, J.R., G. Oldham, R. Janson and K. Purdy (1981). "A New Strategy for Job Enrichment." In D.E. Klingner (ed.) *Public Personnel Management*. Palo Alto: Mayfield Publishing Company.

Haney, C., W.C. Banks and P.G. Zimbardo (1973). "Interpersonal Dynamics in a Simulated Prison." *International Journal of Criminology and Penology*. 1:69-97.

Harding, C., B. Hines, R. Ireland and P. Rawlings (1985). *Imprisonment in England and Wales: A Concise History.* London: Croom Helm Ltd.

Hayes, L.M. (1983). "And Darkness Closes In...A National Study of Jail Suicides." *Criminal Justice and Behavior.* 10:461-484.

Hays, S.W. and T.Z. Reeves (1984). *Personnel Management in the Public Sector.* Boston: Allyn and Bacon, Inc.

Haythorn, W.W. (1973). "The Miniworld of Isolation: Laboratory Studies." In J.E. Rasmussen (ed.) *Man in Isolation and Confinement.* Chicago: Aldine Publishing Company.

Haythorn, W.W. (1970). "Interpersonal Stress in Isolated Groups." In J.E. McGarth (ed.) *Social and Psychological Factors in Stress.* New York: Holt, Rinehart, and Winston.

Haythorn, W.W. and I. Altman (1967). "Together in Isolation." *Transaction.* 4:18-22.

Haythorn, W.W., I. Altman and T.I. Myers (1966). "Emotional Symptomatology and Stress in Isolated Pairs of Men." *Journal of Experimental Research in Personality.* 4:290-306.

Heilig, S. (1973). "Suicides in Jails." In L. Danto (ed.) *Jail House Blues.* Orchard Lake, Michigan: Epic.

Herzberg, F., B. Mausner and B.B. Snyderman (1959). *The Motivation to Work.* New York: John Wiley & Sons, Inc.

Hitchcock, J. and A. Waterhouse (1979). "Expressway Noise and Apartment Tenant Response." *Environment and Behavior.* 11:251-267.

Holt v. Sarver, 442 F.2d 308 (8th Cir. 1971).

Howard, A.E.D. (1982). "The States and the Supreme Court." 31 *Catholic University Law Review* 375.

Howard, D.L. (1960). *The English Prisons: Their Past and Their Future.* London: Methuen and Company, Ltd.

Inmates of the Suffolk County Jail v. Eisenstadt, 360 F. Supp. 676, 679 (1973).

Illinois State Charities Commission (1911). *First Annual Report.* Springfield: Illinois State Journal Company.

Irwin, J. (1985). *The Jail: Managing the Underclass in American Society.* Berkeley, California: University of California Press.

Irwin, J. (1970). *The Felon.* Englewood Cliffs, New Jersey: Prentice-Hall, Inc.

Jacobs, J.B. and H.G. Retsky (1975). "Prison Guard." *Urban Life.* (April):5-21.

Johnston, N. (1973). *The Human Cage: A Brief History of Prison Architecture.* New York: The American Foundation, Inc.

Jones, R.A. (1977). *Self-Fulfilling Prophecies: Social, Psychological and Physiological Effects of Expectancies.* Hillsdale, New Jersey: Lawrence Erlbaum Associates, Publishers.

Jordan, P.D. (1970). *Frontier Law and Order: Ten Essays.* Lincoln, Nebraska: University of Nebraska Press.

Jurik, N.C. and R. Winn (1986). "Describing Correctional Security Dropouts and Rejects: An Individual or Organizational Profile?" Presented at the annual meeting of the Academy of Criminal Justice Sciences in Orlando, Florida, March, 1986.

Kentucky Department of Justice (1981). *Behind Bars: Kentucky Looks at Its County Jails.* Frankfort, Kentucky: Kentucky Department of Justice.

Kerle, K.E. (1985). "The American Woman County Jail Officer." In I.L. Moyer (ed.) *The Changing Role of Women in the Criminal Justice System.* Prospect Heights, Illinois: Waveland Press, Inc.

Kleck, R. (1969). "Physical Stigma and Task Oriented Interactions." *Human Relations.* 22:53-60.

Kryter, K.D. (1970). *The Effects of Noise on Man.* New York: Academic Press.

Lansing, D., J.B. Bogan and L. Karacki (1977). "Unit Management: Implementing a Different Correctional Approach." *Federal Probation.* 41:43-49.

Latham, D.P., L.M. Saari, E.D. Pursell and M.A. Campion (1980). "The Situational Interview." *Journal of Applied Psychology.* 64:422-427.

Latham, G.P. and K.N. Wexley (1981). *Increasing Productivity Through Performance Appraisal.* Reading, Massachusetts: Addison-Wesley Publishing Company.

Law Enforcement Assistance Administration (1971). *National Jail Census—1970.* Washington, DC: U.S. Government Printing Office.

Leroy, C. (1975). "Space in the Prison." In G. DiGennaro (ed.). *Prison Architecture.* Nicholas, New York: Architectural Press.

Lewis, D.A. and M.G. Maxfield (1980). "Fear in the Neighborhood: An Investigation of the Impact of Crime." *Journal of Research in Crime and Delinquency.* 17:160-189.

Ley, D. and R. Cybriwsky (1974). "The Spatial Ecology of Stripped Cars." *Environment and Behavior.* 6:653-668.

Lipsky, M. (1980). *Street Level Bureaucracy.* New York: Russell Sage.

Lorenz, K. (1963). *On Aggression.* New York: Bantam Books, Inc.

Mathews, K.E. and L.K. Canon (1975). "Environmental Noise Level as a Determinant of Helping Behavior." *Journal of Personality and Social Psychology.* 32:571-577.

Mattick, H.W. and A.B. Aikman (1969). "The Cloacal Region of American Corrections." *The Annals of the American Academy of Political and Social Science.* 381:109-118.

Mattick, H.W. (1974). "The Contemporary Jails of the United States: An Unknown and Neglected Area of Justice." In D. Glaser (ed.) *Handbook of Criminology.* Chicago: Rand McNally.

May, E. (1980). "Prison Guards in America—The Inside Story." In B.M. Crouch (ed.) *The Keepers: Prison Guards and Contemporary Corrections.* Springfield, Illinois: Charles C Thomas Publishers.

Mays, G.L. and J.A. Thompson (1988). "Mayberry Revisited: The Characteristics and Operations of America's Small Jails." *Justice Quarterly.* 5:421-440.

McCain, G., V.C. Cox and P.B. Paulus (1980). *The Effect of Prison Crowding on Inmate Behavior.* Washington, DC: National Institute of Justice.

McCain, G., V.C. Cox and P.B. Paulus (1976). "The Relationship Between Illness, Complaints and Degree of Crowding in a Prison Environment." *Environment and Behavior.* 8:283-290.

McReynolds, K.L. (1973). *Physical Components of Correctional Goals.* Ottawa, Canada: Department of the Solicitor General.

McReynolds, K.L. and T.S. Palys (1975). *A Proposal for a Spatial Assessment of the Manitoba Youth Centre.* Ontario, Canada: Thornhill.

McWhorter, W.L. (1981). *Inmate Society: A Study of Inmate Guards.* Saratoga, California: Century Twenty-One Publishing.

Magargee, E.I. (1977). "The Association of Population Density, Reduced Space, and Uncomfortable Temperatures With Misconduct in a Prison Community." *American Journal of Community Psychology.* 5:289-298.

Merton, R.K. (1957). *Social Theory and Social Structure.* (rev. ed.) New York: The Free Press.

Miller, E.E. (1978). *Jail Management: Problems, Programs and Perspectives.* Lexington, Massachusetts: Lexington Books.

Mitford, J. (1973). *Kind and Usual Punishment: The Prison Business.* New York: Alfred A. Knopf.

Moore, J. (1981). "Prison Litigation and the States: A Case Law Review." *State Legislative Report.* 8:1.

Moyer, F.D. (1975). "The Architecture of Closed Institutions." In G. Giuseppe (ed.) *Prison Architecture.* Nichols, New York: Architectural Press.

Moynahan, J.M. and E.K. Stewart (1980). *The American Jail: Its Growth and Development.* Chicago: Nelson-Hall.

Mueller, C.W. (1983). "Environmental Stressors and Aggressive Behavior." In R.G. Green and E.I. Donnerstein (eds.) *Aggression: Theoretical and Empirical Reviews.* Volume 2. New York: Academic Press.

Nacci, P.L., H.E. Teitelbaum and J. Prather (1977). "Population Density and Inmate Misconduct Rates in the Federal Prison System." *Federal Probation.* (June):26-31.

Nagel, W.G. (1973). *The New Red Barn: A Critical Look at the Modern American Prison.* New York: Walker and Company.

National Crime Prevention Institute (1986). *Understanding Crime Prevention.* Louisville, Kentucky: National Crime Prevention Institute.

National Sheriffs' Association (1982). *The State of Our Nation's Jails, 1982.* Washington, DC: National Sheriffs' Association.

Nelson, W.R. (1988a). "Cost Savings in New Generation Jails: The Direct Supervision Approach." *Construction Bulletin.* Washington, DC: National Institute of Justice.

Nelson, W.R. (1988b). "The Origin of the Podular Direct Supervision Concept: A Personal Account." In K. Kerle (ed.) *Proceedings of the 3rd Annual Symposium on*

Direct Supervision Jails. Boulder, Colorado: National Institute of Corrections Jail Center.

Nelson, W.R. and M. O'Toole (1983). *New Generation Jails.* Boulder, Colorado: Library Information Specialists, Inc.

Newman, O. and K. Franck (1980). *Factors Influencing Crime and Instability in Urban Housing Developments.* Washington, DC: U.S. Department of Justice.

Newman, O. (1972). *Defensible Space.* New York: Collier Books.

Newsweek (1975). "Joan Little's Defense." (February 24):86.

Newsweek (1980). "The Scandalous U.S. Jails." (August 18):74-77.

Nogami, G.Y. (1976). "Crowding: Effects of Group Size, Room Size or Density?" *Journal of Applied Social Psychology.* 6:105- 125.

Pablant, P. and J.C. Baxter (1975). "Environmental Correlates of School Vandalism." *Journal of the American Institute of Planners.* (July):270-277.

Page, R.A. (1977). "Noise and Helping Behavior." *Environment and Behavior.* 9:311-334.

Pollack, S. (1977). *Resident Patient Rate in State Mental Hospitals Reduced to One-Fourth the 1955 Rate.* Memorandum No. 6. Rockville, Maryland: National Institute of Mental Health.

Poole, E.D. and R.M. Regoli (1981). "Alienation in Prison." *Criminology.* 12:251-270.

Poulton, E.C. (1978). "A New Look at the Effects of Noise Upon Performance." *British Journal of Psychology.* 69:435-437.

President's Commission on Law Enforcement and Administration of Justice (1967). *Task Force Report: Corrections.* Washington, DC: U.S. Government Printing Office.

Pugh, R.B. (1968). *Imprisonment in Medieval England.* London: Cambridge University Press.

Queen, S.A. (1920). *The Passing of the County Jail.* Menasha, Wisconsin: The Collegiate Press.

Reid, S.T. (1976). *Crime and Criminology.* Hinsdale, Illinois: Dryden Press.

Reston, J., Jr. (1975). "The Joan Little Case." *The New York Times Magazine.* (April 6):40-46.

Richmond, M.S. (1965). "The Jail Blight." *Crime and Delinquency.* 11:132-141.

Robinson, L.N. (1944). *Jails.* Philadelphia: John C. Winston.

Rosenhan, D.L. (1973). "On Being Sane in Insane Places." *Science.* 179:250-258.

Rosenthal, R. and L. Jacobson (1968). *Pygmalion in the Classroom.* New York: Holt, Rinehart and Winston, Inc.

Schettino, A.P. and R.J. Borden (1976). "Sex Differences in Response to Naturalistic Crowding: Affective Reactions to Group Size and Group Density." *Personality and Social Psychology Bulletin.* 2:67-70.

Schrag, C. (1970). "Leadership Among Prison Inmates." In N. Johnson, L. Savitz and M.E. Wolfgang (eds.) *The Sociology of Punishment and Correction.* 2nd Ed. New York: John Wiley & Sons, Inc.

Schrag, C. (1961). "Some Foundations For a Theory of Correction." In D.R. Cressey (ed.) *The Prison: Studies in Institutional Organization and Change.* New York: Holt, Rinehart and Winston, Inc.

Schwartz, I.M., L. Harris and L. Levi (1988). "The Jailing of Juveniles in Minnesota: A Case Study." *Crime and Delinquency.* 34:138-149.

Shamir, B. and A. Drory (1982). "Occupational Tedium Among Prison Officers." *Criminal Justice and Behavior.* 19:79-99.

Sigurdson, H. (1987a). *Pima County Detention Center: A Study of Podular Direct Supervision.* Washington, DC: National Institute of Corrections.

Sigurdson, H. (1987b). *Larimer County Detention Center: A Study of Podular Direct Supervision.* Washington, DC: National Institute of Corrections.

Sigurdson, H. (1985). *The Manhattan House of Detention: A Study of Podular Direct Supervision.* Washington, DC: National Institute of Corrections.

Smith, P.C., L.M. Kendall and C.L. Hulin (1969). *The Measurement of Satisfaction in Work and Retirement.* Chicago: Rand-McNally.

Smith, S. (1969). "Studies of Small Groups in Confinement." In J.P. Zubek (ed.) *Sensory Deprivation: Fifteen Years of Research.* New York: Appleton-Century-Crofts.

Snow, R.E. (1969). "Unfinished Pygmalion." *Contemporary Psychology.* 14:197-199.

Soler, M. (1988). "Litigation on Behalf of Children in Adult Jails." *Crime and Delinquency*. 34:190-208.

Sommer, R. (1972). *Tight Spaces: Hard Architecture and How to Humanize It*. Englewood Cliffs, New Jersey: Prentice-Hall, Inc.

Sommer, R. (1969). *Personal Space: The Behavioral Basis of Design*. Englewood Cliffs, New Jersey: Prentice-Hall, Inc.

Steinhart, D. (1988). "California Legislature Ends the Jailing of Children: The Story of a Policy Reversal." *Crime and Delinquency*. 34:169-189.

Stinchcomb, J.B. (1986). "Correctional Officer Stress: Looking at the Causes; You *May* Be the Cure." Presented at the annual meeting of the Academy of Criminal Justice Sciences, Orlando, Florida, March, 1986.

Stokols, D. (1972). "On the Distinction Between Density and Crowding: Some Implications for Future Research." *Psychological Review*. 79:275.

Stokols, D. and D.G. Marrero (1976). "The Effects of an Environmental Intervention on Racial Polarization in a Youth Training School." In P. Suedfeld, et al. (eds.) *EDRA Conference Proceedings*. Book 1. 125-137.

Suedfeld, P. (1980). *Restricted Environmental Stimulation: Research and Clinical Applications*. New York: John Wiley & Sons, Inc.

Sundstrom, E. (1975). "An Experimental Study of Crowding: Effects of Room Size, Intrusion, and Goal Blocking on Nonverbal Behavior, Self-Disclosure, and Self-Reported Stress." *Journal of Personality and Social Psychology*. 32:645-654.

Sundstrom, E. and I. Altman (1974). "Field Study of Territorial Behavior and Dominance." *Journal of Personality and Social Psychology*. 30:115-124.

Sutton, C. (1874). *The New York Tombs: Its Secrets and Its Mysteries*. Reprint edition, 1973. Montclair, New Jersey: Patterson Smith Publishing Corporation.

Swank, G.E. and D. Winer (1976). "Occurrence of Psychiatric Disorder in a County Jail Population." *American Journal of Psychiatry*. 133:1331-1333.

Sykes, G.M. (1958). *The Society of Captives*. Princeton, New Jersey: Princeton University Press.

Sylvester, S.F., J.H. Reed and D.O. Nelson (1977). *Prison Homicide*. New York. Spectrum.

Thorndike, R.L. (1968). "Review of Pygmalion in the Classroom." *American Educational Research Journal.* 5:708-711.

Time (1975). "A Case of Rape or Seduction?" (July 28):19.

Time (1987). "First the Sentence, Then the Trial." (June 8):69.

Toch, H. (1975). *Men in Crisis: Human Breakdown in Prison.* Chicago: Aldine Publishing Company.

Toch, H. (1977). *Living in Prisons: The Ecology of Survival.* New York: The Free Press.

Toch, H. and J.D. Grant (1982). *Reforming Human Services.* Beverly Hills: Sage Publications.

Daily Home Sun (Talladega, Alabama). "Two Jailers Disciplined For Inmate Death." February 19, 1989:23.

Toch, H. and J. Klofas (1982). "Alienation and Desire for Job Enrichment Among Correction Officers." *Federal Probation.* 46:35-44.

U.S. Congress. House Select Committee on Crime (1970). *Crime in America: Heroin Importation, Distribution, Packaging, and Paraphernalia.* 91st Congress, 2nd Session. 214-222. Testimony of G. McGrath.

U.S. Department of Justice, Bureau of Justice Statistics (1980). *Profile of Jail Inmates: Sociodemographic Findings From the 1978 Survey of Inmates of Local Jails.* Washington, DC: U.S. Government Printing Office.

U.S. Department of Justice, Bureau of Justice Statistics (1983a). *Jail Inmates, 1982.* Washington, DC: U.S. Government Printing Office.

U.S. Department of Justice, Bureau of Justice Statistics (1983b). *Juvenile Suicides in Adult Jails: Findings from a National Survey of Juveniles in Secure Detention Facilities.* Washington, DC: U.S. Government Printing Office.

U.S Department of Justice, Bureau of Justice Statistics (1987). *Jail Inmates, 1986.* Washington, DC: U.S. Government Printing Office.

U.S. Department of Justice, Bureau of Justice Statistics (1988). *Census of Local Jails, 1983.* Washington, DC: U.S. Government Printing Office.

U.S. Department of Justice, Bureau of Justice Statistics (1990). *Census of Local Jails, 1988.* Washington, DC: U.S. Government Printing Office.

U.S. Department of Justice, National Institute of Justice, Office of Justice Programs (1989). *Drug Use Forecasting, April to June, 1989*. Washington, DC: Government Printing Office.

U.S. Department of Justice, National Institute of Justice, Office of Research Programs (1980a). *American Prisons and Jails, Vol. I: Summary and Police Implications of a National Survey*. Washington, DC: U.S. Government Printing Office.

U.S. Department of Justice, National Institute of Justice, Office of Research Programs (1980b). *American Prisons and Jails, Vol. III: Conditions and Costs of Confinement*. Washington, DC: U.S. Government Printing Office.

U.S. General Accounting Office (1980). *Jail Inmates' Mental Health Care Neglected; State and Federal Attention Needed*. Washington, DC: U.S. Government Printing Office.

Vischer, A.L. (1919). *Barbed Wire Disease*. London: John Bale and Davidson.

Waller, I. and N. Okihiro (1978). *Burglary: The Victim and the Public*. Toronto: University of Toronto.

Wener, R. and N. Clark (1976). *User Based Assessment of the Chicago Metropolitan Correctional Center*. Washington, DC: U.S. Bureau of Prisons.

Wener, R. and R. Olsen (1978). *User Based Assessment of the Federal Metropolitan Correctional Centers: Final Report*. Washington, DC: U.S. Bureau of Prisons.

Wener, R. and R. Olsen (1980). "Innovative Correctional Environments: A User Assessment." *Environment and Behavior*. 12:478-493.

Wener, R., W. Frazier and J. Farbstein (1987). "Building Better Jails." *Psychology Today*. 21:40-49.

West, D. (1972). "I Was Afraid to Shut My Eyes." In D.M. Petersen and M. Truzzi (eds.) *Criminal Life: Views From the Inside*. Englewood Cliffs, New Jersey: Prentice-Hall, Inc.

Westin, A.F. (1970). *Privacy and Freedom*. New York: Atheneum.

Whiting, C. and D. DeJoy (1976). "Behavioral Data in Evaluation Research: Use in Correctional Visiting Facilities." *MER Working Paper*. State College, Division of Man-Environment Relations, Pennsylvania State University.

Wilson, J.Q. and G.L. Kelling (1983). "Broken Windows: The Police and Neighborhood Safety." In A.S. Blumberg and E. Niederhoffer (eds.) *The Ambivalent Force*. New York: Holt, Rinehart and Winston, Inc.

Wilson, R. (1980). "Who Will Care for the 'Mad and Bad'." *Corrections Magazine*. (February):4.

Wolff v. McDonnel, 418 U.S. 539 (1974).

Wright, K.N. (1985). "Developing the Prison Environment Inventory." *Journal of Research in Crime and Delinquency*. 22:257-277.

Zimbardo, P.G. (1970). "The Human Choice: Individuation, Reason, and Order Versus Deindividuation, Impulse, and Chaos." In W.J. Arnold and D. Levine (eds.) *Nebraska Symposium on Motivation*. Lincoln, Nebraska: University of Nebraska Press.

Zupan, L.L. and B. Menke (1988). "Implementing Organizational Change: From Traditional to New Generation Jail Operations." *Policy Studies Review*. 7:615-625.

Zupan, L.L. and M. Stohr-Gillmore (1988). "Doing Time in the New Generation Jail: Inmate Perceptions of Gains and Losses." *Policy Studies Review*. 7:626-640.

Index